staining 10/20/15 MA

three&four
ingredient
RECIPES

three&four
ingredient
RECIPES

Over 320 mouthwatering recipes that use four ingredients
or less, shown in more than 1130 step-by-step photographs

JOANNA FARROW & JENNY WHITE

LORENZ BOOKS

This edition is published by Lorenz Books,
an imprint of Anness Publishing Ltd,
Blaby Road, Wigston,
Leicestershire LE18 4SE;
info@anness.com

www.lorenzbooks.com; www.annesspublishing.com

If you like the images in this book and would like to investigate using them for publishing,
promotions or advertising, please visit our website www.practicalpictures.com for more information.

Publisher: Joanna Lorenz
Editorial Director: Judith Simons
Senior Editor: Doreen Gillon
Copy-editors: Bridget Jones and Sally Somers
Photography: Tim Auty, Martin Brigdale, Nicky Dowey, Gus Filgate, Michelle Garrett,
Amanda Heywood, William Lingwood, Craig Robertson, Simon Smith
Home Economist: Jenny White
Home Economist's Assistant: Fergal Connolly
Stylist: Helen Trent
Designer: Paul Oakley
Additional Recipes: Pepita Aris, Alex Barker, Georgina Campbell, Jacqueline Clark, Joanna Farrow,
Brian Glover, Christine Ingram, Becky Johnson, Jane Milton, Jennie Shapter, Marlena Spieler,
Linda Tubby, Kate Whiteman, Jeni Wright
Production Manager: Steve Lang

© Anness Publishing Ltd 2013

A CIP catalogue record for this book is available from the British Library.

This book contains previously published material.

NOTES
Bracketed terms are intended for American readers.
For all recipes, quantities are given in both metric and imperial measures and, where appropriate,
measures are also given in standard cups and spoons. Follow one set, but not a mixture, because
they are not interchangeable.
Standard spoon and cup measures are level. 1 tsp = 5ml, 1 tbsp = 15ml, 1 cup = 250ml/8fl oz.
Australian standard tablespoons are 20ml. Australian readers should use 3 tsp in place of 1 tbsp for
measuring small quantities.
American pints are 16fl oz/2 cups. American readers should use 20fl oz/2.5 cups in place
of 1 pint when measuring liquids.
Electric oven temperatures in this book are for conventional ovens. When using a fan oven,
the temperature will probably need to be reduced by about 10–20°C/20–40°F.
Since ovens vary, you should check with your manufacturer's instruction book for guidance.
Medium (US large) eggs are used unless otherwise stated.

PUBLISHER'S NOTE
Although the advice and information in this book are believed to be accurate and true at the time of
going to press, neither the authors nor the publisher can accept any legal responsibility or liability for
any errors or omissions that may have been made nor for any inaccuracies nor for any loss, harm or
injury that comes about from following instructions or advice in this book.

Contents

Introduction

Just because a dish includes only a few ingredients, it doesn't mean you need to compromise on taste and enjoyment. Reducing the number of ingredients you use in a dish has many benefits. Not only does it make shopping easier and quicker, it also means spending less time on preparation because there's less measuring, peeling, scrubbing and chopping to be done. It also allows you to really enjoy the flavours of the few ingredients used. Fresh food tastes fantastic, so why not let the flavours of a few truly fabulous ingredients shine through rather than masking them with the taste of other ingredients?

Keeping it quick, keeping it simple

In today's busy world, time is of the essence – and no one ever seems to have enough of it. When you're trying to cram as much as possible into a single day, often the first thing that falls by the wayside is cooking. When you're busy, the last thing you feel like doing is spending an hour in the supermarket shopping for ingredients, then going home and preparing them before finally cooking a meal. The temptation is to grab a ready-prepared meal to heat up when you get home, or to pick up a takeaway – but sometimes, when you've had a hectic day at work or your kids have been running you ragged, what you really want is to sit down and relax with a tasty home-cooked meal. This book is devoted to helping you do just this.

The idea of making a dish that requires a huge list of ingredients can often put you off before you've even started – the shopping and preparation alone seeming like an unmanageable task. But the good news is that cooking doesn't need to be this way. It's incredibly easy to make delicious dishes using just a few simple ingredients – but the key to success lies in the ingredients you choose, and how you prepare and cook them.

Above and opposite: You need only three ingredients to make this simple dish of spaghetti with broccoli and spicy chilli. It tastes delicious and can be made in less than 15 minutes.

Using the right ingredients

The recipes in this book combine basic ingredients such as fruit, vegetables, meat, fish, herbs and spices, but they also make good use of ready-made or pre-prepared products such as curry pastes and pastry. Using these convenient products is a great way to save time, both on preparation and shopping, and can sometimes enhance the final dish in a way that the home-made version may not. For example, puff pastry is enormously difficult to make, while the bought varieties are easy to use, give great results and taste delicious.

When buying basic ingredients, always try to buy the freshest, best quality ones you can to get the maximum flavour. Really fresh ingredients also have the benefit of having a higher nutritional content. If you can buy organic produce, do so. The flavour will be better and you will have the knowledge that they do not contain chemical fertilizers and pesticides.

It is also a good idea to buy fruits and vegetables when they're in season. Although most are available all year round, you can really notice the difference between those that have been ripened naturally and those that have been grown out of season. Strawberries may be available in the middle of winter, but when you cut them open they are often white inside with a slightly waxy texture and none of the sweet, juicy, almost perfumed flavour of the summer fruits. There are so many fabulous ingredients at their peak in their own season that you don't have to buy unseasonal ones. Why buy tired-looking asparagus in autumn when there are plenty of mushrooms, squashes and root vegetables around – all of which can be made into a huge number of delicious, varied meals.

When buying pre-prepared or ready-made ingredients such as stocks for soups or custard to make ice cream, try to buy really good-quality, fresh varieties. When an ingredient is playing an integral part in a dish, it needs to be well flavoured with a good texture and consistency. If you use a less good product with an inferior flavour, it will really show in the final dish. The same is true of flavouring ingredients such as curry pastes and spicy sauces – go for quality every time and you will reap the benefits.

About this book

Whether you're an experienced cook or an absolute beginner, you'll find the recipes in this book will suit you perfectly. There are dishes for every occasion: juices to quench your thirst; healthy breakfasts and light lunches to make when time is short. There are also great meat, fish and vegetarian dishes to cook when you have more time on your hands or if you're entertaining guests. There is a selection of divine dishes to eat outside when the weather's sunny, and when you need a sweet treat, there are whole chapters devoted to cookies and cakes and sumptuous hot, cold and iced desserts. No matter what the occasion, how much time you have, how many people you need to feed, or what you're in the mood for – you are sure to find the perfect dish within these pages.

Every recipe has an ingredients list of four items or fewer, and the only other things you will need are basic standbys from the storecupboard: oil or butter to cook with and salt and freshly ground black pepper to season the food. In some cases flavoured oils such as garlic-, lemon-, or herb-infused olive oil are used for cooking or drizzling, so it's well worth keeping a small selection of these oils in the storecupboard.

Appetizers

WHEN A SNACK IS CALLED FOR, OR A LITTLE
SOMETHING TO WHET THE APPETITE BEFORE A MAIN
MEAL, YOU WON'T FIND ANYTHING SIMPLER OR MORE
TASTY THAN THE FOLLOWING RECIPES. FROM
MOUTHWATERING DIPS TO DELICIOUS LITTLE EGGS
MIMOSA, THIS CHAPTER IS PACKED WITH SIMPLE, FUSS-
FREE IDEAS THAT YOU WON'T BE ABLE TO RESIST.

Hummus

This classic Middle Eastern chickpea dip is flavoured with garlic and tahini (sesame seed paste).
A little ground cumin can also be added, and olive oil can be stirred in to enrich the hummus, if you like.
It is delicious served with wedges of toasted pitta bread or crudités.

SERVES FOUR TO SIX

1 Using a potato masher or fork, coarsely mash the chickpeas in a mixing bowl. If you like a smoother purée, process the chickpeas in a food processor or blender until a smooth paste is formed.

2 Mix the tahini into the bowl of chickpeas, then stir in the chopped garlic cloves and lemon juice. Season to taste with salt and freshly ground black pepper, and if needed, add a little water. Serve the hummus at room temperature.

**400g/14oz can
chickpeas, drained**

60ml/4 tbsp tahini

**2–3 garlic cloves,
chopped**

juice of ¹/₂–1 lemon

FROM THE
STORECUPBOARD

**salt and ground
black pepper**

Baba Ghanoush

Adjust the amount of aubergine, garlic and lemon juice in this richly flavoured Middle Eastern aubergine dip depending on how creamy, garlicky or tart you want it to be. The dip can served with a garnish of chopped fresh coriander leaves, olives or pickled cucumbers. Hot pepper sauce or a little ground coriander can be added, too.

1 large or 2 medium aubergines (eggplant)

2–4 garlic cloves, chopped

90–150ml/6–10 tbsp tahini

juice of 1 lemon, or to taste

SERVES TWO TO FOUR

1 Place the aubergine(s) directly over the flame of a gas stove or on the coals of a barbecue. Turn the aubergine(s) fairly frequently until deflated and the skin is evenly charred. Remove from the heat with tongs. Alternatively, place under a hot grill (broiler), turning frequently, until charred.

2 Put the aubergine(s) in a plastic bag and seal the top tightly, or place in a bowl and cover with crumpled kitchen paper. Leave to cool for 30–60 minutes.

3 Peel off the blackened skin from the aubergine(s), reserving the juices. Chop the aubergine flesh, either by hand for a coarse texture or in a food processor for a smooth purée. Put the aubergine in a bowl and stir in the reserved juices.

4 Add the garlic and tahini to the aubergine and stir until smooth. Stir in the lemon juice. If the mixture becomes too thick, add 15–30ml/1–2 tbsp water. Spoon into a serving bowl. Serve at room temperature.

Cannellini Bean Pâté

Serve this simple pâté with melba toast or toasted wholegrain bread as an appetizer or snack. A dusting of paprika gives an extra kick. You can also use other types of canned beans such as kidney beans.

SERVES FOUR

2 x 400g/14oz cans cannellini beans, drained and rinsed

50g/2oz mature Cheddar cheese, finely grated

30ml/2 tbsp chopped fresh parsley

FROM THE STORECUPBOARD

45ml/3 tbsp olive oil

salt and ground black pepper

1 Put the cannellini beans in a food processor with the olive oil, and process to a chunky paste.

2 Transfer to a bowl and stir in the cheese, parsley and some salt and pepper. Spoon into a serving dish and sprinkle a little paprika on top, if you like.

COOK'S TIP *Canned beans are usually in a sugar, salt and water solution so always drain and rinse them thoroughly before use – otherwise the finished pâté may be rather too salty.*

Chicken Liver and Brandy Pâté

This pâté really could not be simpler to make, and tastes so much better than anything you can buy ready-made in the supermarkets. Serve with crispy Melba toast for an elegant appetizer.

SERVES FOUR

1 Heat the butter in a large frying pan until foamy. Add the chicken livers and cook over a medium heat for 3–4 minutes, or until browned and cooked through.

2 Add the brandy and allow to bubble for a few minutes. Let the mixture cool slightly, then tip into a food processor with the cream and some salt and pepper.

3 Process the mixture until smooth and spoon into ramekin dishes. Level the surface and chill overnight to set. Serve garnished with sprigs of parsley to add a little colour.

350g/12oz chicken livers, trimmed and roughly chopped

30ml/2 tbsp brandy

30ml/2 tbsp double (heavy) cream

FROM THE STORECUPBOARD

50g/2oz/¼ cup butter

salt and ground black pepper

Peperonata

This richly flavoured spicy tomato and sweet red pepper dip is delicious served with crisp Italian-style bread sticks – enjoy it with drinks or as a snack while watching television. It also makes a tasty relish served with grilled chicken and fish dishes. It is delicious served either hot, cold or at room temperature and can be stored in the refrigerator for several days.

SERVES FOUR

1 Heat the oil in a large pan over a low heat and add the sliced peppers. Cook very gently, stirring occasionally for 3–4 minutes.

2 Add the chilli flakes to the pan and cook for 1 minute, then pour in the tomatoes and season. Cook gently for 50 minutes to 1 hour, stirring occasionally.

COOK'S TIP *Long, slow cooking helps to bring out the sweetness of the peppers and tomatoes, so don't be tempted to cheat on the cooking time by cooking over a higher heat.*

2 large red (bell) peppers, halved, seeded and sliced

pinch dried chilli flakes

400g/14oz can pomodorino tomatoes

FROM THE STORECUPBOARD

60ml/4 tbsp garlic-infused olive oil

salt and ground black pepper

Artichoke and Cumin Dip

This dip is so easy to make and is unbelievably tasty. Serve with olives, hummus and wedges of pitta bread to make a summery snack selection. Grilled artichokes bottled in oil have a fabulous flavour and can be used instead of canned artichokes. You can also vary the flavourings – try adding chilli powder in place of the cumin and add a handful of basil leaves to the artichokes before blending.

SERVES FOUR

1 Put the artichoke hearts in a food processor with the garlic and ground cumin, and a generous drizzle of olive oil. Process to a smooth purée and season with plenty of salt and ground black pepper to taste.

2 Spoon the purée into a serving bowl and serve with an extra drizzle of olive oil swirled on the top and slices of warm pitta bread for dipping.

2 x 400g/14oz cans artichoke hearts, drained

2 garlic cloves, peeled

2.5ml/½ tsp ground cumin

FROM THE STORECUPBOARD

olive oil

salt and ground black pepper

Sweet and Salty Vegetable Crisps

This delightfully simple snack is perfect to serve with pre-dinner drinks as an informal appetizer. Serve them with a bowl of aioli or a creamy dip such as hummus or taramasalata, and use the crisps to scoop it up. You can cook other sweet root vegetables, such as carrots and sweet potatoes, in the same way. Make a pretty, appetizing snack by making several different types of vegetable crisps, then pile them together in a bowl.

SERVES FOUR

1 Peel the beetroot and, using a mandolin or a vegetable peeler, cut it into very thin slices. Lay the slices on kitchen paper and sprinkle them with sugar and fine salt.

2 Heat 5cm/2in oil in a pan, until a bread cube dropped into the pan turns golden in 1 minute. Cook the slices, in batches, until they float to the surface and turn golden at the edge. Drain on kitchen paper and sprinkle with salt when cool.

1 small fresh beetroot (beet)

caster (superfine) sugar

FROM THE STORECUPBOARD

salt, for sprinkling

olive oil, for frying

Sizzling Prawns

These richly flavoured prawns (shrimp) are a classic Spanish tapas dish, but they also make a perfect appetizer. Traditionally they are brought to the table in little individual earthenware dishes, sizzling frantically in the hot oil with garlic. The addition of fiery chillies gives them an additional kick, but if you prefer a milder appetizer, simply omit the chillies.

SERVES FOUR

1 Split the chillies lengthways and discard the seeds. (Wash your hands with soap and water immediately.)

2 Heat the olive oil in a large frying pan and stir-fry the garlic and chillies for 1 minute, until the garlic begins to turn brown.

3 Add the whole prawns and stir-fry for 3–4 minutes, coating them well with the flavoured oil.

4 Remove the pan from the heat and divide the prawns among four dishes. Spoon over the flavoured oil and serve immediately. (Remember to provide a plate for the heads and shells, plus plenty of napkins.)

1–2 dried chillies (to taste)

3 garlic cloves, finely chopped

16 large raw prawns (shrimp), in the shell

FROM THE STORECUPBOARD

60ml/4 tbsp olive oil

Potted Shrimps with Cayenne Pepper

Cayenne pepper adds a hint of spiciness to this traditional English seaside favourite. Serve with crusty bread or brown toast. The potted shrimps can be stored in the refrigerator for up to 3 days.

SERVES SIX

1 Put the butter, mace and cayenne pepper into a small pan and warm over a gentle heat until melted.

2 Add the peeled shrimps and stir gently until warmed through. Butter six small ramekin dishes.

3 Remove the mace from the shrimp mixture and divide the shrimps and butter evenly between the six ramekins, patting down gently with the back of a spoon. Chill until set.

4 When the butter in the shrimp mixture has set, put the clarified butter in a small pan and melt over a gentle heat. Pour a layer of clarified butter over the top of each ramekin to cover the shrimps and chill again to set.

2 blades of mace

a pinch of cayenne pepper

600ml/1 pint/2¹⁄₂ cups peeled brown shrimps

FROM THE STORECUPBOARD

115g/4oz/¹⁄₂ cup butter, plus extra for greasing

90ml/6 tbsp clarified butter

Marinated Feta with Lemon and Oregano

The longer the cheese is left to marinate, the better the flavour will be. Serve with tomato and red onion salad and some crisp flatbreads.

SERVES FOUR

1 Drain the feta and pat dry with kitchen paper. Cut it into cubes and arrange in a non-metallic bowl or dish with the lemon wedges and oregano sprigs.

2 Pour the olive oil over the top and cover with clear film (plastic wrap). Chill for at least 3 hours, then serve with a selection of flat breads and salads.

200g/7oz Greek feta cheese

1 lemon, cut into wedges

a small handful of fresh oregano sprigs

FROM THE STORECUPBOARD

300ml/¹⁄₂ pint/1¹⁄₄ cups extra virgin olive oil

COOK'S TIP

Feta cheese is a salty, crumbly Greek cheese that is usually bought packed in brine. Use a good quality brand and drain thoroughly before using.

Mushroom Caviar

The name caviar refers to the dark colour and texture of this dish of chopped mushrooms. Serve the mushroom mixture in individual serving dishes with toasted rye bread rubbed with cut garlic cloves, to accompany. Chopped hard-boiled egg, spring onion and parsley, the traditional garnishes for caviar, can be added as a garnish.

SERVES FOUR

1 Heat the oil in a large pan, add the mushrooms, shallots and garlic, and cook, stirring occasionally, until browned. Season with salt, then continue cooking until the mushrooms give up their liquor.

2 Continue cooking, stirring frequently, until the liquor has evaporated and the mushrooms are brown and dry.

3 Put the mixture in a food processor or blender and process briefly until a chunky paste is formed. Spoon the mushroom caviar into dishes and serve.

450g/1lb mushrooms, coarsely chopped

5–10 shallots, chopped

4 garlic cloves, chopped

FROM THE STORECUPBOARD

45ml/3 tbsp olive or vegetable oil

EXTRAS

For a rich wild mushroom caviar, soak 10–15g/¼–½oz dried porcini in about 120ml/4fl oz/ ½ cup water for about 30 minutes. Add the porcini and their soaking liquid to the browned mushrooms in step 2. Continue as in the recipe. Serve with wedges of lemon, for their tangy juice.

Brandade of Salt Cod

There are many versions of this creamy French salt cod purée: some contain mashed potatoes, others truffles. Serve the brandade with warmed crispbread or crusty bread for a tasty appetizer, or for a light lunch serve the brandade and bread with a tomato and basil salad. You can omit the garlic from the brandade, if you prefer, and serve toasted slices of French bread rubbed with garlic instead.

SERVES SIX

200g/7oz salt cod

250ml/8fl oz/1 cup extra virgin olive oil

4 garlic cloves, crushed

250ml/8fl oz/1 cup double (heavy) or whipping cream

1 Soak the fish in cold water for 24 hours, changing the water frequently. Drain the fish well. Cut the fish into pieces, place in a shallow pan and pour in enough cold water to cover. Heat the water until it is simmering and poach the fish for 8 minutes, until it is just cooked. Drain the fish, then remove the skin and bones.

2 Combine the extra virgin olive oil and crushed garlic cloves in a small pan and heat gently. In another pan, heat the double cream until it just starts to simmer.

3 Put the cod into a food processor, process it briefly, then gradually add alternate amounts of the garlic-flavoured olive oil and cream, while continuing to process the mixture. The aim is to create a purée with the consistency of mashed potato.

4 Season to taste with freshly ground black pepper, then scoop the brandade into a serving bowl or on to individual serving plates and serve with crispbread or crusty bread.

Chopped Egg and Onions

This dish is one of the oldest dishes in Jewish culinary history. It is delicious served sprinkled with chopped parsley and onion rings on crackers, piled on toast, or used as a sandwich or bagel filling. Serve chopped egg and onion as part of a buffet with a selection of dips and toppings.

SERVES FOUR TO SIX

1 Put the eggs in a large pan and cover with cold water. Bring the water to the boil and when it boils, reduce the heat and simmer over a low heat for 10 minutes.

2 Hold the boiled eggs under cold running water (if too hot to handle, place the eggs in a strainer and hold under the running water). When cool, remove the shells from the eggs and discard. Dry the eggs and chop coarsely.

3 Place the chopped eggs in a large bowl, add the onions, season generously with salt and black pepper and mix well. Add enough mayonnaise or chicken fat to bind the mixture together. Stir in the mustard, if using, and chill before serving.

8–10 eggs

6–8 spring onions (scallions) and/or 1 yellow or white onion, very finely chopped, plus extra to garnish

60–90ml/4–6 tbsp mayonnaise or rendered chicken fat

mild French wholegrain mustard, to taste (optional if using mayonnaise)

FROM THE STORECUPBOARD

salt and ground black pepper

Israeli Cheese with Green Olives

In Israel, mild white cheeses spiked with seasonings, such as this one that is flavoured with piquant green olives, are served with drinks and little crackers or toast. It is also very good served for brunch – spread generously on chunks of fresh, crusty bread or bagels.

SERVES FOUR

175–200g/6–7oz soft white (farmer's) cheese

65g/2½ oz feta cheese, preferably sheep's milk, lightly crumbled

20–30 pitted green olives, some chopped, the rest halved or quartered

2–3 large pinches of fresh thyme, plus extra to garnish

1 Place the soft white cheese in a mixing bowl and stir with the back of a spoon or a fork until soft and smooth. Add the crumbled feta cheese and stir the two cheeses together until they are thoroughly combined.

2 Add the chopped, halved and quartered olives and the pinches of fresh thyme to the cheese mixture and mix thoroughly.

3 Spoon the mixture into a bowl, sprinkle with thyme and serve with crackers, toast, chunks of bread or bagels.

Bacon-rolled Enokitake Mushrooms

The Japanese name for this dish is *Obimaki enoki*: an *obi* (belt or sash) is made from bacon and wrapped around enokitake mushrooms before they are grilled. The strong, smoky flavour of the bacon complements the subtle flavour of mushrooms. Small heaps of ground white pepper can be offered with these savouries, if you like.

SERVES FOUR

450g/1lb fresh enokitake mushrooms

6 rindless smoked streaky (fatty) bacon rashers (strips)

4 lemon wedges

1 Cut off the root part of each enokitake cluster 2cm/¾in from the end. Do not separate the stems. Cut the bacon rashers in half lengthways.

2 Divide the enokitake into 12 equal bunches. Take one bunch, then place the middle of the enokitake near the edge of one bacon rasher, with 2.5–4cm/1–1½in of enokitake protruding at each end.

3 Carefully roll up the bunch of enokitake in the bacon. Tuck any straying short stems into the bacon and slide the bacon slightly upwards at each roll to cover about 4cm/1½in of the enokitake. Secure the end of the bacon roll with a cocktail stick (toothpick). Repeat using the remaining enokitake and bacon to make 11 more rolls.

4 Preheat the grill (broiler) to high. Place the enokitake rolls on an oiled wire rack. Grill (broil) both sides until the bacon is crisp and the enokitake start to char. This takes 10–13 minutes.

5 Remove the enokitake rolls and place on a board. Using a fork and knife, chop each roll in half in the middle of the bacon belt. Arrange the top part of the enokitake roll standing upright, the bottom part lying down next to it. Add a wedge of lemon to each portion and serve.

Walnut and Goat's Cheese Bruschetta

The combination of toasted walnuts and melting goat's cheese is lovely in this simple appetizer, served with a pile of salad leaves. Toasting the walnuts helps to enhance their flavour. Walnut bread is readily available in most large supermarkets and makes an interesting alternative to ordinary crusty bread, although this can be used if walnut bread is unavailable.

SERVES FOUR

1 Preheat the grill (broiler). Lightly toast the walnut pieces, then remove and set aside. Put the walnut bread on a foil-lined grill rack and toast on one side. Turn the slices over and drizzle each with 15ml/1 tbsp of the French dressing.

2 Cut the goat's cheese into twelve slices and place three on each piece of bread. Grill (broil) for about 3 minutes, until the cheese is melting and beginning to brown.

3 Transfer the bruschetta to serving plates, sprinkle with the toasted walnuts and drizzle with the remaining French dressing. Serve the bruschetta immediately with salad leaves.

50g/2oz/¹/₂ cup walnut pieces

4 thick slices walnut bread

120ml/4fl oz/¹/₂ cup French dressing

200g/7oz chèvre or other semi-soft goat's cheese

COOK'S TIP *Use walnut bread slices from a slender loaf, so that the portions are not too wide. If you can buy only a large loaf, cut the slices in half to make neat, chunky pieces.*

Party Snacks

WHEN YOU WANT LITTLE PARTY SNACKS WITH THE MINIMUM OF FUSS, THINK SIMPLICITY. FROM MOUTHWATERING CANAPÉS SUCH AS BLINIS WITH CAVIAR AND CRÈME FRAÎCHE TO MOREISH SALT COD AND POTATO FRITTERS, THIS CHAPTER IS PACKED WITH FUSS-FREE IDEAS THAT YOU WON'T BE ABLE TO RESIST. SERVE GOLDEN, MELT-IN-THE-MOUTH PARMESAN TUILES OR GOLDEN GRUYÈRE AND BASIL TORTILLAS WITH DRINKS, OR ENJOY CRAB AND WATER-CHESTNUT WONTONS AS AN APPETIZER.

Spanish Salted Almonds

Served with a glass of chilled dry sherry, these delicious salted nuts make a perfect tapas dish or pre-dinner snack.

SERVES FOUR TO SIX

1 Preheat the oven 200°C/400°F/Gas 6. Whisk the egg white in a bowl until it forms stiff peaks.

2 Add the almonds to the egg white, and stir until the nuts are thoroughly coated. Tip the mixture on to a baking sheet and spread out evenly in a single layer.

1 egg white

200g/7oz/generous 1 cup shelled unblanched almonds

a good handful of flaked sea salt

3 Sprinkle the salt over the almonds and bake for about 15 minutes, or until the egg white and salt are crusty. Leave to cool completely, then serve in bowls with a selection of other nibbles, dips and pâtés.

Golden Gruyère and Basil Tortillas

These simple fried tortilla wedges make a great late-night snack with sweet chilli sauce. If you have a few slices of ham or salami in the refrigerator, add these to the tortillas as well.

SERVES TWO

1 Heat the oil in a frying pan, over a medium heat. Add one of the tortillas, arrange the Gruyère cheese slices and basil leaves on top and season with salt and pepper.

2 Place the remaining tortilla on top to make a sandwich and flip the whole thing over with a metal spatula. Cook for a few minutes, until the underneath is golden.

3 Slide the tortilla sandwich on to a chopping board or plate and cut into wedges. Serve immediately.

2 soft flour tortillas

115g/4oz Gruyère cheese, thinly sliced

a handful of fresh basil leaves

FROM THE STORECUPBOARD

15ml/1 tbsp olive oil

salt and ground black pepper

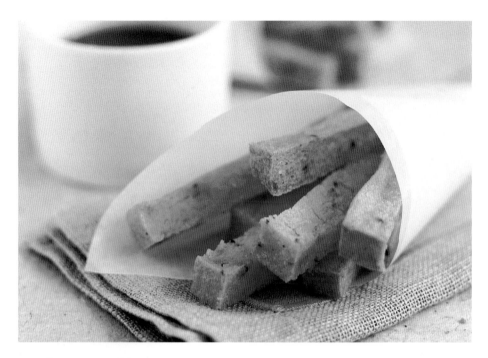

Polenta Chips

These tasty Parmesan-flavoured batons are best served warm from the oven with a spicy, tangy dip.
A bowl of Thai chilli dipping sauce or a creamy, chilli-spiked guacamole are perfect for dipping into.

MAKES ABOUT EIGHTY

1 Put 1.5 litres/2½ pints/6¼ cups water into a large heavy pan and bring to the boil. Reduce the heat, add the salt and pour in the polenta in a steady stream, stirring constantly with a wooden spoon. Cook over a low heat for about 5 minutes, stirring, until the mixture thickens and comes away from the sides of the pan.

2 Remove the pan from the heat and add the cheese and butter. Season to taste. Stir well until the mixture is smooth. Pour on to a smooth surface, such as a marble slab or a baking sheet.

3 Using a metal spatula, spread out the polenta to a thickness of 2cm/¾in and shape into a rectangle. Leave to stand for at least 30 minutes until cold. Meanwhile preheat the oven to 200°C/400°F/Gas 6 and lightly oil two or three baking sheets.

4 Cut the polenta slab in half, then carefully cut into even-size strips. Bake for 40–50 minutes, or until dark golden brown and crunchy, turning from time to time. Serve warm.

375g/13oz/3¼ cups instant polenta

150g/5oz/1½ cups freshly grated Parmesan cheese

FROM THE STORECUPBOARD

10ml/2 tsp salt, plus extra

90g/3½oz/7 tbsp butter

10ml/2 tsp cracked black pepper

olive oil, for brushing

Parmesan Tuiles

These lacy tuiles look very impressive and make splendid nibbles for a party, but they couldn't be easier to make. Believe or not, they use only a single ingredient – Parmesan cheese.

MAKES EIGHT TO TEN

1 Preheat the oven to 200°C/400°F/Gas 6. Line two baking sheets with baking parchment. Grate the cheese using a fine grater, pulling it down slowly to make long strands.

2 Spread the grated cheese in 7.5–9cm/3–3½in rounds on the baking parchment, forking it into shape. Do not spread the cheese too thickly; it should just cover the parchment. Bake for 5–7 minutes, or until bubbling and golden brown.

3 Leave the tuiles on the baking sheet for about 30 seconds and then carefully transfer, using a metal spatula, to a wire rack to cool completely. Alternatively, drape over a rolling pin to make a curved shape.

| **115g/4oz Parmesan cheese**

COOK'S TIP

Tuiles can be made into little cup shapes by draping over an upturned egg cup. These little cups can be filled to make tasty treats to serve with drinks. Try a little cream cheese flavoured with herbs.

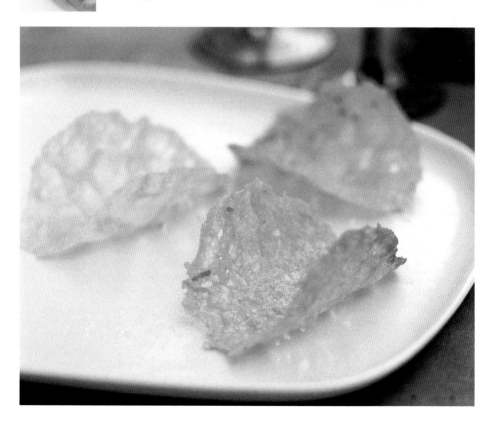

Yogurt Cheese in Olive Oil

In Greece, sheep's yogurt is hung in muslin to drain off the whey before being patted into balls of soft cheese. Here the cheese is bottled in extra virgin olive oil with dried chillies and fresh herbs to make a wonderful gourmet gift or aromatic appetizer. It is delicious spread on thick slices of toast as a snack or a light lunch.

FILLS TWO 450G/1LB JARS

1 Sterilize a 30cm/12in square of muslin (cheesecloth) by soaking it in boiling water. Drain and lay it over a large plate. Season the yogurt with salt and tip on to the centre of the muslin. Bring up the sides of the muslin and tie with string.

2 Hang the bag on a kitchen cupboard handle or suitable position where it can be suspended over a bowl to catch the whey. Leave for 2–3 days until the yogurt stops dripping.

3 Sterilize two 450g/1lb glass preserving jars by heating them in the oven at 150°C/300°F/Gas 2 for 15 minutes.

4 Mix the crushed dried chillies and herbs. Take teaspoonfuls of the cheese and roll into balls with your hands. Lower into the jars, sprinkling each layer with the herb mixture.

5 Pour the oil over the cheese until completely covered. Store in the refrigerator for up to 3 weeks. To serve, spoon the cheese out of the jars with a little of the flavoured olive oil and spread on slices of lightly toasted bread.

1 litre/1³⁄₄ pints/4 cups Greek sheep's (US strained plain) yogurt

10ml/2 tsp crushed dried chillies or chilli powder

30ml/2 tbsp chopped fresh herbs, such as rosemary, and thyme or oregano

FROM THE STORECUPBOARD

about 300ml/¹⁄₂ pint/ 1¹⁄₄ cups extra virgin olive oil, preferably garlic-flavoured

salt and ground black pepper

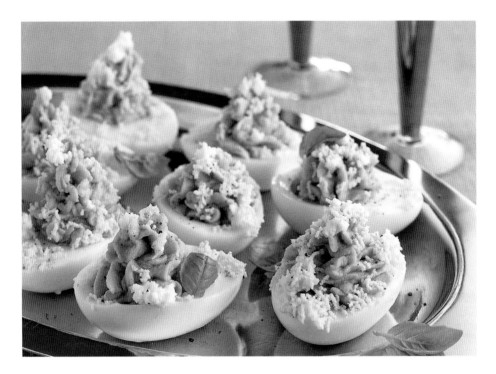

Eggs Mimosa

Mimosa describes the fine yellow and white grated egg in this dish, which looks very similar to the flower of the same name. The eggs taste delicious when garnished with black pepper and basil leaves. Grated egg yolk can also be used as a garnish for a variety of other savoury dishes, such as sauces, soups and rice dishes.

MAKES TWENTY

1 Reserve two of the hard-boiled eggs and halve the remainder. Carefully remove the yolks with a teaspoon and blend them with the avocados, garlic and oil, adding freshly ground black pepper and salt to taste. Spoon or pipe the mixture into the halved egg whites using a piping (pastry) bag with a 1cm/½in or pipe star nozzle.

2 Sieve the remaining egg whites and sprinkle over the filled eggs. Sieve the yolks and arrange on top. Arrange the filled egg halves on a serving platter.

12 eggs, hard-boiled and peeled

2 ripe avocados, halved and stoned (pitted)

1 garlic clove, crushed

FROM THE STORECUPBOARD

15ml/1 tbsp olive oil

Marinated Smoked Salmon with Lime and Coriander

If you want an elegant appetizer that is really quick to put together, then this is the one for you. The tangy lime juice and aromatic coriander leaves contrast perfectly with the delicate yet distinct flavour of the salmon. Serve with thinly sliced brown bread and butter.

SERVES SIX

200g/7oz smoked salmon

a handful of fresh coriander (cilantro) leaves

grated rind and juice of 1 lime

FROM THE STORECUPBOARD

15ml/1 tbsp extra virgin olive oil

ground black pepper

1 Using a sharp knife or pair of kitchen scissors, cut the salmon into strips and arrange on a serving platter.

2 Sprinkle the coriander leaves and lime rind over the salmon and squeeze over the lime juice. Drizzle with the olive oil and season with black pepper. Cover with clear film (plastic wrap) and chill for 1 hour before serving.

COOK'S TIP *You can make this dish up to 1 hour before serving. However, do not leave it for longer than this because the lime juice will discolour the salmon and spoil the look of the dish.*

Blinis with Caviar and Crème Fraîche

Classic Russian blinis are made with buckwheat flour, which gives them a very distinctive taste. They are available ready-made in large supermarkets and make a tasty first course or snack to serve with drinks, topped with crème fraîche and caviar. Caviar is expensive, but a very small amount goes a long way and the exquisite flavour is well worth it.

SERVES TWELVE

1 Put the crème fraîche in a bowl and season with salt and ground black pepper to taste. Place a teaspoonful of the mixture on each blini.

2 Top each spoonful of crème fraîche with a teaspoon of caviar and serve immediately.

200g/7oz/scant 1 cup crème fraîche

12 ready-made blinis

60ml/4 tbsp caviar

FROM THE STORECUPBOARD

salt and ground black pepper

VARIATION *For a stunning effect, top half the blinis with orange salmon or trout roe and the other half with black caviar.*

Marinated Anchovies

These tiny fish tend to lose their freshness very quickly so marinating them in garlic and lemon juice is the perfect way to enjoy them. It is probably the simplest way of preparing these fish, because it requires no cooking. Serve them scattered with parsley for a decorative finish.

SERVES FOUR

225g/8oz fresh anchovies, heads and tails removed, and split open along the belly

juice of 3 lemons

2 garlic cloves, finely chopped

FROM THE STORECUPBOARD

30ml/2 tbsp extra virgin olive oil

flaked sea salt

1 Turn the anchovies on to their bellies, and press down along their spine with your thumb. Using the tip of a small knife, carefully remove the backbones from the fish, and arrange the anchovies skin side down in a single layer on a large plate.

2 Squeeze two-thirds of the lemon juice over the fish and sprinkle them with the salt. Cover and leave to stand for 1–24 hours, basting occasionally with the juices, until the flesh is white and no longer translucent.

3 Transfer the anchovies to a serving plate and drizzle with the olive oil and the remaining lemon juice. Scatter the fish with the chopped garlic, then cover with clear film (plastic wrap) and chill until ready to serve.

Chilli Prawn Skewers

Try to get the freshest prawns you can for this recipe. If you buy whole prawns, you will need to remove the heads and shells, leaving the tail section intact. Serve with extra lime wedges.

SERVES FOUR

1 Place eight bamboo skewers in cold water and leave to soak for at least 10 minutes, then preheat the grill (broiler) to high.

2 Thread a prawn on to each skewer, then a lime wedge, then another prawn. Brush the sweet chilli sauce over the prawns and lime wedges.

3 Arrange the skewers on a baking sheet and grill (broil) for about 2 minutes, turning them once, until cooked through. Serve immediately with more chilli sauce for dipping.

16 giant raw prawns (shrimp), shelled with the tail section left intact

1 lime, cut into 8 wedges

60ml/4 tbsp sweet chilli sauce

Salt Cod and Potato Fritters

These little fritters are extremely easy to make and taste delicious. Serve them simply with a wedge of fresh lemon and some watercress or green salad. Offer a bowl of garlic mayonnaise for dipping.

MAKES ABOUT TWENTY FOUR

450g/1lb salt cod fillets

500g/1¹/₄lb floury potatoes, unpeeled

plain (all-purpose) flour, for coating

FROM THE STORECUPBOARD

vegetable oil, for deep-frying

salt and ground black pepper

1 Put the salt cod in a bowl, pour over cold water and leave to soak for 24 hours, changing the water every 6–8 hours. Drain, rinse and place in a pan of cold water. Slowly bring to the boil and simmer for 5 minutes, then drain and cool. When cooled, remove any bones and skin and mash the fish with a fork.

2 Cook the potatoes in their skins in a pan of salted boiling water for 20–25 minutes, or until just tender. Peel and mash.

3 Add the fish to the potatoes and mix well. Season to taste with salt and pepper. Break off walnut-sized pieces of the mixture and roll into balls. Place on a floured plate, cover and chill for 20–30 minutes. Roll each ball lightly in flour, dusting off any excess.

4 Heat enough oil for deep-frying in a large pan and fry the balls for 5–6 minutes, or until golden. Remove with a slotted spoon and drain on kitchen paper. Serve hot or warm.

Asian-style Crab Cakes

You could serve these patties as a simple supper, or an appetizer for eight people. Use a mixture of white and brown crab meat, as the dark adds a depth of flavour and texture. Serve with sweet chilli sauce.

MAKES SIXTEEN

450g/1lb/2²/₃ cups fresh crab meat, white and brown

15ml/1 tbsp grated fresh root ginger

15–30ml/1–2 tbsp plain (all-purpose) flour

FROM THE STORECUPBOARD

60ml/4 tbsp sunflower oil

salt and ground black pepper

1 Put the crab meat in a bowl and add the ginger, some salt and ground black pepper and the flour. Stir well until thoroughly mixed.

2 Using floured hands, divide the mixture into 16 equal-sized pieces and shape roughly into patties.

3 Heat the sunflower oil in a frying pan and add the patties, four at a time. Cook for 2–3 minutes on each side, until golden. Remove with a metal spatula and leave to drain on kitchen paper for a few minutes.

4 Keep the cooked crab cakes warm while you cook the remaining patties in the same way. Serve immediately.

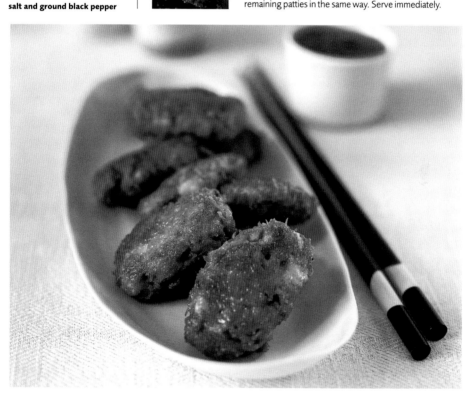

Crab and Water-chestnut Wontons

Serve these mouthwatering parcels as part of a dim sum selection or with a bowl of soy sauce for dipping as a first course for a Chinese meal. They are also perfect for serving as snacks with drinks at parties as they can be prepared in advance, then steamed at the last minute. Wonton wrappers are available in most Asian food stores and need to be soaked in cold water for a few minutes before use.

SERVES FOUR

1 Finely chop the water chestnuts, mix them with the crab meat and season with salt and pepper.

2 Place about a teaspoonful of the mixture along the centre of each wonton wrapper. Roll up the wontons, tucking in the sides as you go to form a neat parcel.

3 Fill the bottom part of a steamer with boiling water and place the wontons, seam down, in the steamer basket. Sit the basket on top of the water and cover with a tight-fitting lid. Steam for 5–8 minutes, or until the wonton wrappers are tender. Serve hot or warm.

50g/2oz/⅓ cup drained, canned water chestnuts

115g/4oz/generous ½ cup fresh or canned white crab meat

12 wonton wrappers

FROM THE STORECUPBOARD

salt and ground black pepper

Chilli-spiced Chicken Wings

These crispy chicken wings are always the perfect snack for parties and go incredibly well with cold beer! If you like your food spicy, use red hot cayenne pepper in place of the chilli powder. To make a milder version that will be a hit with kids, use sweet paprika in place of the chilli powder. Serve with a fresh tomato and onion salsa for dipping.

SERVES FOUR

12 chicken wings

30ml/2 tbsp plain (all-purpose) flour

15ml/1 tbsp chilli powder

FROM THE STORECUPBOARD

a pinch of salt

sunflower oil, for deep-frying

1 Pat the chicken wings dry with kitchen paper. Mix the flour, chilli powder and salt together and put into a large plastic bag. Add the chicken wings, seal the bag and shake well to coat the chicken wings in the seasoned flour.

2 Heat enough sunflower oil for deep-frying in a large pan and add the chicken wings, three or four at a time. Fry for 8–10 minutes, or until golden and cooked through.

3 Remove the chicken wings with a slotted spoon and drain on kitchen paper. Keep warm in a low oven. Repeat with the remaining chicken wings and serve hot.

Vietnamese Spring Rolls with Pork

You will often find these little spring rolls on the menu in Vietnamese restaurants, called "rice paper rolls". Serve with a chilli dipping sauce.

SERVES FOUR

1 Heat the oil in a frying pan and add the pork. Fry for 5–6 minutes, or until browned. Season well with salt and pepper, stir in the oyster sauce and remove from the heat. Leave to cool.

2 Lay the rice paper wrappers on a clean work surface. Place one-eighth of the pork mixture down one edge of each wrapper. Roll up the wrappers, tucking in the ends as you go to form a roll, and then serve immediately.

350g/12oz/1½ cups minced (ground) pork

30ml/2 tbsp oyster sauce

8 rice-paper roll wrappers

FROM THE STORECUPBOARD

15ml/1 tbsp sunflower oil

salt and ground black pepper

Curried Lamb Samosas

Filo pastry is perfect for making samosas. Once you've mastered folding them, you'll be amazed how quick they are to make.

MAKES TWELVE SAMOSAS

225g/8oz/1 cup minced (ground) lamb

30ml/2 tbsp mild curry paste

12 filo pastry sheets

FROM THE STORECUPBOARD

25g/1oz/2 tbsp butter

salt and ground black pepper

1 Heat a little of the butter in a large pan and add the lamb. Fry for 5–6 minutes, stirring occasionally until browned. Stir in the curry paste and cook for 1–2 minutes. Season and set aside. Preheat the oven to 190°C/375°F/Gas 5.

2 Melt the remaining butter in a pan. Cut the pastry sheets in half lengthways. Brush one strip of pastry with butter, then lay another strip on top and brush with more butter.

3 Place a spoonful of lamb in the corner of the strip and fold over to form a triangle at one end. Keep folding over in the same way to form a triangular package. Brush with butter and place on a baking sheet. Repeat using the remaining pastry. Bake for 15–20 minutes until golden. Serve hot.

Soups

SOUP IS ONE OF THE MOST VERSATILE DISHES AROUND AND
CAN BE SERVED AS AN ELEGANT APPETIZER OR A LIGHT
MEAL. FROM CHILLED SUMMER SOUPS TO WARMING
WINTER BROTHS, THEY ARE INCREDIBLY EASY TO MAKE
AND ONLY NEED A FEW INGREDIENTS AND FLAVOURINGS
TO CREATE FABULOUS, MOUTHWATERING RESULTS.

Avocado Soup

This delicious soup has a fresh, delicate flavour and a wonderful colour. For added zest, add a generous squeeze of lime juice or spoon 15ml/1 tbsp salsa into the soup just before serving. Choose ripe avocados for this soup – they should feel soft when gently pressed. Keep very firm avocados at room temperature for 3–4 days until they soften. To speed ripening, place in a brown paper bag.

SERVES FOUR

1 Cut the avocados in half, remove the peel and lift out the stones (pits). Chop the flesh coarsely and place it in a food processor with 45–60ml/3–4 tbsp of the sour cream. Process until smooth.

2 Heat the chicken stock in a pan. When it is hot, but still below simmering point, stir in the rest of the cream.

3 Gradually stir the avocado mixture into the hot stock. Heat but do not let the mixture approach boiling point.

4 Chop the coriander. Ladle the soup into individual heated bowls and sprinkle each portion with chopped coriander and black pepper. Serve immediately.

2 large ripe avocados

300ml/¹/₂ pint/1¹/₄ cups sour cream

1 litre/1³/₄ pints/4 cups well-flavoured chicken stock

small bunch of fresh coriander (cilantro)

FROM THE STORECUPBOARD

ground black pepper

Vichyssoise

This classic, chilled summer soup of leeks and potatoes was first created in the 1920s by Louis Diat, chef at the New York Ritz-Carlton. He named it after Vichy near his home in France. The soup can be sharpened with lemon juice, enriched with swirls of cream and garnished with chives.

SERVES FOUR TO SIX

1 Melt the unsalted butter in a heavy pan and cook the leeks, covered, for 15–20 minutes, until they are soft but not browned.

2 Add the potato chunks and cook over a low heat, uncovered, for a few minutes.

3 Stir in the stock or water and milk, with salt and pepper to taste. Bring to the boil, then reduce the heat and partly cover the pan. Simmer for 15 minutes, or until the potatoes are soft.

4 Cool, then process the soup until smooth in a blender or food processor. Sieve the soup into a bowl. Taste and adjust the seasoning and add a little iced water if the consistency of the soup seems too thick.

5 Chill the soup for at least 4 hours or until very cold. Taste the chilled soup for seasoning again before serving. Pour the soup into bowls and serve.

600g/1lb 5oz leeks, white parts only, thinly sliced

250g/9oz floury potatoes (such as King Edward or Maris Piper), peeled and cut into chunks

1.5 litres/2 ½ pints/6 ½ cups half and half light chicken stock or water and milk

FROM THE STORECUPBOARD

50g/2oz/¼ cup unsalted (sweet) butter

salt and ground black pepper

EXTRAS
To make a fabulous chilled leek and sorrel or watercress soup, add about 50g/2oz/1 cup shredded sorrel to the soup at the end of cooking. Finish and chill as in the main recipe, then serve the soup garnished with a little pile of finely shredded sorrel. The same quantity of watercress can also be used.

Avgolemono

The name of this popular Greek soup means egg and lemon, the two essential ingredients that produce a light, nourishing soup. The soup also contains orzo, which is Greek, rice-shaped pasta, but you can use any small shape. Serve the soup with thin slices of lightly toasted bread and add a garnish of very thin lemon slices for a pretty appearance on special occasions.

SERVES FOUR TO SIX

1 Pour the chicken stock into a large pan and bring to the boil. Add the orzo pasta or other small pasta shapes and cook for 5 minutes, or according to the packet instructions.

2 Beat the eggs until they are frothy, then add the lemon juice and a tablespoon of cold water. Slowly stir in a ladleful of the hot chicken stock, then add one or two more. Remove the pan from the heat, then pour in the egg mixture and stir well. Season to taste with salt and freshly ground black pepper and serve immediately. (Do not let the soup boil once the egg, lemon juice and stock mixture has been added, or it will curdle.)

**1.75 litres/3 pints/
7½ cups chicken stock**

**115g/4oz/½ cup
orzo pasta**

3 eggs

juice of 1 large lemon

FROM THE STORECUPBOARD

salt and ground black pepper

Simple Cream of Onion Soup

This wonderfully soothing soup has a deep, buttery flavour that is achieved with only a few ingredients and the minimum of fuss. It makes delicious comfort food on a cold day. Use home-made stock if you have it, or buy fresh stock for the best flavour. Crisp croûtons or chopped chives complement the smooth soup when sprinkled over just before serving.

SERVES FOUR

1kg/2¼lb yellow onions, sliced

1 litre/1¾ pints/4 cups good chicken or vegetable stock

150ml/¼ pint/⅔ cup double (heavy) cream

FROM THE STORECUPBOARD

115g/4oz/ ½ cup unsalted (sweet) butter

salt and ground black pepper

1 Melt 75g/3oz/6 tbsp of the unsalted butter in a large, heavy pan. Set about 200g/7oz of the onions aside and add the rest to the pan. Stir to coat in the butter, then cover and cook very gently for about 30 minutes. The onions should be very soft and tender, but not browned.

2 Add the chicken or vegetable stock, 5ml/1 tsp salt and freshly ground black pepper to taste. Bring to the boil, reduce the heat and simmer for 5 minutes, then remove from the heat.

3 Leave the soup to cool, then process it in a blender or food processor. Return the soup to the rinsed pan.

4 Meanwhile, melt the remaining butter in another pan and cook the remaining onions over a low heat, covered, until soft but not browned. Uncover and continue to cook the onions gently until they turn golden yellow.

5 Add the cream to the soup and reheat it gently until hot, but do not allow it to boil. Taste and adjust the seasoning. Add the buttery onions and stir for 1–2 minutes, then ladle the soup into bowls. Serve the soup immediately.

Cappelletti in Broth

This soup is traditionally served in northern Italy on Santo Stefano (St Stephen's Day, the day after Christmas) and on New Year's Day as a welcome light change from all the special celebration food. Cappelletti are little stuffed pasta shapes that resemble hats.

SERVES FOUR

1 Pour the chicken stock into a large pan and bring to the boil. Drop in the pasta.

2 Stir well and bring back to the boil. Lower the heat to a simmer and cook according to the instructions on the packet, until the pasta is *al dente*, that is, tender but still firm to the bite.

3 Swirl in the finely chopped fresh flat leaf parsley, if using, then taste and adjust the seasoning, if necessary. Ladle into four warmed soup plates, then sprinkle with the freshly grated Parmesan cheese and serve immediately.

**1.2 litres/2 pints/
5 cups chicken stock**

**90–115g/3½–4oz/
1 cup fresh or dried
cappelletti**

**about 45ml/3 tbsp
finely chopped
fresh flat leaf
parsley (optional)**

**about 30ml/2 tbsp
freshly grated
Parmesan cheese**

COOK'S TIP *If you don't have home-made stock use two 300g/11oz cans of condensed beef consommé, adding water as instructed, or chilled commercial stock.*

Tiny Pasta in Broth

This Italian soup is ideal for a light supper served with ciabatta bread and also makes a delicious first course for an *al fresco* supper. A wide variety of different types of *pastina* or soup pasta are available including stellette (stars), anellini (tiny thin rounds), risoni (rice-shaped) and farfalline (little butterflies). Choose just one shape or a combination of different varieties for an interesting result.

SERVES FOUR

**1.2 litres/2 pints/
5 cups beef stock**

**75g/3oz/¾ cup dried
tiny soup pasta**

**2 pieces bottled
roasted red (bell)
pepper, about 50g/2oz**

**coarsely shaved
Parmesan cheese**

1 Bring the beef stock to the boil in a large pan. Drop in the dried soup pasta. Stir well and bring the stock back to the boil.

2 Reduce the heat so that the soup simmers and cook for 7–8 minutes, or according to the packet instructions, until the pasta is *al dente*, that is, tender but still firm to the bite.

3 Drain the pieces of roasted pepper and dice them finely. Place them in the base of four warmed soup plates. Taste the soup for seasoning before ladling it into the soup plates. Serve immediately, topped with shavings of Parmesan.

Potato and Roasted Garlic Broth

Roasted garlic takes on a mellow, sweet flavour that is subtle, not overpowering, in this delicious vegetarian soup. Choose floury potatoes for this soup, such as Maris Piper, Estima, Cara or King Edward – they will give the soup a delicious velvety texture. Serve the broth piping hot with melted Cheddar or Gruyère cheese on French bread, as the perfect winter warmer.

SERVES FOUR

1 Preheat the oven to 190°C/375°F/Gas 5. Place the unpeeled garlic bulbs or bulb in a small roasting pan and bake for 30 minutes until soft in the centre.

2 Meanwhile, par-boil the potatoes in a large pan of boiling water for 10 minutes.

3 Simmer the stock in another pan for 5 minutes. Drain the potatoes and add them to the stock.

4 Squeeze the garlic pulp into the soup, reserving a few whole cloves and stir. Simmer for 15 minutes and serve topped with whole garlic cloves and parsley.

2 small or 1 large whole head of garlic (about 20 cloves)

4 medium potatoes (about 500g/1¼lb in total), diced

1.75 litres/3 pints/ 7½ cups good-quality hot vegetable stock

chopped flat leaf parsley, to garnish

Winter Squash Soup with Tomato Salsa

Creamy butternut squash makes good soup with very few additional ingredients. Select a really good bought salsa for this soup and add a sprinkling of chopped fresh oregano or marjoram as a garnish.

SERVES FOUR TO FIVE

1 butternut squash

2 onions, chopped

60–120ml/4–8 tbsp tomato salsa

FROM THE STORECUPBOARD

75ml/5 tbsp garlic-flavoured olive oil

1 Preheat the oven to 220°C/425°F/Gas 7. Halve and seed the butternut squash and place it on a baking sheet and brush with some of the oil and roast for 25 minutes. Reduce the temperature to 190°C/375°F/Gas 5 and cook for 20–25 minutes more, or until it is tender.

2 Heat the remaining oil in a large, heavy pan and cook the chopped onions over a low heat for about 10 minutes, or until softened.

3 Meanwhile, scoop the squash out of its skin, adding it to the pan. Pour in 1.2 litres/2 pints/5 cups water and stir in 5ml/1 tsp salt and plenty of black pepper. Bring to the boil, cover and simmer for 10 minutes.

4 Cool the soup slightly, then process it in a blender or food processor to a smooth purée. Alternatively, press the soup through a fine sieve with the back of a spoon. Reheat without boiling, then ladle it into warmed bowls. Top each serving with a spoonful of salsa and serve.

Butter Bean, Sun-dried Tomato and Pesto Soup

This soup is so quick and easy to make: the key is to use a good-quality home-made or bought fresh stock for the best result. Using plenty of pesto and sun-dried tomato purée (paste) gives it a rich, minestrone-like flavour. As an alternative to butter beans, haricot (navy) or cannellini beans will make good substitutes.

SERVES FOUR

1 Put the stock in a pan with the butter beans and bring just to the boil. Reduce the heat and stir in the tomato purée and pesto. Cook gently for 5 minutes.

2 Transfer six ladlefuls of the soup to a blender or food processor, scooping up plenty of the beans. Process until smooth, then return the purée to the pan.

3 Heat gently, stirring frequently, for 5 minutes. Ladle into four warmed soup bowls and serve with warm crusty bread or breadsticks.

900ml/1½ pints/ 3¾ cups chicken or vegetable stock

2 x 400g/14oz cans butter (lima) beans, drained and rinsed

60ml/4 tbsp sun-dried tomato purée (paste)

75ml/5 tbsp pesto

Stilton and Watercress Soup

A good creamy Stilton and plenty of peppery watercress bring maximum flavour to this rich, smooth soup, which is superlative in small portions. Rocket (arugula) can be used as an alternative to watercress – both leaves are an excellent source of iron. When choosing any salad leaves, look for crisp, fresh leaves and reject any wilted or discoloured greens.

SERVES FOUR TO SIX

1 Pour the stock into a pan and bring almost to the boil. Remove and discard any very large stalks from the watercress. Add the watercress to the pan and simmer gently for 2–3 minutes, until tender.

600ml/1 pint/2½ cups chicken or vegetable stock

225g/8oz watercress

2 Crumble the cheese into the pan and simmer for 1 minute more, until the cheese has started to melt. Process the soup in a blender or food processor, in batches if necessary, until very smooth. Return the soup to the pan.

150g/5oz Stilton or other blue cheese

150ml/¼ pint/⅔ cup single (light) cream

3 Stir in the cream and check the seasoning. The soup will probably not need any extra salt, as the blue cheese is already quite salty. Heat the soup gently, without boiling, then ladle it into warm bowls.

Light Lunches

WHAT COULD BE BETTER THAN A TASTY MEAL IN THE
MIDDLE OF THE DAY THAT HAS TAKEN ONLY MINUTES
TO PREPARE AND NEEDS JUST THREE OR FOUR
INGREDIENTS? WHATEVER YOU'RE IN THE MOOD FOR,
WHETHER IT'S A HEALTHY SALAD, A GOURMET
SANDWICH OR A BOWL OF PASTA, THERE'S SOMETHING
HERE FOR YOU. THE RECIPES ARE ALL SO SIMPLE THAT
YOU CAN EASILY REDUCE OR INCREASE THE
PROPORTIONS TO MAKE A QUICK LUNCH FOR ONE,
OR A HEALTHY MEAL FOR THE WHOLE FAMILY.

Baked Eggs with Creamy Leeks

This simple but elegant appetizer is perfect for last-minute entertaining or quick dining. Garnish the baked eggs with crisp, fried fresh sage leaves and serve with warm, fresh crusty bread for a special meal. Small- to medium-sized leeks (less than 2.5cm/1in in diameter) are best for this dish as they have the most tender flavour and only require a short cooking time.

SERVES FOUR

1 Preheat the oven to 190°C/375°F/Gas 5. Generously butter the base and sides of four ramekins.

2 Melt the butter in a frying pan and cook the leeks over a medium heat, stirring frequently, for 3–5 minutes, until softened and translucent, but not browned.

3 Add 45ml/3 tbsp of the cream and cook over a low heat for 5 minutes, until the leeks are very soft and the cream has thickened a little. Season to taste.

4 Place the ramekins in a small roasting pan and divide the leeks among them. Break an egg into each, spoon over the remaining cream and season.

5 Pour boiling water into the roasting pan to come about halfway up the sides of the ramekins. Transfer the pan to the oven and bake in the preheated oven for about 10 minutes, until just set. Serve piping hot.

225g/8oz small leeks, thinly sliced

75–90ml/5–6 tbsp whipping cream

4 small–medium (US medium–large) eggs

FROM THE STORECUPBOARD

15g/¹⁄₂oz/1 tbsp butter, plus extra for greasing

salt and ground black pepper

Red Onion and Olive Pissaladière

For a taste of the Mediterranean, try this French-style pizza – it makes a delicious and easy snack. Cook the sliced red onions slowly until they are caramelized and sweet before piling them into the pastry cases. To prepare the recipe in advance, pile the cooled onions on to the pastry round and chill the pissaladière until you are ready to bake it.

SERVES SIX

1 Preheat the oven to 220°C/425°F/Gas 7. Heat the oil in a large, heavy frying pan and cook the onions gently, stirring frequently, for 15–20 minutes, until they are soft and golden. Season to taste.

2 Roll out the pastry thinly on a floured surface. Cut out a 33cm/13in round and transfer it to a lightly dampened baking sheet.

3 Spread the onions over the pastry in an even layer to within 1cm/½in of the edge. Sprinkle the olives on top. Bake the tart for 20–25 minutes, until the pastry is risen and deep golden. Cut into wedges and serve warm.

500g/1¼lb small red onions, thinly sliced

500g/1¼lb puff pastry, thawed if frozen

75g/3oz/¾ cup small pitted black olives

FROM THE STORECUPBOARD

75ml/5 tbsp extra virgin olive oil

Figs with Prosciutto and Roquefort

Fresh figs are a delicious treat, whether you choose dark purple, yellowy green or green-skinned varieties. When they are ripe, you can split them open with your fingers to reveal the soft, sweet flesh full of edible seeds. In this easy, stylish dish figs and honey balance the richness of the ham and cheese. Serve with warm bread for a simple appetizer before any rich main course.

SERVES FOUR

1 Preheat the grill (broiler). Quarter the figs and place on a foil-lined grill rack. Tear each slice of prosciutto into two or three pieces and crumple them up on the foil beside the figs. Brush the figs with 15ml/1 tbsp of the clear honey and cook under the grill until lightly browned.

2 Crumble the Roquefort cheese and divide among four plates, setting it to one side. Add the honey-grilled figs and ham and pour over any cooking juices caught on the foil. Drizzle the remaining honey over the figs, ham and cheese, and serve seasoned with plenty of freshly ground black pepper.

8 fresh figs

75g/3oz prosciutto

**45ml/3 tbsp
clear honey**

75g/3oz Roquefort cheese

FROM THE STORECUPBOARD

ground black pepper

Pea and Mint Omelette

Serve this deliciously light omelette with crusty bread and a green salad for a fresh and tasty lunch. If you're making the omelette for a summer lunch when peas are in season, use freshly shelled peas instead of frozen ones.

SERVES TWO

1 Cook the peas in a large pan of salted boiling water for 3–4 minutes until tender. Drain well and set aside. Break the eggs into a large bowl and beat with a fork. Season well with salt and pepper, then stir in the peas and chopped mint.

2 Heat the butter in a medium frying pan until foamy. Pour in the egg mixture and cook over a medium heat for 3–4 minutes, drawing in the cooked egg from the edges from time to time, until the mixture is nearly set.

3 Finish off cooking the omelette under a hot grill (broiler) until set and golden. Carefully fold the omelette over, cut it in half and serve immediately.

50g/2oz/¹⁄₂ cup frozen peas

4 eggs

30ml/2 tbsp chopped fresh mint

FROM THE STORECUPBOARD

knob (pat) of butter

salt and ground black pepper

Warm Penne with Fresh Tomatoes and Basil

This dish is fresh, healthy and ready in minutes. It is the perfect way to use up a glut of ripe summer tomatoes.

SERVES FOUR

500g/1¼lb dried penne

5 very ripe plum tomatoes

1 small bunch of fresh basil

FROM THE STORECUPBOARD

60ml/4 tbsp extra virgin olive oil

salt and ground black pepper

1 Cook the pasta in plenty of salted, boiling water according to the instructions on the packet. Meanwhile, roughly chop the tomatoes, pull the basil leaves from their stems and tear up the leaves.

2 Drain the pasta thoroughly and toss with the tomatoes, basil and olive oil. Season with salt and freshly ground black pepper and serve immediately.

COOK'S TIP

If you cannot find ripe tomatoes, roast them to bring out their flavour. Put the tomatoes in a roasting pan, drizzle with oil and roast at 190°C/375°F/ Gas 5 for 20 minutes, then mash roughly.

Broccoli and Chilli Spaghetti

The contrast between the hot chilli and the mild broccoli is delicious and goes perfectly with spaghetti. To add extra flavour and texture, sprinkle the spaghetti and broccoli with toasted pine nuts and grated or shaved Parmesan cheese just before serving.

SERVES FOUR

350g/12oz dried spaghetti

450g/1lb broccoli, cut into small florets

1 fat red chilli, seeded and finely chopped

FROM THE STORECUPBOARD

150ml/¼ pint/⅔ cup garlic-infused olive oil

salt and ground black pepper

1 Bring a large pan of lightly salted water to the boil. Add the spaghetti and broccoli and cook for 8–10 minutes, until both are tender. Drain thoroughly.

2 Using the back of a fork crush the broccoli roughly, taking care not to mash the spaghetti strands at the same time.

3 Meanwhile, warm the oil and finely chopped chilli in a small pan over a low heat and cook very gently for 5 minutes.

4 Pour the chilli and oil over the spaghetti and broccoli and toss together to combine. Season to taste. Divide between four warmed bowls and serve immediately.

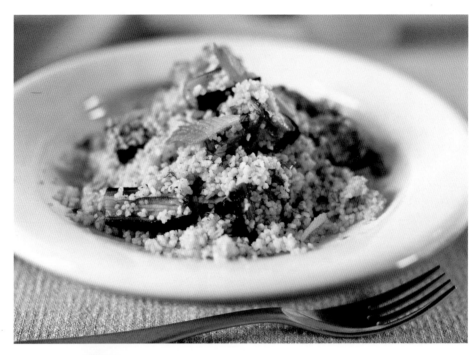

Grilled Aubergine, Mint and Couscous Salad

Packets of flavoured couscous are available in most supermarkets – you can use whichever you like, but garlic and coriander is particularly good for this recipe. Serve with a crisp green salad.

SERVES TWO

1 large aubergine (eggplant)

115g/4oz packet garlic-and-coriander (cilantro) flavoured couscous

30ml/2 tbsp chopped fresh mint

FROM THE STORECUPBOARD

30ml/2 tbsp olive oil

salt and ground black pepper

1 Preheat the grill (broiler) to high. Cut the aubergine into large chunky pieces and toss them with the olive oil. Season with salt and pepper to taste and spread the aubergine pieces on a non-stick baking sheet. Grill for 5–6 minutes, turning occasionally, until golden brown.

2 Meanwhile, prepare the couscous according to the instructions on the packet. Stir the grilled aubergine and chopped mint into the couscous, toss thoroughly and serve immediately.

Marinated Courgette and Flageolet Bean Salad

Serve this healthy salad as a light lunch or as an accompaniment to meat and chicken dishes. It has a wonderful bright green colour and is perfect for a summer lunch.

SERVES FOUR

2 courgettes (zucchini), halved lengthways and sliced

400g/14oz can flageolet beans, drained and rinsed

grated rind and juice of 1 unwaxed lemon

FROM THE STORECUPBOARD

45ml/3 tbsp garlic-infused olive oil

salt and ground black pepper

1 Cook the courgettes in boiling salted water for 2–3 minutes, or until just tender. Drain well and refresh under cold running water.

2 Transfer the drained courgettes into a bowl with the beans and stir in the oil, lemon rind and juice and some salt and pepper. Chill for 30 minutes before serving.

VARIATION

To add extra flavour to the salad add 30ml/2 tbsp chopped fresh herbs before chilling. Basil and mint both have fresh, distinctive flavours that will work very well.

Roasted Pepper and Hummus Wrap

Wraps make a tasty change to sandwiches and have the bonus that they can be made a few hours in advance without going soggy in the way that bread sandwiches often can. You can introduce all kinds of variation to this basic combination. Try using roasted aubergine (eggplant) in place of the red peppers, or guacamole in place of the hummus. As well as plain flour tortillas, you can also buy flavoured tortillas from most supermarkets.

SERVES TWO

1 large red (bell) pepper, halved and seeded

4 tbsp hummus

2 soft flour tortillas

FROM THE STORECUPBOARD

15ml/1 tbsp olive oil

salt and ground black pepper

1 Preheat the grill (broiler) to high. Brush the pepper halves with the oil and place cut side down on a baking sheet. Grill for 5 minutes, until charred. Put the pepper halves in a sealed plastic bag and leave to cool.

2 When cooled, remove the peppers from the bag and carefully peel away the charred skin and discard. Thinly slice the flesh using a sharp knife.

3 Spread the hummus over the tortillas in a thin, even layer and top with the roasted pepper slices. Season with salt and plenty of ground black pepper, then roll them up and cut in half to serve.

Focaccia with Sardines and Roast Tomatoes

Fresh sardines not only have a lovely flavour and texture, but they are also cheap to buy – so make an economical yet utterly delicious lunch.

SERVES FOUR

1 Preheat the oven to 190°C/375°F/Gas 5. Put the cherry tomatoes in a small roasting pan and drizzle 30ml/2 tbsp of the oil over the top. Season with salt and pepper and roast for 10–15 minutes, or until tender and slightly charred. Remove from the oven and set aside.

20 cherry tomatoes

12 fresh sardine fillets

1 focaccia loaf

FROM THE STORECUPBOARD

45ml/3 tbsp herb-infused olive oil

salt and ground black pepper

2 Preheat the grill (broiler) to high. Brush the sardine fillets with the remaining oil and lay them on a baking sheet. Grill for 4–5 minutes on each side, until cooked through.

3 Split the focaccia in half horizontally and cut each piece in half to give four equal pieces. Toast the cut side under the grill until golden. Top with the sardines and tomatoes and an extra drizzle of oil. Season with black pepper then serve.

Jansson's Temptation

This traditional Swedish gratin is utterly moreish. The name probably does not refer to a specific Jansson but means "everyone's temptation", as Jansson is a common Swedish surname.

SERVES FOUR TO SIX

1 Preheat the oven to 200°C/400°F/Gas 6. Cut the potatoes into thin slices, then cut the slices into matchstick strips. Sprinkle half of them in the base of a greased shallow 1.5 litre/2½ pint/6¼ cup baking dish.

2 Lay half of the onions on top of the potatoes, and season with black pepper. Lay the anchovies on top of the onions, then add the remaining onions and potatoes.

3 Mix the cream with 30ml/2 tbsp cold water and pour over the potatoes and onions. Cover with foil and bake for 1 hour, then reduce the oven temperature to 180°C/350°F/Gas 4 and uncover the dish. Bake for a further 40–50 minutes, or until the potatoes are golden and tender when tested with a knife.

900g/2lb potatoes

2 large, sweet onions, sliced

2 x 50g/2oz cans anchovies in olive oil, drained

450ml/¾ pint/scant 2 cups whipping cream or half and half double (heavy) and single (light) cream

Crisp Fried Whitebait

This must be one of the simplest of all classic fish dishes and it is absolutely delicious with lemon wedges and thinly sliced brown bread and butter. If you prefer, serve the whitebait with a simple lemon and herb dip – mix 150ml/¼ pint/⅔ cup natural (plain) yogurt with the rind of one lemon and 45ml/ 3 tbsp chopped fresh herbs. Serve chilled.

SERVES FOUR

150ml/¹⁄₄ pint/²⁄₃ cup milk

115g/4oz/1 cup plain (all-purpose) flour

450g/1lb whitebait

FROM THE STORECUPBOARD

oil, for deep-frying

COOK'S TIP
Most whitebait are sold frozen. Thaw them before use and dry them thoroughly on kitchen paper before flouring.

1 Heat the oil in a large pan or deep-fryer. Put the milk in a shallow bowl and spoon the flour into a paper bag. Season the flour well with salt and pepper.

2 Dip a handful of the whitebait into the bowl of milk, drain them well, then put them into the paper bag. Shake to coat them evenly in the seasoned flour, then transfer to a plate. Repeat until all the fish have been coated. Don't add too many whitebait at once to the bag, or they will stick together.

3 Heat the oil for deep-frying to 190°C/375°F or until a cube of stale bread, dropped into the oil, browns in about 20 seconds. Add a batch of whitebait, preferably in a frying basket, and deep-fry for 2–3 minutes, until crisp and golden brown. Drain and keep hot while you cook the rest. Serve very hot.

Seared Tuna Niçoise

A traditional tuna Niçoise consists of tuna, olives, green beans, potatoes and eggs, but this modern version using fresh tuna is a simplified one – although just as tasty. Serve it with a green salad.

SERVES FOUR

1 Put the tuna steaks in a shallow non-metallic dish. Mix the oil and vinegar together and season with salt and pepper.

2 Pour the mixture over the tuna steaks and turn them to coat in the marinade. Cover and chill for up to 1 hour.

3 Heat a griddle pan until smoking hot. Remove the tuna steaks from the marinade and lay them on the griddle pan. Cook for 2–3 minutes on each side, so that they are still pink in the centre. Remove from the pan and set aside.

4 Meanwhile, cook the eggs in a pan of boiling water for 5–6 minutes, then cool under cold running water. Shell the eggs and cut in half lengthways.

5 Pour the marinade on to the griddle pan and cook until it starts to bubble. Divide the tuna steaks among four serving plates and top each with half an egg. Drizzle the marinade over the top and serve immediately.

**4 tuna steaks, about 150g/
5oz each**

30ml/2 tbsp sherry vinegar

2 eggs

FROM THE STORECUPBOARD

**45ml/3 tbsp garlic-infused
olive oil**

salt and ground black pepper

Creamy Parmesan-Baked Eggs

These eggs are delicious as they are but can easily be "dressed up" with additional ingredients. Try adding chopped smoked ham and parsley before you cook them. Serve with thinly sliced bread and butter.

SERVES TWO

1 Preheat the oven to 160°C/325°F/Gas 3. Break the eggs into four ramekin dishes and spoon the cream over the top. Season with salt and ground black pepper and sprinkle the Parmesan cheese on top.

2 Bake the eggs for about 10 minutes, or until they are just set, and serve immediately.

COOK'S TIPS
Serve these rich and creamy eggs with a leafy green salad flavoured with fresh tarragon. For the best results, be sure to serve the eggs as soon as they are cooked.

4 large (US extra large) eggs

**60ml/4 tbsp double (heavy)
cream**

**30ml/2 tbsp freshly grated
Parmesan cheese**

FROM THE STORECUPBOARD

salt and ground black pepper

Toasted Sourdough with Goat's Cheese

Choose a good-quality, firm goat's cheese for this recipe because it needs to keep its shape during cooking. Serve with fresh rocket leaves.

SERVES TWO

2 thick sourdough bread slices

30ml/2 tbsp chilli jam

2 firm goat's cheese slices, about 90g/3½oz each

FROM THE STORECUPBOARD

30ml/2 tbsp garlic-infused olive oil

ground black pepper

1 Preheat the grill (broiler) to high. Brush the sourdough bread on both sides with the oil, and grill (broil) one side until golden. Spread the un-toasted side of each slice with the chilli jam and top with the goat's cheese.

2 Return the bread to the grill and cook for 3–4 minutes, or until the cheese is beginning to melt and turn golden and bubbling. Season with ground black pepper and serve immediately with rocket (arugula) leaves.

Steak and Blue Cheese Sandwiches

Many people like their rib eye steaks cooked quite rare in the centre, but how you like yours is up to you. Add a couple of minutes to the cooking time if you prefer them more well done.

SERVES TWO

1 Bake the ciabatta according to the instructions on the packet. Remove from the oven and leave to rest for a few minutes. Cut the loaf in half and split each half horizontally.

2 Heat a griddle pan until hot. Brush the steaks with the olive oil and lay them on the griddle pan. Cook for 2–3 minutes on each side, depending on the thickness of the steaks.

3 Remove the steaks from the pan and set aside to rest for a few minutes. Cut them in half and place in the sandwiches with the cheese. Season with salt and pepper, and serve.

1 ready-to-bake ciabatta bread

2 rib eye steaks, about 200g/7oz each

115g/4oz Gorgonzola cheese, sliced

FROM THE STORECUPBOARD

15ml/1 tbsp olive oil

salt and ground black pepper

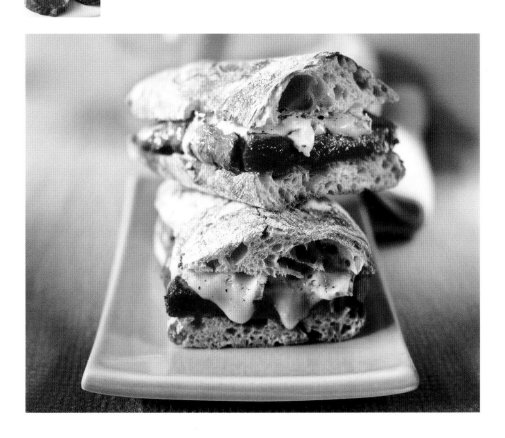

Spicy Chorizo Sausage and Spring Onion Hash

Use up leftover boiled potatoes for this recipe. Fresh chorizo sausages are available from good butchers and Spanish delis.

SERVES FOUR

1 Heat a large frying pan over a medium heat and add the sausages. Cook for 8–10 minutes, turning occasionally, until cooked through. Remove from the pan and set aside.

2 Add the olive oil to the sausage fat in the pan and then add the potatoes. Cook over a low heat for 5–8 minutes, turning occasionally until golden. Meanwhile, cut the sausages into bite-size chunks and add to the pan.

3 Add the spring onions to the pan and cook for a couple more minutes, until they are piping hot. Season with salt and pepper, and serve immediately.

450g/1lb fresh chorizo sausages

450g/1lb cooked potatoes, diced

1 bunch of spring onions (scallions), sliced

FROM THE STORECUPBOARD

15ml/1 tbsp olive oil

salt and ground black pepper

Baked Sweet Potatoes with Leeks and Gorgonzola

This dish tastes wonderful and looks stunning if you buy the beautiful orange-fleshed sweet potatoes.

SERVES FOUR

4 large sweet potatoes, scrubbed

2 large leeks, washed and sliced

115g/4oz Gorgonzola cheese, sliced

FROM THE STORECUPBOARD

30ml/2 tbsp olive oil

salt and ground black pepper

1 Preheat the oven to 190°C/375°F/Gas 5. Dry the sweet potatoes with kitchen paper and rub them all over with 15ml/1 tbsp of the oil. Place them on a baking sheet and sprinkle with salt. Bake for 1 hour, or until tender.

2 Meanwhile, heat the remaining oil in a frying pan and add the sliced leeks. Cook for 3–4 minutes, or until softened and just beginning to turn golden.

3 Cut the potatoes in half lengthways and place them cut side up on the baking sheet. Top with the cooked leeks and season.

4 Lay the cheese slices on top and grill (broil) under a hot grill for 2–3 minutes, until the cheese is bubbling. Serve immediately.

Fish and Shellfish

THE DELICATE TASTE OF FISH AND SHELLFISH IS PERFECTLY
SUITED TO SUBTLE, SIMPLE FLAVOURINGS SUCH AS FRESH
HERBS, CITRUS JUICE, SUCCULENT TOMATOES OR SMOKY
BACON. THE FABULOUS RECIPES IN THIS CHAPTER MAKE
THE MOST OF SIMPLE, SEASONAL INGREDIENTS TO ACHIEVE
TRULY WONDERFUL DISHES.

Mussels in White Wine

This simple yet delicious dish is perfect for informal entertaining. Serve with a big bowl of chips (US fries) to share. To make a variation, cook the mussels in beer instead of wine – they taste fantastic.

SERVES TWO

300ml/¹/₂ pint/1¹/₄ cups dry white wine

1kg/2¹/₄lb mussels, cleaned

45ml/3 tbsp chopped fresh parsley

FROM THE STORECUPBOARD

25g/1oz/2 tbsp butter

salt and ground black pepper

1 Heat the butter in a large pan until foaming, then pour in the wine. Bring to the boil. Discard any open mussels that do not close when sharply tapped, and add the remaining ones to the pan. Cover with a tight-fitting lid and cook over a medium heat for 4–5 minutes, shaking the pan every now and then. By this time, all the mussels should have opened. Discard any that are still closed.

2 Line a large sieve with kitchen paper and strain the mussels and their liquid through it. Transfer the mussels to warmed serving bowls. Pour the liquid into a small pan and bring to the boil. Season with salt and pepper and stir in the parsley. Pour over the mussels and serve immediately.

Crab and Cucumber Wraps

This dish is a modern twist on the ever-popular Chinese classic, crispy Peking duck with pancakes. In this quick and easy version, crisp, refreshing cucumber and full-flavoured dressed crab are delicious with spicy-sweet hoisin sauce in warm tortilla wraps. Serve the wraps as an appetizer for four people, or as a main course for two.

SERVES TWO

1 Cut the cucumber into small even-sized batons. Scoop the dressed crab into a small mixing bowl, add a little freshly ground black pepper and mix lightly to combine.

2 Heat the tortillas gently, one at a time, in a heavy frying pan until they begin to colour on each side.

3 Spread a tortilla with 30ml/2 tbsp hoisin sauce, then sprinkle with one-quarter of the cucumber. Arrange one-quarter of the seasoned crab meat down the centre of each tortilla and roll up. Repeat with the remaining ingredients. Serve immediately.

$^1/_2$ **cucumber**

1 medium dressed crab

4 small wheat tortillas

120ml/8 tbsp hoisin sauce

FROM THE STORECUPBOARD

ground black pepper

Scallops with Fennel and Bacon

This dish is a delicious combination of succulent scallops and crispy bacon, served on a bed of tender fennel and melting mascarpone. If you can't get large scallops (known as king scallops), buy the smaller queen scallops and serve a dozen per person. If you buy scallops in the shell, wash and keep the pretty fan-shaped shells to serve a range of fish dishes in.

SERVES TWO

1 Trim, halve and slice the fennel, reserving and chopping any feathery tops. Blanch the slices in boiling water for about 3 minutes, until softened, then drain.

2 Preheat the grill (broiler) to moderate. Place the fennel in a shallow flameproof dish. Dot with the mascarpone and grill (broil) for about 5 minutes, until the cheese has melted and the fennel is lightly browned.

3 Meanwhile, pat the scallops dry on kitchen paper and season lightly. Cook the bacon in a large, heavy frying pan, until crisp and golden, turning once. Drain and keep warm. Fry the scallops in the bacon fat for 1–2 minutes on each side, until cooked through.

4 Transfer the fennel to serving plates and crumble or snip the bacon into bite size pieces over the top. Pile the scallops on the bacon and sprinkle with any reserved fennel tops.

2 small fennel bulbs

130g/4¹/₂oz/ generous ¹/₂ cup mascarpone cheese

8 large scallops, shelled

75g/3oz thin smoked streaky (fatty) bacon rashers (strips)

Prawn and New Potato Stew

New potatoes with plenty of flavour, such as Jersey Royals, Maris Piper or Nicola, are essential for this effortless stew. Use a good quality jar of tomato and chilli sauce; there are now plenty available in the supermarkets. For a really easy supper dish, serve with warm, crusty bread to mop up the delicious sauce, and a mixed green salad.

SERVES FOUR

675g/1¹/₂lb small new potatoes, scrubbed

15g/¹/₂oz/¹/₂ cup fresh coriander (cilantro)

350g/12oz jar tomato and chilli sauce

300g/11oz cooked peeled prawns (shrimp), thawed and drained if frozen

1 Cook the potatoes in boiling water for 15 minutes, until tender. Drain and return to the pan.

2 Finely chop half the coriander and add to the pan with the tomato and chilli sauce and 90ml/6 tbsp water. Bring to the boil, reduce the heat, cover and simmer gently for 5 minutes.

3 Stir in the prawns and heat briefly until they are warmed through. Do not overheat the prawns or they will quickly shrivel, becoming tough and tasteless. Spoon into shallow bowls and serve sprinkled with the remaining coriander, torn into pieces.

Haddock with Fennel Butter

Fresh fish tastes fabulous cooked in a simple herb butter. Here the liquorice flavour of fennel complements the haddock beautifully to make a simple dish ideal for a dinner party. If you can buy only small haddock fillets, fold them in half before baking, or use cod as an alternative. Serve tiny new potatoes and a herb salad with the fish to make a light, summery main course.

SERVES FOUR

1 Preheat the oven to 220°C/425°F/Gas 7. Season the fish on both sides with salt and pepper. Melt one-quarter of the butter in a frying pan, preferably non-stick, and cook the fish over a medium heat briefly on both sides.

2 Transfer the fish to a shallow ovenproof dish. Cut four wafer-thin slices from the lemon and squeeze the juice from the remainder over the fish. Place the lemon slices on top and then bake for 15–20 minutes, or until the fish is cooked.

3 Meanwhile, melt the remaining butter in the frying pan and add the fennel and a little seasoning.

4 Transfer the cooked fish to plates and pour the cooking juices into the herb butter. Heat gently for a few seconds, then pour the herb butter over the fish. Serve immediately.

675g/1¹/₂lb haddock fillet, skinned and cut into 4 portions

1 lemon

45ml/3 tbsp coarsely chopped fennel

FROM THE STORECUPBOARD

50g/2oz/¹/₄ cup butter

salt and ground black pepper

Baked Salmon with Caraway Seeds

This classic Czech way of cooking salmon is very easy and gives excellent results. The fish cooks in its own juices, taking on the lovely warm flavour of the caraway seeds. Serve sprinkled with flat leaf parsley and wedges of lemon for squeezing over the fish.

SERVES FOUR

1.8kg/4lb whole salmon, cleaned

2.5–5ml/¹/₂–1 tsp caraway seeds

45ml/3 tbsp lemon juice

FROM THE STORECUPBOARD

115g/4oz/¹/₂ cup butter, melted

1 Preheat the oven to 180°C/350°F/Gas 4. Scale the salmon, remove the head and tail and slice off the fins with a sharp knife, then cut the fish in half lengthways.

2 Place the salmon, skin-side down, in a lightly greased roasting pan. Brush with the melted butter. Season with salt and pepper, sprinkle over the caraway seeds and drizzle with lemon juice.

3 Cover the salmon loosely with foil and bake for 25 minutes. Remove it from the oven, lift off the foil and test the fish. (The flesh should be opaque and flake easily. Return to the oven if necessary.)

4 Remove the foil and carefully lift the fish on to a serving plate. It may be served hot or cold.

Sea Bass in a Salt Crust

Baking fish in a crust of sea salt seals in and enhances its flavour. Any firm fish can be cooked in this way. Decorate with a garnish of seaweed or blanched samphire and lemon slices, and break open the crust at the table to release the glorious aroma. Serve the fish with baby new potatoes roasted with olive oil and a sprinkling of dried rosemary, and steamed green vegetables such as broccoli or green beans.

SERVES FOUR

1 Preheat the oven to 240°C/475°F/Gas 9. Fill the cavity of the fish with the sprigs of fresh fennel, rosemary and thyme, and grind over some of the mixed peppercorns.

2 Spread half the salt in an ovenproof dish (ideally oval) and lay the sea bass on it. Cover the fish all over with a 1cm/½in layer of salt, pressing it down firmly. Moisten the salt lightly by spraying with water from an atomizer. Bake the fish for 30–40 minutes, until the salt crust is just beginning to colour.

3 Bring the sea bass to the table in its salt crust. Use a sharp knife to break open the crust and cut into four portions.

1 sea bass, about 1kg/2¼lb, cleaned and scaled

1 sprig each of fresh fennel, rosemary and thyme

mixed peppercorns

2kg/4½lb coarse sea salt

Roast Cod Wrapped in Prosciutto with Vine Tomatoes

Wrapping chunky fillets of cod in wafer-thin slices of prosciutto keeps the fish succulent and moist, at the same time adding flavour and visual impact. Serve with baby new potatoes and a herb salad for a stylish supper or lunch dish.

SERVES FOUR

1 Preheat the oven to 220°C/425°F/Gas 7. Pat the fish dry on kitchen paper and remove any stray bones. Season.

2 Place one fillet in an ovenproof dish and drizzle 15ml/ 1 tbsp of the oil over it. Cover with the second fillet, laying the thick end on top of the thin end of the lower fillet to create an even shape. Lay the ham over the fish, overlapping the slices to cover the fish in an even layer. Tuck the ends of the ham under the fish and tie it in place at intervals with fine string.

3 Using kitchen scissors, snip the vines into four portions and add to the dish. Drizzle the tomatoes and ham with the remaining oil and season lightly. Roast for 35 minutes, until the tomatoes are lightly coloured and the fish is cooked through. Test the fish by piercing one end of the parcel with the tip of a knife to check that it flakes easily.

4 Slice the fish and transfer the portions to warm plates, adding the tomatoes. Spoon over the cooking juices from the dish and serve immediately.

2 thick skinless cod fillets, each weighing about 375g/13oz

75g/3oz prosciutto, thinly sliced

400g/14oz tomatoes, on the vine

FROM THE STORECUPBOARD

75ml/5 tbsp extra virgin olive oil

salt and ground black pepper

Grilled Hake with Lemon and Chilli

Choose firm hake fillets, as thick as possible. This is an ideal recipe if you are counting the calories, because it is low in fat. Serve with new potatoes and steamed fine green beans. Or, if you're not counting calories, serve with creamy mashed potatoes with plenty of butter stirred in.

SERVES FOUR

4 hake fillets, each 150g/5oz

finely grated rind and juice of 1 unwaxed lemon

15ml/1 tbsp crushed chilli flakes

FROM THE STORECUPBOARD

30ml/2 tbsp olive oil

salt and ground black pepper

1 Preheat the grill (broiler) to high. Brush the hake fillets all over with the olive oil and place them skin side up on a baking sheet.

2 Grill (broil) the fish for 4–5 minutes, until the skin is crispy, then carefully turn them over using a metal spatula.

3 Sprinkle the fillets with the lemon rind and chilli flakes and season with salt and ground black pepper.

4 Grill the fillets for a further 2–3 minutes, or until the hake is cooked through. (Test using the point of a sharp knife; the flesh should flake.) Squeeze over the lemon juice just before serving.

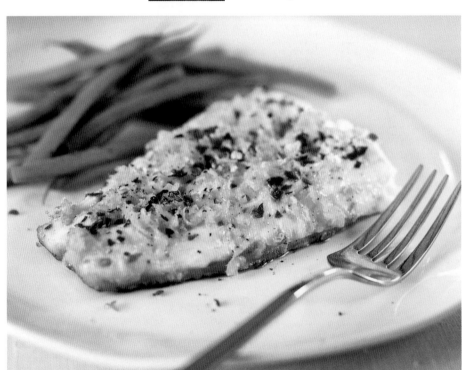

Trout with Grilled Serrano Ham

Traditionally in this Spanish recipe, the trout would have come from mountain streams and been stuffed and wrapped in locally cured ham. One of the beauties of this method is that the skins come off in one piece, leaving the succulent, moist flesh to be eaten with the crisped, salt ham.

SERVES FOUR

1 Extend the belly cavity of each trout, cutting up one side of the backbone. Slip a knife behind the rib bones to loosen them (sometimes just flexing the fish makes them pop up). Snip these off from both sides with scissors, and season the fish well inside.

2 Preheat the grill (broiler) to high, with a shelf in the top position. Line a baking tray with foil and butter it.

3 Working with the fish on the foil, fold a piece of ham into each belly. Use smaller or broken bits of ham for this, and reserve the eight best slices.

4 brown or rainbow trout, about 250g/9oz each, cleaned

16 thin slices Serrano ham, about 200g/7oz

buttered potatoes, to serve (optional)

FROM THE STORECUPBOARD

50g/2oz/¼ cup melted butter, plus extra for greasing

salt and ground black pepper

4 Brush each trout with a little butter, seasoning the outside lightly with salt and pepper. Wrap two ham slices round each one, crossways, tucking the ends into the belly. Grill (broil) the trout for 4 minutes, then carefully turn them over with a metal spatula, rolling them across on the belly so the ham doesn't come loose, and grill for a further 4 minutes.

5 Serve the trout very hot, with any spare butter spooned over the top. Diners should open the trout on their plates, and eat them from the inside, pushing the flesh off the skin.

Poached Fish in Spicy Tomato Sauce

A selection of white fish fillets are used in this Middle-Eastern dish – cod, haddock, hake or halibut are all good. Serve the fish with flat breads, such as pitta, and a spicy tomato relish. It is also good with couscous or rice and a green salad with a refreshing lemon juice dressing.

SERVES EIGHT

1 Heat the tomato sauce with the harissa and coriander in a large pan. Add seasoning to taste and bring to the boil.

2 Remove the pan from the heat and add the fish to the hot sauce. Return to the heat and bring the sauce to the boil again. Reduce the heat and simmer very gently for about 5 minutes, or until the fish is tender. (Test with a fork: if the flesh flakes easily, then it is cooked.)

3 Taste the sauce and adjust the seasoning, adding more harissa if necessary. Serve hot or warm.

600ml/1 pint/2¹/₂ cups fresh tomato sauce

2.5–5ml/¹/₂–1 tsp harissa

60ml/4 tbsp chopped fresh coriander (cilantro) leaves

1.5kg/3¹/₄lb mixed white fish fillets, cut into chunks

FROM THE STORECUPBOARD

salt and ground black pepper

COOK'S TIP
Harissa is a chilli paste spiced with cumin, garlic and coriander. It is fiery and should be used with care until you are familiar with the flavour. Start by adding a small amount and then add more after tasting the sauce.

Fish with Tomato and Pine Nuts

Whole fish marinated in lemon juice and cooked with pine nuts in a spicy tomato sauce is a speciality of Jewish cooking, particularly as a festival treat for Rosh Hashanah, the Jewish New Year. The fish may be cooked and served with head and tail on, as here, or if you like, with these removed. A simple garnish of flat leaf parsley improves the appearance of this delicious dish.

SERVES SIX TO EIGHT

1–1.5kg/2¹/₄–3¹/₄lb fish, such as snapper, cleaned, with head and tail left on

juice of 2 lemons

65g/2¹/₂oz/scant ³/₄ cup pine nuts, toasted

350ml/12fl oz/1¹/₂ cups spicy tomato sauce

FROM THE STORECUPBOARD

salt and ground black pepper

1 Prick the fish all over with a fork and rub with 2.5ml/ ½ tsp salt. Put the fish in a roasting pan or large dish and pour over the lemon juice. Leave to stand for 2 hours.

2 Preheat the oven to 180°C/350°F/Gas 4. Sprinkle half of the pine nuts over the base of an ovenproof dish, top with half of the sauce, then add the fish and its marinade. Add the remaining tomato sauce and the remaining pine nuts.

3 Cover the ovenproof dish tightly with a lid or foil and bake in the preheated oven for 30 minutes, or until the fish is tender. Serve the fish immediately, straight from the dish.

Teriyaki Salmon

Bottles of teriyaki sauce – a lovely rich Japanese glaze – are available in most large supermarkets and Asian stores. Serve the salmon with sticky rice or soba noodles.

SERVES FOUR

4 salmon fillets, 150g/5oz each

75ml/5 tbsp teriyaki marinade

5cm/2in piece of fresh root ginger, peeled and cut into matchsticks

FROM THE STORECUPBOARD

150ml/¹/₄ pint/²/₃ cup sunflower oil

1 Put the salmon in a shallow, non-metallic dish and pour over the teriyaki marinade. Cover and chill for 2 hours.

2 Meanwhile, heat the sunflower oil in a small pan and add the ginger. Fry for 1–2 minutes, or until golden and crisp. Remove with a slotted spoon and drain on kitchen paper.

3 Heat a griddle pan until smoking hot. Remove the salmon from the marinade and add, skin side down, to the pan. Cook for 2–3 minutes, then turn over and cook for a further 1–2 minutes, or until cooked through. Remove from the pan and divide among four serving plates. Top the salmon fillets with the crispy fried ginger.

4 Pour the marinade into the pan and cook for 1–2 minutes. Pour over the salmon and serve.

Roast Mackerel with Spicy Chermoula Paste

Chermoula is a spice mix used widely in Moroccan and North African cooking. It is now readily available in most large supermarkets.

SERVES FOUR

4 whole mackerel, cleaned and gutted

2–3 tbsp chermoula

2 red onions, sliced

FROM THE STORECUPBOARD

75ml/5 tbsp olive oil

salt and ground black pepper

1 Preheat the oven to 190°C/375°F/Gas 5. Place each mackerel on a large sheet of baking parchment. Using a sharp knife, slash each fish several times.

2 In a small bowl, mix the chermoula with the olive oil, and spread over the mackerel, rubbing the mixture into the cuts.

3 Scatter the red onions over the mackerel, and season with salt and pepper. Scrunch the ends of the paper together to seal the fish and place on a baking tray. Bake for 20 minutes, until the mackerel is cooked through. Serve in the paper parcels, to be unwrapped at the table.

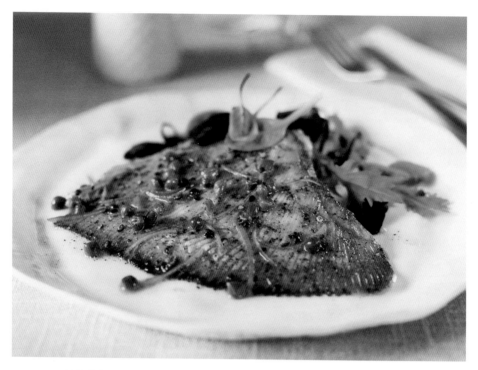

Pan-fried Skate Wings with Capers

This sophisticated way of serving skate is perfect for a dinner party. Serve with a light, green salad.

SERVES SIX

6 small skate wings

grated rind and juice of 2 limes

30ml/2 tbsp salted capers, rinsed and drained

FROM THE STORECUPBOARD

50g/2oz/¹/₄ cup butter

salt and ground black pepper

1 Heat the butter in a large frying pan and add one of the skate wings. Fry for 4–5 minutes on each side, until golden and cooked through.

2 Using a fish slice (metal spatula) carefully transfer the cooked skate wing to a warmed serving plate and keep warm while you cook each of the remaining skate wings in the same way.

3 Return the pan to the heat and add the lime rind and juice, and capers. Season with salt and freshly ground black pepper to taste and allow to bubble for 1–2 minutes. Spoon a little of the juices and the capers over each skate wing and serve immediately.

Sea Bass with Parsley and Lime Butter

The delicate but firm, sweet flesh of sea bass goes beautifully with citrus flavours. Serve with roast fennel and sautéed diced potatoes.

SERVES SIX

6 sea bass fillets, about 150g/5oz each

grated rind and juice of 1 large lime

30ml/2 tbsp chopped fresh parsley

FROM THE STORECUPBOARD

50g/2oz/¹/₄ cup butter

salt and ground black pepper

1 Heat the butter in a large frying pan and add three of the sea bass fillets, skin side down. Cook for 3–4 minutes, or until the skin is crisp and golden. Flip the fish over and cook for a further 2–3 minutes, or until cooked through.

2 Remove the fillets from the pan with a metal spatula. Place each on a serving plate and keep them warm. Cook the remaining fish in the same way and transfer to serving plates.

3 Add the lime rind and juice to the pan with the parsley, and season with salt and black pepper. Allow to bubble for 1–2 minutes, then pour a little over each fish portion and serve immediately.

Meat

WITH THE SIMPLE ADDITION OF A FEW WELL-CHOSEN
INGREDIENTS, MEAT DISHES CAN BE TRANSFORMED INTO
EXCITING, INNOVATIVE DISHES. FROM STEAK TO PORK,
THIS CHAPTER INCLUDES A WONDERFUL SELECTION OF
DISHES THAT ARE EQUALLY SUITED TO A QUICK FAMILY
SUPPER, A LONG SUNDAY LUNCH OR AN INSPIRED
DINNER PARTY.

Beef Patties with Onions and Peppers

This is a firm family favourite. It is easy to make and delicious, and it can be varied by adding other vegetables, such as sliced red peppers, broccoli or mushrooms. These patties are very versatile and can be served in a variety of ways – with chunky home-made chips (French fries), with crusty bread, or with rice and a ready-made tomato sauce.

SERVES FOUR

1 Place the minced beef, chopped onion and 15ml/1 tbsp garlic-flavoured oil in a bowl and mix well. Season well and form into four large or eight small patties.

2 Heat the remaining oil in a large non-stick pan, then add the patties and cook on both sides until browned. Sprinkle over 15ml/1 tbsp water and add a little seasoning.

3 Cover the patties with the sliced onions and peppers. Sprinkle in another 15ml/1 tbsp water and a little seasoning, then cover the pan. Reduce the heat to very low and braise for 20–30 minutes.

4 When the onions are turning golden brown, remove the pan from the heat. Serve with onions and peppers.

500g/1¼lb lean minced (ground) beef

4 onions, 1 finely chopped and 3 sliced

2–3 green (bell) peppers, seeded and sliced lengthways into strips

FROM THE STORECUPBOARD

30ml/2 tbsp garlic-flavoured olive oil or olive oil

salt and ground black pepper

Steak with Warm Tomato Salsa

A refreshing, tangy salsa of tomatoes, spring onions and balsamic vinegar makes a colourful topping for chunky, pan-fried steaks. Choose rump, sirloin or fillet – whichever is your favourite – and if you do not have a non-stick pan, grill the steak instead for the same length of time. Serve with potato wedges and a mixed leaf salad with a mustard dressing.

SERVES TWO

1 Trim any excess fat from the steaks, then season on both sides with salt and pepper. Heat a non-stick frying pan and cook the steaks for about 3 minutes on each side for medium rare. Cook for a little longer if you like your steak well cooked.

2 Meanwhile, put the tomatoes in a heatproof bowl, cover with boiling water and leave for 1–2 minutes, until the skins start to split. Drain and peel the tomatoes, then halve them and scoop out the seeds. Dice the tomato flesh. Thinly slice the spring onions.

3 Transfer the steaks to plates and keep warm. Add the vegetables, balsamic vinegar, 30ml/2 tbsp water and a little seasoning to the cooking juices in the pan and stir briefly until warm, scraping up any meat residue. Spoon the salsa over the steaks to serve.

2 steaks, about 2cm/³/₄in thick

4 large plum tomatoes

2 spring onions (scallions)

30ml/2 tbsp balsamic vinegar

FROM THE STORECUPBOARD

salt and ground black pepper

Meatballs in Tomato Sauce

Cook meatballs in their sauce, rather than frying them first, because this helps keep them nice and moist. Serve in the traditional way with spaghetti and shavings of Parmesan cheese.

SERVES FOUR

1 Put the minced beef in a bowl and season with salt and pepper. Remove the sausages from their skins and mix thoroughly into the beef.

2 Shape the mixture into balls about the size of large walnuts and arrange in a single layer in a shallow baking dish. Cover and chill for 30 minutes.

3 Preheat the oven to 180°C/350°F/Gas 4. Process the tomatoes in a food processor until just smooth, and season. Pour over the meatballs, making sure they are all covered.

4 Bake the meatballs for 40 minutes, stirring once or twice until they are cooked through, then serve.

225g/8oz/1 cup minced (ground) beef

4 Sicilian-style sausages

2 x 400g/14oz cans pomodorino tomatoes

FROM THE STORECUPBOARD

salt and ground black pepper

Beef Cooked in Red Wine

Shin of beef is traditionally quite a tough cut that needs long, slow cooking, and marinating the beef in red wine gives a tender result. Sprinkle the stew with rosemary and serve with mashed potatoes.

SERVES FOUR TO SIX

675g/1¹/₂lb boned and cubed shin of beef

3 large garlic cloves, finely chopped

1 bottle fruity red wine

FROM THE STORECUPBOARD

salt and ground black pepper

1 Put the beef in a casserole dish with the garlic and some black pepper, and pour over the red wine. Stir to combine, then cover and chill for at least 12 hours.

2 Preheat the oven to 160°C/325°F/Gas 3. Cover the casserole with a tight-fitting lid and transfer to the oven. Cook for 2 hours, or until the beef is very tender. Season with salt and pepper to taste, and serve piping hot.

VARIATION *Marinate the beef in a mixture of half port and half beef stock instead of the red wine. Port cooks down to produce a lovely rich sauce, but be sure to dilute it with stock because it can be quite overpowering on its own. A half-and-half mixture will give the perfect balance of taste.*

Pan-fried Gaelic Steaks

A good steak is always popular and top quality raw materials plus timing are the keys to success. Choose small, thick steaks rather than large, thin ones if you can. Traditional accompaniments include potato chips, fried onions, mushrooms and peas.

SERVES FOUR

4 x 225–350g/8–12oz sirloin steaks, at room temperature

50ml/2fl oz/¼ cup Irish whiskey

300ml/½ pint/1¼ cups double (heavy) cream

FROM THE STORECUPBOARD

15g/1/2oz/1 tbsp butter

5ml/1 tsp oil

salt and ground black pepper

1 Season the steaks with pepper. Heat a heavy pan, over high heat. When it is hot, add the oil and butter. Add the steaks one at a time, to seal the meat quickly. Lower the heat to moderate. Allowing 3–4 minutes for rare, 4–5 minutes for medium or 5–6 minutes for well-done steaks, leave undisturbed for half of the specified cooking time; thick steaks will take longer than thin ones. Turn only once.

2 When the steaks are cooked to your liking, transfer them to warmed plates to keep warm. Pour off the fat from the pan and discard. Add the whiskey and stir to remove the sediment at the base of the pan. Allow the liquid to reduce a little, then add the cream and simmer over low heat for a few minutes, until the cream thickens. Season to taste, pour the sauce around or over the steaks, as preferred, and serve immediately.

Thai-style Rare Beef and Mango Salad

This simplified version of Thai beef salad is especially tasty served with little bowls of fresh coriander (cilantro) leaves, chopped spring onions (scallions) and peanuts for sprinkling at the table.

SERVES FOUR

450g/1lb sirloin steak

45ml/3 tbsp soy sauce

2 mangoes, peeled, stoned (pitted) and finely sliced

FROM THE STORECUPBOARD

45ml/3 tbsp garlic-infused olive oil

ground black pepper

1 Put the steak in a shallow, non-metallic dish and pour over the oil and soy sauce. Season with pepper and turn the steaks to coat in the marinade. Cover and chill for 2 hours.

2 Heat a griddle pan until hot. Remove the steak from the marinade and place on the griddle pan. Cook for 3–5 minutes on each side, moving the steak halfway through if you want a criss-cross pattern.

3 Transfer the steak to a board and leave to rest for 5–10 minutes. Meanwhile, pour the marinade into the pan and cook for a few seconds, then remove from the heat. Thinly slice the steak and arrange on four serving plates with the mangoes. Drizzle over the pan juices to serve.

North African Lamb

This dish is full of contrasting flavours that create a rich, spicy and fruity main course. For best results, use lamb that still retains some fat, as this will help keep the meat moist and succulent during roasting. Serve the lamb with couscous or mixed white and wild rice, sprinkled with chopped coriander (cilantro). Roasted chunks of red and yellow (bell) peppers, aubergine (eggplant) and courgettes (zucchini), cooked in the oven with the lamb, complete the meal.

SERVES FOUR

1 Preheat the oven to 200°C/400°F/Gas 6. Heat a frying pan, preferably non-stick, and cook the lamb on all sides until beginning to brown. Transfer to a roasting pan, reserving any fat in the frying pan.

2 Peel the onions and cut each into six wedges. Toss with the lamb and roast for about 30-40 minutes, until the lamb is cooked through and the onions are deep golden brown.

3 Tip the lamb and onions back into the frying pan. Mix the harissa with 250ml/8fl oz/1 cup boiling water and add to the roasting pan. Scrape up any residue in the pan and pour the mixture over the lamb and onions. Stir in the prunes and heat until just simmering. Cover and simmer for 5 minutes, then serve.

675g/1¹/₂lb lamb fillet or shoulder steaks, cut into chunky pieces

5 small onions

7.5ml/1¹/₂ tsp harissa

115g/4oz ready-to-eat pitted prunes, halved

Lamb Steaks with Redcurrant Glaze

This classic, simple dish is absolutely delicious and is an excellent, quick recipe for cooking on the barbecue. The tangy flavour of redcurrants is a traditional accompaniment to lamb. It is good served with new potatoes and fresh garden peas tossed in butter.

SERVES FOUR

1 Reserve the tips of the rosemary and chop the remaining leaves. Rub the chopped rosemary, salt and pepper all over the lamb.

2 Preheat the grill (broiler). Heat the redcurrant jelly gently in a small pan with 30ml/2 tbsp water. Stir in the vinegar.

3 Place the steaks on a foil-lined grill (broiler) rack and brush with a little of the redcurrant glaze. Cook for about 5 minutes on each side, until deep golden, brushing with more glaze.

4 Transfer the lamb to warmed plates. Tip any juices from the foil into the remaining glaze and heat through. Pour the glaze over the lamb and serve, garnished with the reserved rosemary.

4 large fresh rosemary sprigs

4 lamb leg steaks

75ml/5 tbsp redcurrant jelly

30ml/2 tbsp raspberry or red wine vinegar

FROM THE STORECUPBOARD

salt and ground black pepper

Lamb Chops with a Mint Jelly Crust

Mint and lamb are classic partners, and the breadcrumbs used here add extra texture. Serve the chops with sweet potatoes baked in their skins and some steamed green vegetables.

SERVES FOUR

1 Preheat the oven to 190°C/375°F/Gas 5. Place the lamb chops on a baking sheet and season with plenty of salt and ground black pepper.

2 Put the breadcrumbs and mint jelly in a bowl and mix together to combine. Spoon the breadcrumb mixture on top of the chops, pressing down firmly with the back of a spoon making sure they stick to the chops.

3 Bake the chops for 20–30 minutes, or until they are just cooked through. Serve immediately.

8 lamb chops, about 115g/4oz each

50g/2oz/1 cup fresh white breadcrumbs

30ml/2 tbsp mint jelly

FROM THE STORECUPBOARD

salt and ground black pepper

Marinated Lamb
with Oregano and Basil

Lamb leg steaks are chunky with a sweet flavour and go well with oregano and basil. However, you could also use finely chopped rosemary or thyme. Serve with couscous.

SERVES FOUR

1 Put the lamb in a shallow, non-metallic dish. Mix 45ml/3 tbsp of the oil with the oregano, basil and some salt and pepper, reserving some of the herbs for garnish. Pour over the lamb and turn to coat in the marinade. Cover and chill for up to 8 hours.

2 Heat the remaining oil in a large frying pan. Remove the lamb from the marinade and fry for 5–6 minutes on each side, until slightly pink in the centre. Add the marinade and cook for 1–2 minutes until warmed through. Garnish with the reserved herbs and serve.

4 large or 8 small lamb leg steaks

1 small bunch of fresh oregano, roughly chopped

1 small bunch of fresh basil, torn

FROM THE STORECUPBOARD

60ml/4 tbsp garlic-infused olive oil

salt and ground black pepper

Roast Shoulder of Lamb with Whole Garlic Cloves

The potatoes catch the lamb fat as it cooks, giving garlicky, juicy results. Return the potatoes to the oven to keep warm while you leave the lamb to rest before carving. Serve with seasonal vegetables.

SERVES FOUR TO SIX

675g/1¹/₂lb waxy potatoes, peeled and cut into large dice

12 garlic cloves, unpeeled

1 whole shoulder of lamb

FROM THE STORECUPBOARD

45ml/3 tbsp olive oil

salt and ground black pepper

1 Preheat the oven to 180°C/350°F/Gas 4. Put the potatoes and garlic cloves into a large roasting pan and season with salt and pepper. Pour over 30ml/2 tbsp of the oil and toss the potatoes and garlic to coat.

2 Place a rack over the roasting pan, so that it is not touching the potatoes. Place the lamb on the rack and drizzle over the remaining oil. Season with salt and pepper.

3 Roast the lamb and potatoes for 2–2¹/₂ hours, or until the lamb is cooked through. Halfway through the cooking time, carefully take the lamb and the rack off the roasting pan and turn the potatoes to ensure even cooking.

Roast Leg of Lamb with Rosemary and Garlic

This is a classic combination of flavours, and always popular. Serve as a traditional Sunday lunch with roast potatoes and vegetables. Leaving the lamb to rest before carving ensures a tender result.

SERVES FOUR TO SIX

1 leg of lamb, approx 1.8kg/4lb

2 garlic cloves, finely sliced

leaves from 2 sprigs of fresh rosemary

FROM THE STORECUPBOARD

30ml/2 tbsp olive oil

salt and ground black pepper

1 Preheat the oven to 190°C/375°F/Gas 5. Using a small sharp knife, make slits at 4cm/1¹/₂in intervals over the lamb, deep enough to hold a piece of garlic. Push the garlic and rosemary leaves into the slits.

2 Drizzle the olive oil over the top of the lamb and season with plenty of salt and ground black pepper. Roast for 25 minutes per 450g/1lb of lamb, plus another 25 minutes.

3 Remove the lamb from the oven and leave to rest for about 15 minutes before carving.

Sweet-and-sour Lamb

Buy lamb loin chops from your butcher and ask him to French trim them for you. Serve with steamed carrots or green beans.

SERVES FOUR

8 French-trimmed lamb loin chops

90ml/6 tbsp balsamic vinegar

30ml/2 tbsp caster (superfine) sugar

FROM THE STORECUPBOARD

30ml/2 tbsp olive oil

salt and ground black pepper

1 Put the lamb chops in a shallow, non-metallic dish and drizzle over the balsamic vinegar. Sprinkle with the sugar and season with salt and black pepper. Turn the chops to coat in the mixture, then cover with clear film (plastic wrap) and chill for 20 minutes.

2 Heat the olive oil in a large frying pan and add the chops, reserving the marinade. Cook for 3–4 minutes on each side.

3 Pour the marinade into the pan and leave to bubble for about 2 minutes, or until reduced slightly. Remove from the pan and serve immediately.

Roast Lamb with Figs

Lamb fillet is an expensive cut of meat, but because it is very lean there is very little waste. To make a more economical version of this dish, use leg of lamb instead. It has a stronger flavour but is equally good. Serve with steamed green beans.

SERVES SIX

1kg/2¼lb lamb fillet

9 fresh figs

150ml/¹/₄ pint/²/₃ cup ruby port

FROM THE STORECUPBOARD

30ml/2 tbsp olive oil

salt and ground black pepper

1 Preheat the oven to 190°/375°F/Gas 5. Heat the oil in a roasting pan over a medium heat. Add the lamb fillet and sear on all sides until evenly browned.

2 Cut the figs in half and arrange around the lamb. Season the lamb with salt and ground black pepper and roast for 30 minutes. Pour the port over the figs.

3 Return the lamb to the oven and roast for a further 30–45 minutes. The meat should still be slightly pink in the middle so be careful not to overcook.

4 Transfer the lamb to a board and leave to rest for about 5 minutes. Carve into slices and serve.

Paprika Pork

This chunky, goulash-style dish is rich with peppers and paprika. Grilling the peppers before adding them to the meat really brings out their sweet, vibrant flavour. Rice or buttered boiled potatoes go particularly well with the rich pork.

SERVES FOUR

2 red, 1 yellow and 1 green (bell) pepper, seeded

500g/1¼lb lean pork fillet (tenderloin)

45ml/3 tbsp paprika

300g/11oz jar or tub of tomato sauce with herbs or garlic

FROM THE STORECUPBOARD

salt and ground black pepper

1 Preheat the grill (broiler). Cut the peppers into thick strips and sprinkle in a single layer on a foil-lined grill rack. Cook under the grill for 20–25 minutes, until the edges of the strips are lightly charred.

2 Meanwhile, cut the pork into chunks. Season and cook in a frying pan for about 5 minutes, until beginning to brown.

3 Transfer the meat to a heavy pan and add the paprika, tomato sauce, 300ml/½ pint/1¼ cups water and a little seasoning. Bring to the boil, reduce the heat, cover and simmer gently for 30 minutes.

4 Add the grilled (broiled) peppers and cook for a further 10–15 minutes, until the meat is tender. Taste for seasoning and serve immediately.

Pork Kebabs

The word kebab comes from Arabic and means on a skewer. Use pork fillet (tenderloin) for these kebabs because it is lean and tender, and cooks very quickly. They are good served with rice, or stuffed into warmed pitta bread with some shredded lettuce leaves.

SERVES FOUR

1 Cut the pork into 2.5cm/1in cubes. Cut the spring onions into 2.5cm/1in long sticks.

2 Preheat the grill (broiler) to high. Oil the wire rack and spread out the pork cubes on it. Grill (broil) the pork until the juices drip, then dip the pieces in the barbecue sauce and put back on the grill. Grill for 30 seconds on each side, repeating the dipping process twice more. Set aside and keep warm.

3 Gently grill (broil) the spring onions until soft and slightly brown outside. Do not dip in the barbecue sauce. Thread about four pieces of pork and three spring onion pieces on to each of eight bamboo skewers.

4 Arrange the skewers on a platter. Cut the lemon into wedges and squeeze a little lemon juice over each skewer. Serve immediately, offering the remaining lemon wedges separately.

500g/1¼lb lean pork fillet (tenderloin)

8 large, thick spring onions (scallions), trimmed

120ml/4fl oz/½ cup barbecue sauce

1 lemon

COOK'S TIP *If you are cooking the pork on a barbecue, soak the skewers overnight in water. This prevents them burning. Keep the skewer handles away from the fire and turn them frequently.*

Fragrant Lemon Grass and Ginger Pork Patties

Lemon grass lends a fragrant citrus flavour to pork, enhanced by the fresh zing of ginger. Serve the patties in burger buns with thick slices of juicy tomato, crisp, refreshing lettuce and a splash of chilli sauce.

SERVES FOUR

450g/1lb/2 cups minced (ground) pork

15ml/1 tbsp fresh root ginger, grated

1 lemon grass stalk

FROM THE STORECUPBOARD

30ml/2 tbsp sunflower oil

salt and ground black pepper

1 Put the pork in a bowl and stir in the ginger. Season with salt and pepper. Remove the tough outer layers from the lemon grass stalk and discard. Chop the centre part as finely as possible and mix into the pork. Shape into four patties and chill for about 20 minutes.

2 Heat the oil in a large, non-stick frying pan and add the patties. Fry for 3–4 minutes on each side over a gentle heat, until cooked through. Remove from the pan with a metal spatula and drain on kitchen paper, then serve.

Pan-fried Gammon with Cider

Gammon and cider are a delicious combination with the sweet, tangy flavour of cider complementing the gammon perfectly. Serve with mustard mashed potatoes.

4 gammon steaks (smoked or cured ham), 225g/8oz each

150ml/¹/₄ pint/²/₃ cup dry (hard) cider

45ml/3 tbsp double (heavy) cream

FROM THE STORECUPBOARD

30ml/2 tbsp sunflower oil

salt and ground black pepper

SERVES FOUR

1 Heat the oil in a large frying pan until hot. Neatly snip the rind on the gammon steaks to stop them curling up and add them to the pan.

2 Cook the steaks for 3–4 minutes on each side, then pour in the cider. Allow to boil for a couple of minutes, then stir in the cream and cook for 1–2 minutes, or until thickened. Season with salt and pepper, and serve immediately.

Caramelized Onion and Sausage Tarte Tatin

Toulouse sausages have a garlicky flavour and meaty texture that is delicious with fried onions. Serve with a green salad of bitter leaves.

SERVES FOUR

450g/1lb Toulouse sausages

2 large onions, sliced

250g/9oz ready-made puff pastry, thawed if frozen

FROM THE STORECUPBOARD

45ml/3 tbsp sunflower oil

salt and ground black pepper

1 Heat the oil in a 23cm/9in non-stick frying pan with an ovenproof handle, and add the sausages. Cook over a gentle heat, turning occasionally, for 7–10 minutes, or until golden and cooked through. Remove from the pan and set aside.

2 Preheat the oven to 190°C/375°F/Gas 5. Pour the remaining oil into the frying pan and add the onions. Season with salt and pepper and cook over a gentle heat for 10 minutes, stirring occasionally, until caramelized and tender.

3 Slice each sausage into four or five chunks and stir into the onions. Remove from the heat and set aside.

4 Roll out the puff pastry and cut out a circle slightly larger than the frying pan. Lay the pastry over the sausages and onions, tucking the edges in all the way around. Bake for 20 minutes, or until the pastry is risen and golden. Turn out on to a board, pastry side down, cut into wedges and serve.

Roast Pork with Juniper Berries and Bay

Juniper berries have a strong, pungent taste and are a great flavouring for rich, fatty meats such as pork, while bay leaves add a lovely aroma. Serve with roast potatoes and lightly cooked leafy green vegetables.

SERVES FOUR TO SIX

1kg/2¼lb boned leg of pork

5 fresh bay leaves

6 juniper berries

FROM THE STORECUPBOARD

15ml/1 tbsp olive oil

salt and ground black pepper

1 Preheat the oven to 180°C/350°F/Gas 4. Open out the pork and season with plenty of salt and black pepper.

2 Lay the bay leaves on the pork and sprinkle over the juniper berries. Carefully roll up the pork to enclose the bay leaves and juniper berries and tie with string to secure.

3 Rub the skin with the oil and then rub in plenty of salt. Roast the pork for 20 minutes per 450g/1lb, plus an extra 20 minutes.

4 Remove the pork from the oven and leave to rest for about 10 minutes before carving, then serve immediately.

Sticky Glazed Pork Ribs

These spare ribs have a lovely sweet-and-sour flavour and are always as popular with children as they are with adults, making them the perfect choice for a family meal. They're also great for cooking over a barbecue; make sure you leave them to marinate for at least 30 minutes before cooking. To enjoy sticky ribs at their best you need to get stuck in and eat them with your fingers, so make sure you serve them with plenty of paper napkins.

SERVES FOUR

1 Preheat the oven to 190°C/375°F/Gas 5. Put the spare ribs in a roasting pan and season well with plenty of salt and ground black pepper.

2 In a small bowl, mix together the honey and soy sauce and pour over the ribs. Turn the ribs several times, spooning over the mixture until thoroughly coated.

3 Bake the spare ribs for 30 minutes, then increase the oven temperature to 220°C/425°F/Gas 7 and cook for a further 10 minutes, or until the honey and soy sauce marinade turns into a thick, sticky glaze.

900g/2lb pork spare ribs

75ml/5 tbsp clear honey

75ml/5 tbsp light soy sauce

FROM THE STORECUPBOARD

salt and ground black pepper

Chinese Spiced Pork Chops

Five-spice powder is a fantastic ingredient for perking up dishes and adding a good depth of flavour. The five different spices – Szechuan pepper, cinnamon, cloves, fennel seeds and star anise – are perfectly balanced, with the aniseed flavour of star anise predominating. Serve the chops with lightly steamed pak choi (bok choy) and plain boiled rice.

SERVES FOUR

4 large pork chops, about 200g/7oz each

15ml/1 tbsp Chinese five-spice powder

30ml/2 tbsp soy sauce

FROM THE STORECUPBOARD

30ml/2 tbsp garlic-infused olive oil

1 Arrange the pork chops in a single layer in a non-metallic roasting pan or baking dish.

2 Sprinkle the five-spice powder over the chops, then drizzle over the soy sauce and garlic infused oil. (Alternatively, mix together the garlic-infused olive oil, soy sauce and five-spice powder, and pour over the chops.)

3 Using your hands, rub the mixture into the meat. Cover the dish with clear film (plastic wrap) and chill for 2 hours.

4 Preheat the oven to 160°C/325°F/Gas 3. Uncover the dish and bake for 30–40 minutes, or until the pork is cooked through and tender. Serve immediately.

Poultry and Game

WITH THE SIMPLE ADDITION OF A FEW WELL-CHOSEN
INGREDIENTS, POULTRY CAN BE TRANSFORMED INTO
EXCITING, INNOVATIVE DISHES. FROM DUCK TO PHEASANT,
THIS CHAPTER INCLUDES A WONDERFUL SELECTION OF
DISHES THAT ARE EQUALLY SUITED TO A QUICK FAMILY
SUPPER OR A DINNER PARTY.

Pot-roasted Chicken with Preserved Lemons

Roasting chicken and potatoes in this way gives an interesting variety of textures. The chicken and potatoes on the top crisp up, while underneath they stay soft and juicy. Serve with steamed carrots or curly kale.

SERVES FOUR TO SIX

675g/1¹/₂lb potatoes, unpeeled and cut into chunks

6–8 pieces of preserved lemon

1.3kg/3lb corn-fed chicken, jointed

FROM THE STORECUPBOARD

30ml/2 tbsp olive oil

salt and ground black pepper

1 Preheat the oven to 190°C/375°F/Gas 5. Drizzle the olive oil into the bottom of a large roasting pan. Spread the chunks of potato in a single layer in the pan and tuck in the pieces of preserved lemon.

2 Pour about 1cm/¹/₂in of cold water into the roasting pan. Arrange the chicken pieces on top and season with plenty of salt and black pepper. Roast for 45 minutes–1 hour, or until the chicken is cooked through, and serve.

Honey Mustard Chicken

Chicken thighs have a rich flavour, but if you want to cut down on fat, use four chicken breast portions instead and cook for 20–25 minutes. Serve with a chunky tomato and red onion salad.

SERVES FOUR

1 Preheat the oven to 190°C/375°F/Gas 5. Put the chicken thighs in a single layer in a roasting pan.

2 Mix together the mustard and honey, season with salt and ground black pepper to taste and brush the mixture all over the chicken thighs.

3 Cook for 25–30 minutes, brushing the chicken with the pan juices occasionally, until cooked through. (To check the chicken is cooked through, skewer it with a sharp knife; the juices should run clear.)

8 chicken thighs

60ml/4 tbsp wholegrain mustard

60ml/4 tbsp clear honey

FROM THE STORECUPBOARD

salt and ground black pepper

Drunken Chicken

In this traditional Chinese dish, cooked chicken is marinated in sherry, fresh root ginger and spring onions for several days. Because of the lengthy preparation time, it is important to use a very fresh bird from a reputable supplier. Fresh herbs can be added as an additional garnish, if you like.

SERVES FOUR TO SIX

1 Rinse and dry the chicken inside and out. Place the ginger and spring onions in the body cavity. Put the chicken in a large pan or flameproof casserole and just cover with water. Bring to the boil, skim off any scum and cook for 15 minutes.

2 Turn off the heat, cover the pan or casserole tightly and leave the chicken in the cooking liquid for 3–4 hours, by which time it will be cooked. Drain well, reserving the stock. Pour 300ml/¹/₂ pint/1¹/₄ cups of the stock into a jug (pitcher).

3 Remove the skin and cut the chicken into neat pieces. Divide each leg into a drumstick and thigh. Make two more portions from the wings and some of the breast. Finally, cut away the remainder of the breast pieces (still on the bone) and divide each piece into two even-size portions.

4 Arrange the chicken portions in a shallow dish. Rub salt into the chicken and cover with clear film (plastic wrap). Leave in a cool place for several hours or overnight in the refrigerator.

5 Later, lift off any fat from the stock, add the sherry and pour over the chicken. Cover again and leave in the refrigerator to marinate for 2–3 days, turning occasionally.

6 When ready to serve, cut the chicken through the bone into chunky pieces and arrange on a large serving platter. Garnish the chicken with spring onion shreds.

1 chicken, about 1.3kg/3lb

1cm/¹/₂ in piece of fresh root ginger, thinly sliced

2 spring onions (scallions), trimmed, plus extra to garnish

300ml/¹/₂ pint/1¹/₄ cups dry sherry

FROM THE STORECUPBOARD

salt

VARIATION *To serve as a cocktail snack, take the meat off the bones, cut it into bitesize pieces, then spear each piece on a cocktail stick (toothpick).*

Soy-marinated Chicken

Two simple flavours, soy sauce and orange, combine to make this mouthwatering dish. Serving the chicken on a bed of asparagus turns the dish into a special treat. Wilted spinach or shredded greens work well as an everyday alternative. Boiled egg noodles or steamed white rice make a good accompaniment.

SERVES FOUR

4 skinless, chicken breast fillets

1 large orange

30ml/2 tbsp dark soy sauce

400g/14oz medium asparagus spears

1 Slash each chicken portion diagonally and place them in a single layer in a shallow, ovenproof dish. Halve the orange, squeeze the juice from one half and mix it with the soy sauce. Pour this over the chicken. Cut the remaining orange into wedges and place these on the chicken. Cover and leave to marinate for several hours.

2 Preheat the oven to 180°C/350°F/Gas 4. Turn the chicken over and bake, uncovered, for 20 minutes. Turn the chicken over again and bake for a further 15 minutes, or until cooked through.

3 Meanwhile, cut off any tough ends from the asparagus and place in a frying pan. Pour in enough boiling water just to cover and cook gently for 3–4 minutes, until just tender. Drain and arrange on warmed plates, then top with the chicken and orange wedges. Spoon over the cooking juices. Serve immediately.

Stir-fried Chicken with Thai Basil

Thai basil, sometimes called holy basil, has purple-tinged leaves and a more pronounced, slightly aniseedy flavour than the usual varieties. It is available in most Asian food stores but if you can't find any, use a handful of ordinary basil instead. Serve this fragrant stir-fry with plain steamed rice or boiled noodles and soy sauce on the side.

SERVES FOUR

1 Using a sharp knife, slice the chicken breast portions into strips. Halve the peppers, remove the seeds, then cut each piece of pepper into strips.

2 Heat the oil in a wok or large frying pan. Add the chicken and red peppers and stir-fry over a high heat for about 3 minutes, until the chicken is golden and cooked through. Season with salt and ground black pepper.

3 Roughly tear up the basil leaves, add to the chicken and peppers and toss briefly to combine. Serve immediately.

4 skinless chicken breast fillets, cut into strips

2 red (bell) peppers

1 small bunch of fresh Thai basil

FROM THE STORECUPBOARD

30ml/2 tbsp garlic-infused olive oil

salt and ground black pepper

Crème Fraîche and Coriander Chicken

Boneless chicken thighs are used for this recipe but you can substitute breast portions if you like. Be generous with the coriander leaves, as they have a wonderful fragrant flavour, or use chopped parsley instead. Serve with creamy mashed potatoes. To make a lower fat version of this dish, use chicken breast portions and low-fat crème fraîche.

SERVES FOUR

6 skinless chicken thigh fillets

60ml/4 tbsp crème fraîche

1 small bunch of fresh coriander (cilantro), roughly chopped

FROM THE STORECUPBOARD

15ml/1 tbsp sunflower oil

salt and ground black pepper

1 Cut each chicken thigh into three or four pieces. Heat the oil in a large frying pan, add the chicken and cook for about 6 minutes, turning occasionally, until cooked through.

2 Add the crème fraîche to the pan and stir until melted, then allow to bubble for 1–2 minutes.

3 Add the chopped coriander to the chicken and stir to combine. Season with salt and ground black pepper to taste, and serve immediately.

Chicken Escalopes with Lemon and Serrano Ham

Chicken escalopes are flattened chicken breast fillets – they cook quicker than normal breast portions and absorb flavours more readily. In this light summery dish, the chicken absorbs the delicious flavours of the ham and lemon. It can be assembled in advance, so is good for entertaining.

SERVES FOUR

1 Preheat the oven to 180°C/350°F/Gas 4. Beat the butter with plenty of freshly ground black pepper and set aside. Place the chicken portions on a large sheet of clear film (plastic wrap), spacing them well apart. Cover with a second sheet, then beat with a rolling pin until the portions are half their original thickness.

2 Transfer the chicken to a large, shallow ovenproof dish and crumple a slice of ham on top of each. Cut eight thin slices from the lemon and place two on each slice of ham.

3 Dot with the pepper butter and bake for about 30 minutes, until the chicken is cooked. Transfer to serving plates and spoon over any juices from the dish.

4 skinless chicken breast fillets

4 slices Serrano ham

1 lemon

FROM THE STORECUPBOARD

40g/1¹/₂oz/3 tbsp butter, softened

salt and ground black pepper

Roast Chicken with Herb Cheese, Chilli and Lime Stuffing

Whether you are entertaining guests or cooking a family meal, a tasty chicken is a sure winner every time. This is a modern twist on the classic roast chicken – the stuffing is forced under the chicken skin, which helps to produce a wonderfully flavoured, succulent flesh.

SERVES FIVE TO SIX

1 Preheat the oven to 200°C/400°F/Gas 6. Using first the point of a knife and then your fingers, separate the skin from the meat across the chicken breast and over the tops of the legs. Use the knife to loosen the first piece of skin, then carefully run your fingers underneath, taking care not to tear the skin.

2 Grate the lime and beat the rind into the cream cheese together with the chopped chilli. Pack the cream cheese stuffing under the skin, using a teaspoon, until fairly evenly distributed. Push the skin back into place, then smooth your hands over it to spread the stuffing in an even layer.

3 Put the chicken in a roasting pan and squeeze the juice from the lime over the top. Roast for 1½ hours, or until the juices run clear when the thickest part of the thigh is pierced with a skewer. If necessary, cover the chicken with foil towards the end of cooking if the top starts to become too browned.

4 Carve the chicken and arrange on a warmed serving platter. Spoon the pan juices over it and serve immediately.

1.8kg/4lb chicken

1 lime

115g/4oz/¹/₂ cup cream cheese with herbs and garlic

1 mild fresh red chilli, seeded and finely chopped

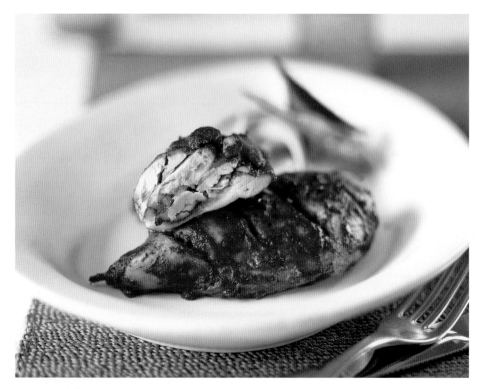

Tandoori Chicken

If you have time, prepare this dish when you get up in the morning, so that it's ready to cook for supper. Serve with a red onion and cucumber salad and warmed naan bread.

SERVES FOUR

4 skinless chicken breast fillets and 4 skinless chicken thigh fillets

200ml/7fl oz/scant 1 cup Greek (US strained plain) yogurt

45ml/3 tbsp tandoori curry paste

FROM THE STORECUPBOARD

salt and ground black pepper

1 Using a sharp knife, slash the chicken breasts and thighs and place in a shallow, non-metallic dish.

2 Put the curry paste and yogurt in a bowl and mix together. Season with salt and pepper, then pour over the chicken and toss to coat well. Cover the dish with clear film (plastic wrap) and chill for at least 8 hours.

3 Preheat the oven to 190°C/375°F/Gas 5. Remove the clear film from the chicken and transfer the dish to the oven. Bake for 20–30 minutes, or until the chicken is cooked through. Serve immediately.

Roast Chicken with Black Pudding and Sage

The combination of juicy roast chicken and black pudding is wonderful. Serve as part of a Sunday roast or simply with a salad.

SERVES FOUR

1 medium oven-ready chicken

115g/4oz black pudding (blood sausage), skinned

30ml/2 tbsp fresh sage leaves

FROM THE STORECUPBOARD

25g/1oz/2 tbsp softened butter

salt and ground black pepper

1 Preheat the oven to 190°C/375°F/Gas 5. Carefully push your fingers between the skin and the flesh at the neck end of the bird to loosen it, making sure you don't tear the skin.

2 Shape the black pudding into a flat, roundish shape, to fit the space between the skin and the breast meat. Push it under the skin with half the sage leaves.

3 Smooth the skin back and tuck underneath. Tie the legs together and place the chicken in a roasting pan. Spread the butter over the breast and thighs, and season. Sprinkle over the remaining sage leaves and roast for 1$^{1}/_{2}$ hours, or until the chicken is cooked through. Remove to a board and leave to rest for 10 minutes before carving.

Spatchcock Poussins with Herb Butter

Spatchcock is said to be a distortion of an 18th-century Irish expression "dispatch cock" for providing an unexpected guest with a quick and simple meal. A young chicken was prepared without frills or fuss by being split, flattened and fried or grilled.

SERVES TWO

2 poussins, each weighing about 450g/1lb

2 garlic cloves, crushed

45ml/3 tbsp chopped mixed fresh herbs, such as flat leaf parsley, sage, rosemary and thyme

FROM THE STORECUPBOARD

75g/3oz/6 tbsp butter, softened

salt and ground black pepper

1 To spatchcock a poussin, place it breast down on a chopping board and split it along the back. Open out the bird and turn it over, so that the breast side is uppermost. Press the bird as flat as possible, then thread two metal skewers through it, across the breast and thigh, to keep it flat. Repeat with the second poussin and place the skewered birds on a large grill pan.

2 Add the crushed garlic and chopped mixed herbs to the butter with plenty of seasoning, and then beat well. Dot the butter over the spatchcock poussins.

3 Preheat the grill to high and cook the poussins for 30 minutes, turning them over halfway through. Turn again and baste with the cooking juices, then cook for a further 5–7 minutes on each side.

Chilli-spiced Poussin

When you are short of time these spicy poussins make a quick alternative to a traditional roast. Serve with a leafy salad.

SERVES FOUR

2 poussins, 675g/1¹/₂lb each

15ml/1 tbsp chilli powder

15ml/1 tbsp ground cumin

FROM THE STORECUPBOARD

45ml/3 tbsp olive oil

salt and ground black pepper

1 Spatchcock one poussin: remove the wishbone and split the bird along each side of the backbone and remove it. Press down on the breastbone to flatten the bird. Push a metal skewer through the wings and breast to keep the bird flat, then push a second skewer through the thighs and breast. Spatchcock the second poussin in the same way.

2 Combine the chilli, cumin, oil and seasoning. Brush over the poussins. Preheat the grill (broiler). Lay the birds, skin side down, on a grill rack and grill (broil) for 15 minutes. Turn over and grill for a further 15 minutes until cooked through.

3 Remove the skewers and split each bird in half along the breastbone. Serve drizzled with the pan juices.

Turkey Patties

So much better than store-bought burgers, these light patties are delicious served hamburger-style in split and toasted buns with relish, salad leaves and chunky fries. They can also be made using minced chicken, lamb, pork or beef. If you are making them for children, shape the mixture into 12 equal-sized rounds and serve in mini-rolls or in rounds stamped out from sliced bread.

SERVES SIX

675g/1¹/₂lb minced (ground) turkey

1 small red onion, finely chopped

small handful of fresh thyme leaves

FROM THE STORECUPBOARD

30ml/2 tbsp lime-flavoured olive oil

1 Mix together the turkey, onion, thyme, 15ml/1 tbsp of the oil and seasoning. Cover and chill for up to 4 hours to let the flavours infuse (steep), then divide the mixture into six equal portions and shape into round patties.

2 Preheat a griddle pan. Brush the patties with half of the remaining lime-flavoured olive oil, then place them on the pan and cook for 10–12 minutes. Turn the patties over, brush with more oil, and cook for 10–12 minutes on the second side, or until cooked right through. Serve the patties immediately.

Guinea Fowl with Whisky Sauce

Served with creamy, sweet mashed potato and lightly boiled whole baby leeks, guinea fowl is magnificent with a rich, creamy whisky sauce. If you don't like the flavour of whisky, then substitute brandy, Madeira or Marsala. Or, to make a non-alcoholic version, use freshly squeezed orange juice instead. Garnish with fresh thyme sprigs or other fresh herbs.

SERVES FOUR

2 guinea fowl, each weighing about 1kg/2¹/₄lb

90ml/6 tbsp whisky

**150ml/¹/₄ pint/²/₃ cup well-flavoured
chicken stock**

150ml/¹/₄ pint/²/₃ cup double (heavy) cream

FROM THE STORECUPBOARD

salt and ground black pepper

1 Preheat the oven to 200°C/400°F/Gas 6. Brown the guinea fowl on all sides in a roasting pan on the hob (stove-top), then turn it breast uppermost and transfer the pan to the oven. Roast for about 1 hour, until the guinea fowl are golden and cooked through. Transfer the guinea fowl to a warmed serving dish, cover with foil and keep warm.

2 Pour off the excess fat from the pan, then heat the juices on the hob and stir in the whisky. Bring to the boil and cook until reduced. Add the stock and cream and simmer again until reduced slightly. Strain and season to taste.

3 Carve the guinea fowl and serve on individual plates, arranged around the chosen vegetable accompaniments. Sprinkle with plenty of freshly ground black pepper. Spoon a little of the sauce over each portion and serve the rest separately.

Pheasant Cooked in Port with Mushrooms

This warming dish is delicious served with mashed root vegetables and shredded cabbage or leeks. Marinating the pheasant in port helps to moisten and tenderize the meat, which can often be slightly dry. If you prefer, marinate the pheasant in a full-bodied red wine and use button (white) mushrooms.

SERVES FOUR

2 pheasants, cut into portions

300ml/¹/₂ pint/1¹/₄ cups port

300g/11oz chestnut mushrooms, halved if large

FROM THE STORECUPBOARD

50g/2oz/¹/₄ cup butter

salt and ground black pepper

1 Place the pheasant in a bowl and pour over the port. Cover and marinate for 3–4 hours or overnight, turning the portions occasionally.

2 Drain the meat thoroughly, reserving the marinade. Pat the portions dry on kitchen paper and season lightly with salt and pepper. Melt three-quarters of the butter in a frying pan and cook the pheasant portions on all sides for about 5 minutes, until deep golden. Drain well, transfer to a plate, then cook the mushrooms in the fat remaining in the pan for 3 minutes.

3 Return the pheasant to the pan and pour in the reserved marinade with 200ml/7fl oz/scant 1 cup water. Bring to the boil, reduce the heat and cover, then simmer gently for about 45 minutes, until the pheasant is tender.

4 Using a slotted spoon, carefully remove the pheasant portions and mushrooms from the frying pan and keep warm. Bring the cooking juices to the boil and boil vigorously for 3–5 minutes, until they are reduced and slightly thickened. Strain the juices through a fine sieve and return them to the pan. Whisk in the remaining butter over a gentle heat until it has melted, season to taste, then pour the juices over the pheasant and mushrooms and serve.

Roast Pheasant with Sherry and Mustard Sauce

Use only young pheasants for roasting – older birds are too tough and only suitable for casseroles. Serve with potatoes braised in wine with garlic and onions, Brussels sprouts and bread sauce.

SERVES FOUR

2 young oven-ready pheasants

200ml/7fl oz/scant 1 cup sherry

15ml/1 tbsp Dijon mustard

FROM THE STORECUPBOARD

50g/2oz/¹⁄₄ cup softened butter

salt and ground black pepper

1 Preheat the oven to 200°C/400°F/Gas 6. Put the pheasants in a roasting pan and spread the butter all over both birds. Season with salt and pepper.

2 Roast the pheasants for 50 minutes, basting often to stop the birds from drying out. When the pheasants are cooked, take them out of the pan and leave to rest on a board, covered with foil.

3 Meanwhile, place the roasting pan over a medium heat. Add the sherry and season with salt and pepper. Simmer for 5 minutes, until the sherry has slightly reduced, then stir in the mustard. Carve the pheasants and serve with the sherry and mustard sauce.

Marmalade and Soy Roast Duck

Sweet-and-sour flavours, such as marmalade and soy sauce, complement the rich, fatty taste of duck beautifully. Serve these robustly flavoured duck breast portions with simple accompaniments such as steamed sticky rice and lightly cooked pak choi (bok choy).

SERVES SIX

6 duck breast portions

45ml/3 tbsp fine-cut marmalade

45ml/3 tbsp light soy sauce

FROM THE STORECUPBOARD

salt and ground black pepper

1 Preheat the oven 190°C/375°F/Gas 5. Place the duck breasts skin side up on a grill (broiler) rack and place in the sink. Pour boiling water all over the duck. This shrinks the skin and helps it crisp during cooking. Pat the duck dry with kitchen paper and transfer to a roasting pan.

2 Combine the marmalade and soy sauce, and brush over the duck. Season with a little salt and some black pepper and roast for 20–25 minutes, basting occasionally with the marmalade mixture in the pan.

3 Remove the duck breasts from the oven and leave to rest for 5 minutes. Slice the duck breasts and serve drizzled with any juices left in the pan.

Duck with Plum Sauce

Sharp plums cut the rich flavour of duck wonderfully well in this updated version of an old English dish. Duck is often considered to be a fatty meat but modern breeding methods have made leaner ducks widely available. For an easy dinner party main course, serve the duck with creamy mashed potatoes and celeriac and steamed broccoli.

SERVES FOUR

1 Prick the duck skin all over with a fork to release the fat during cooking and help give a crisp result, then place the portions in a heavy frying pan, skin side down.

2 Cook the duck pieces for 10 minutes on each side, or until golden brown and cooked right through. Remove the duck from the frying pan using a slotted spoon and keep warm.

3 Pour away all but 30ml/2 tbsp of the duck fat, then stir-fry the onion for 5 minutes, or until golden. Add the plums and cook for 5 minutes, stirring frequently. Add the jelly and mix well.

4 Replace the duck portions and cook for a further 5 minutes, or until thoroughly reheated. Serve immediately.

4 duck quarters

1 large red onion, finely chopped

500g/1¼lb ripe plums, stoned (pitted) and quartered

30ml/2 tbsp redcurrant jelly

COOK'S TIP *It is important that the plums used in this dish are very ripe, otherwise the mixture will be too dry and the sauce will be extremely sharp.*

Pasta and Rice

PASTA AND RICE ARE THE PERFECT STAPLES UPON WHICH
TO BASE SIMPLE, TASTY MEALS. YOU NEED ONLY A FEW
INGREDIENTS TO RUSTLE UP DELICIOUS DISHES, FROM A
SIMPLE MIDWEEK SUPPER TO MORE ELEGANT DISHES FOR
ENTERTAINING. WHETHER YOU CHOOSE A SUBSTANTIAL
BOWL OF PASTA OR A FRAGRANT SEAFOOD RISOTTO –
THE RECIPES IN THIS CHAPTER ARE SURE TO DELIGHT.

Minty Courgette Linguine

Sweet, mild courgettes and refreshing mint are a great combination and are delicious with pasta. Dried linguine has been used here but you can use any type of pasta you like. Couscous also works well in place of pasta if you prefer.

SERVES FOUR

450g/1lb dried linguine

4 small courgettes (zucchini), sliced

1 small bunch of fresh mint, roughly chopped

FROM THE STORECUPBOARD

75ml/5 tbsp garlic-infused olive oil

salt and ground black pepper

1 Cook the linguine in plenty of salted, boiling water according to the instructions on the packet.

2 Meanwhile, heat 45ml/3 tbsp of the oil in a large frying pan and add the courgettes. Fry for 2–3 minutes, stirring occasionally, until they are tender and golden.

3 Drain the pasta well and toss with the courgettes and chopped mint. Season with salt and pepper, drizzle over the remaining oil and serve immediately.

Pasta with Roast Tomatoes and Goat's Cheese

Roasting tomatoes brings out their flavour and sweetness, which contrasts perfectly with the sharp taste and creamy texture of goat's cheese. Serve with a crisp green salad flavoured with herbs.

SERVES FOUR

8 large ripe tomatoes

450g/1lb any dried pasta shapes

200g/7oz firm goat's cheese, crumbled

FROM THE STORECUPBOARD

60ml/4 tbsp garlic-infused olive oil

salt and ground black pepper

1 Preheat the oven to 190°C/375°F/Gas 5. Place the tomatoes in a roasting pan and drizzle over 30ml/2 tbsp of the oil. Season well with salt and pepper and roast for 20–25 minutes, or until soft and slightly charred.

2 Meanwhile, cook the pasta in plenty of salted, boiling water, according to the instructions on the packet. Drain well and return to the pan.

3 Roughly mash the tomatoes with a fork, and stir the contents of the roasting pan into the pasta. Gently stir in the goat's cheese and the remaining oil and serve.

Linguine with Anchovies and Capers

This is a fantastic storecupboard recipe. Use salted capers if you can find them, as they have a better flavour than the bottled ones, but remember that you need to rinse them thoroughly before using. Be sure to chop the anchovies finely so that they "melt" into the sauce.

SERVES FOUR

450g/1lb dried linguine

8 anchovy fillets, drained

30ml/2 tbsp salted capers, thoroughly rinsed and drained

FROM THE STORECUPBOARD

75ml/5 tbsp garlic-infused olive oil

salt and ground black pepper

1 Cook the linguine in plenty of salted, boiling water according to the instructions on the packet.

2 Meanwhile, finely chop the anchovy fillets and place in a small pan with the oil and some black pepper. Heat very gently for 5 minutes, stirring occasionally, until the anchovies start to disintegrate.

3 Drain the pasta thoroughly and toss with the anchovies, oil and capers. Season with a little salt and plenty of black pepper to taste. Divide between warmed bowls and serve immediately.

Home-made Potato Gnocchi

These classic Italian potato dumplings are very simple to make – it just requires a little patience when it comes to shaping them. Serve them as soon as they are cooked, tossed in melted butter and fresh sage leaves, sprinkled with grated Parmesan cheese and plenty of black pepper. They make a fabulous alternative to pasta.

900g/2lb floury potatoes, cut into large chunks

2 eggs, beaten

150–175g/5–6oz/1¼–1½ cups plain (all-purpose) flour

FROM THE STORECUPBOARD

10ml/2 tsp salt

SERVES TWO

1 Cook the potatoes in salted, boiling water for 15 minutes, until tender. Drain well and return to the pan, set it over a low heat and dry the potatoes for 1–2 minutes.

2 Mash the potatoes until smooth, then gradually stir in the eggs and salt. Work in enough flour to form a soft dough.

3 Break off small pieces of the dough and roll into balls, using floured hands. Press the back of a fork into each ball to make indentations. Repeat until all the dough has been used. Leave the gnocchi to rest for 15–20 minutes before cooking.

4 Bring a large pan of water to a gentle boil. Add the gnocchi, about ten at a time, and cook for 3–4 minutes, or until they float to the surface. Drain thoroughly and serve as soon as all the gnocchi have been cooked.

VARIATION To make herb-flavoured gnocchi, add 45ml/3 tbsp chopped fresh herbs, such as basil, parsley and sage, to the potato and flour dough and combine well. Serve with butter and grated Parmesan.

Spaghettini with Roasted Garlic

If you have never tried roasting garlic, then this is the recipe that will convert you to its delicious mellowed sweetness. Spaghettini is very fine spaghetti, but any long thin pasta can be used in this dish – try spaghetti, linguine, tagliatelle or capellini. This simple pasta dish is very good served with a mixed leaf salad dressed with lemon juice and extra virgin olive oil.

SERVES FOUR

1 Preheat the oven to 180°C/350°F/Gas 4. Place the garlic in an oiled roasting pan and roast it for 30 minutes.

2 Leave the garlic to cool, then lay it on its side and slice off the top one-third with a sharp knife.

3 Hold the garlic over a bowl and dig out the flesh from each clove with the point of the knife. When all the flesh has been added to the bowl, pour in the oil and add plenty of black pepper. Mix well.

4 Cook the pasta in a pan of salted boiling water according to the instructions on the packet. Drain the pasta and return it to the clean pan. Pour in the oil and garlic mixture and toss the pasta vigorously over a medium heat until all the strands are thoroughly coated. Serve immediately, with shavings of Parmesan.

1 whole head of garlic

400g/14oz fresh or dried spaghettini

coarsely shaved Parmesan cheese

FROM THE STORECUPBOARD

120ml/4fl oz/¹/₂ cup extra virgin olive oil

salt and ground black pepper

Spaghetti with Lemon

This is the dish to make when you get home and find there's nothing to eat. If you keep spaghetti and olive oil in the store cupboard (pantry), and garlic and lemons in the vegetable rack, you can prepare this delicious meal in minutes. You can also add some freshly grated Parmesan cheese if you have some.

SERVES FOUR

1 Cook the pasta in a pan of salted boiling water according to the instructions on the packet, then drain well and return to the pan.

2 Pour the olive oil and lemon juice over the cooked pasta, sprinkle in the slivers of garlic and add seasoning to taste. Toss the pasta over a medium to high heat for 1–2 minutes. Serve immediately in four warmed bowls.

350g/12oz dried spaghetti

juice of 1 large lemon

2 garlic cloves, cut into very thin slivers

FROM THE STORECUPBOARD

90ml/6 tbsp extra virgin olive oil

salt and ground black pepper

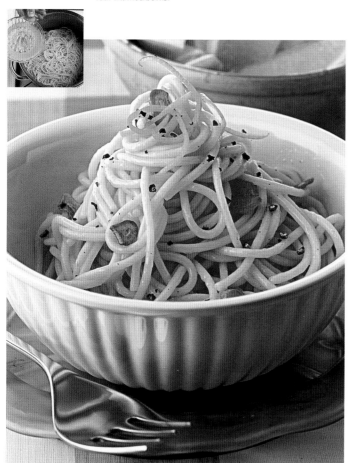

COOK'S TIP *Spaghetti is the best type of pasta for this recipe, because the olive oil and lemon juice cling to its long thin strands. If you are out of spaghetti, use another dried long pasta shape instead, such as spaghettini, linguine or tagliatelle.*

Fettuccine all'Alfredo

This simple recipe was invented by a Roman restaurateur called Alfredo, who became famous for serving it with a gold fork and spoon. Today's busy cooks will find cartons of long-life cream invaluable for this type of recipe. If you can't get fettucine, any long ribbon-like pasta can be used in this dish – try tagliatelle or slightly wider pappardelle instead.

SERVES FOUR

1 Melt the butter in a large pan. Add the cream and bring it to the boil. Simmer for 5 minutes, stirring constantly, then add the Parmesan cheese, with salt and freshly ground black pepper to taste, and turn off the heat under the pan.

2 Bring a large pan of salted water to the boil. Drop in the pasta all at once and quickly bring the water back to the boil, stirring occasionally. Cook the pasta for 2–3 minutes, or according to the instructions on the packet. Drain well.

3 Turn on the heat under the pan of cream to low, add the cooked pasta all at once and toss until it is well coated in the sauce. Taste the sauce for seasoning. Serve immediately, with extra grated Parmesan handed around separately.

200ml/7fl oz/scant 1 cup double (heavy) cream

50g/2oz/²/₃ cup freshly grated Parmesan cheese, plus extra to serve

350g/12oz fresh fettuccine

FROM THE STORECUPBOARD

50g/2oz/¹/₄ cup butter

salt and ground black pepper

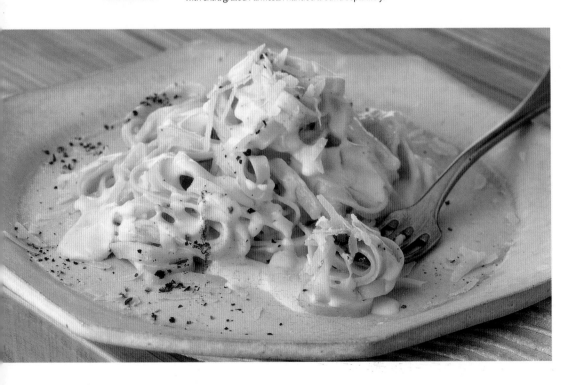

Pansotti with Walnut Sauce

Walnuts and cream make a rich and luscious sauce for stuffed pasta, particularly the types filled with cheese and herbs. Serve this indulgent dish with warm walnut bread and a light, fruity white wine.

SERVES FOUR

1 Put the walnuts and garlic oil in a food processor and process to a paste, adding up to 120ml/4fl oz/½ cup warm water through the feeder tube to slacken the consistency. Spoon the mixture into a large bowl and add the cream. Beat well to mix, then season to taste with salt and black pepper.

2 Cook the pansotti or stuffed pasta in a large pan of salted boiling water for 4–5 minutes, or according to the instructions on the packet. Meanwhile, put the walnut sauce in a large warmed bowl and add a ladleful of the pasta cooking water to thin it.

3 Drain the pasta and tip it into the bowl of walnut sauce. Toss well, then serve immediately.

90g/3¹/₂ oz/scant 1 cup shelled walnuts

120ml/4fl oz/¹/₂ cup double (heavy) cream

350g/12oz cheese and herb-filled pansotti or other stuffed pasta

FROM THE STORECUPBOARD

60ml/4 tbsp garlic-flavoured olive oil

salt and ground black pepper

Fettuccine with Butter and Parmesan

Very few ingredients are needed to make up this incredibly simple dish. It comes from northern Italy, where butter and cheese are the most popular ingredients for serving with pasta. Children love it.

SERVES FOUR

1 Cook the pasta in a pan of salted boiling water according to the instructions on the packet. Drain thoroughly, then tip into a warmed bowl.

2 Add the butter and Parmesan a third at a time, tossing the pasta after each addition until it is evenly coated. Season to taste and serve.

400g/14oz fresh or dried fettuccine

115g/4oz/1¹/₃ cups freshly grated Parmesan cheese

FROM THE STORECUPBOARD

50g/2oz/¹/₄ cup unsalted butter, cubed

salt and ground black pepper

Penne with Cream and Smoked Salmon

This modern way of serving pasta is popular all over Italy and in many Italian restaurants. The three essential ingredients combine beautifully, and the dish is very quick and easy to make.

SERVES FOUR

1 Cook the pasta in a saucepan of salted boiling water according to the instructions on the packet.

2 Meanwhile, using kitchen scissors, cut the smoked salmon into thin strips, about 5mm/¼in wide. Strip the leaves from the thyme sprigs.

3 Melt the butter in a large saucepan. Stir in the cream with about a quarter of the salmon and thyme leaves, then season with pepper. Heat gently for 3–4 minutes, stirring all the time. Do not allow to boil. Taste the sauce for seasoning.

4 Drain the pasta and toss it in the cream and salmon sauce. Divide among four warmed bowls and top with the remaining salmon and thyme leaves. Serve immediately.

350g/12oz/3 cups dried penne

115g/4oz thinly sliced smoked salmon

2–3 fresh thyme sprigs

150ml/¼ pint/²/₃ cup extra-thick single cream

FROM THE STORECUPBOARD

25g/1oz/2 tbsp butter

salt and ground black pepper

Oven-baked Porcini Risotto

This risotto is easy to make because you don't have to stand over it stirring constantly as it cooks, as you do with a traditional risotto.

SERVES FOUR

25g/1oz/¹/₂ cup dried porcini mushrooms

1 onion, finely chopped

225g/8oz/generous 1 cup risotto rice

FROM THE STORECUPBOARD

30ml/2 tbsp garlic-infused olive oil

salt and ground black pepper

1 Put the mushrooms in a heatproof bowl and pour over 750ml/1¹/₄ pints/3 cups boiling water. Leave to soak for 30 minutes. Drain the mushrooms through a sieve lined with kitchen paper, reserving the soaking liquor. Rinse the mushrooms thoroughly under running water to remove any grit, and dry on kitchen paper.

2 Preheat the oven to 180°C/350°F/Gas 4. Heat the oil in a roasting pan on the hob and add the onion. Cook for 2–3 minutes, or until softened but not coloured.

3 Add the rice and stir for 1–2 minutes, then add the mushrooms and stir. Pour in the mushroom liquor and mix well. Season with salt and pepper, and cover with foil.

4 Bake in the oven for 30 minutes, stirring occasionally, until all the stock has been absorbed and the rice is tender. Divide between warm serving bowls and serve immediately.

Persian Baked Rice

In this Persian-style dish, rice is cooked slowly over a low heat so that a crust forms on the bottom. The mild flavours of saffron and almonds go perfectly together. This dish is an ideal accompaniment for lamb.

SERVES FOUR

450g/1lb basmati rice

a good pinch of saffron strands

50g/2oz/¹/₂ cup flaked (sliced) almonds

FROM THE STORECUPBOARD

50g/2oz/¹/₄ cup butter

salt and ground black pepper

1 Cook the rice in a pan of boiling salted water for 5 minutes, then drain thoroughly. Meanwhile, put the saffron in a small bowl with 30ml/2 tbsp warm water and leave to infuse for at least 5 minutes.

2 Heat the butter in a large flameproof pan and add the almonds. Cook over a medium heat for 2–3 minutes, or until golden, stirring occasionally. Add the rice and stir well, then stir in the saffron and its liquid, plus 1 litre/1³/₄ pints/ 4 cups water. Season and cover with a tight-fitting lid.

3 Cook over a very low heat for 30 minutes, or until the rice is tender and a crust has formed on the bottom of the pan. Fork up the rice to mix in the crust before serving.

Rosemary Risotto with Borlotti Beans

Select a high-quality risotto in a subtle flavour as the base for this recipe. The savoury beans, heady rosemary and creamy mascarpone will transform a simple product into a feast. For an even more authentic risotto flavour, substitute half the water with dry white wine. Serve with a simple salad of rocket (arugula) and Parmesan shavings dressed with balsamic vinegar and plenty of freshly ground black pepper.

SERVES THREE TO FOUR

400g/14oz can
borlotti beans

275g/10oz packet
vegetable or
chicken risotto

60ml/4 tbsp
mascarpone cheese

5ml/1 tsp finely
chopped fresh
rosemary

1 Drain the beans, rinse under cold water and drain again. Process about two-thirds of the beans to a fairly coarse purée in a food processor or blender. Set the remaining beans aside.

2 Make up the risotto according to the packet instructions, using the suggested quantity of water.

3 Immediately the rice is cooked, stir in the bean purée. Add the reserved beans, with the mascarpone and rosemary. Stir thoroughly, then cover and leave to stand for about 5 minutes so that the risotto absorbs the flavours fully.

VARIATION

Fresh thyme or marjoram could be used for this risotto instead of rosemary, if you like. One of the great virtues of risotto is that it lends itself well to many variations. Experiment with plain or saffron risotto and add different herbs to make your own speciality dish.

Pancetta and Broad Bean Risotto

This moist risotto makes a satisfying, balanced meal, especially when served with cooked fresh seasonal vegetables or a mixed green salad. Add some chopped fresh herbs and Parmesan shavings as a garnish, if you like. Pancetta is dry cured pork and is the Italian equivalent of streaky (fatty) bacon – either can be used in this recipe.

SERVES FOUR

1 Place the pancetta in a non-stick or heavy pan and cook gently, stirring occasionally, for about 5 minutes, until the fat runs.

2 Add the risotto rice to the pan and cook for 1 minute, stirring constantly. Add a ladleful of the simmering stock and cook, stirring constantly, until the liquid has been absorbed.

3 Continue adding the simmering stock, a ladleful at a time, until the rice is tender, and almost all the liquid has been absorbed. This will take 30–35 minutes.

4 Meanwhile, cook the broad beans in a pan of lightly salted, boiling water for about 3 minutes until tender. Drain well and stir into the risotto. Season to taste. Spoon into a bowl and serve.

175g/6oz smoked pancetta, diced

350g/12oz/1³⁄₄ cups risotto rice

1.5 litres/2¹⁄₂ pints/ 6¹⁄₄ cups simmering herb stock

225g/8oz/2 cups frozen baby broad (fava) beans

FROM THE STORECUPBOARD

salt and ground black pepper

COOK'S TIP

If the broad beans are large, or if you prefer skinned beans, remove the outer skin after cooking them.

Mussel Risotto

The addition of freshly cooked mussels, aromatic coriander and a little cream to a packet of instant risotto can turn a simple meal into a decadent treat. Serve with a side salad for a splendid supper. Other types of cooked shellfish, such as clams or prawns (shrimp), can be used instead of mussels.

SERVES THREE TO FOUR

1 Scrub the mussels, discarding any that do not close when sharply tapped. Place in a large pan. Add 120ml/4fl oz/½ cup water and seasoning, then bring to the boil. Cover the pan and cook the mussels, shaking the pan occasionally, for 4–5 minutes, until they have opened. Drain, reserving the liquid and discarding any that have not opened. Shell most of the mussels, reserving a few in their shells for garnish. Strain the mussel liquid.

2 Make up the packet risotto according to the instructions, using the cooking liquid from the mussels and making it up to the required volume with water.

3 When the risotto is about three-quarters cooked, add the mussels to the pan. Add the coriander and re-cover the pan without stirring in these ingredients.

4 Remove the risotto from the heat, stir in the cream, cover and leave to rest for a few minutes. Spoon into a warmed serving dish, garnish with the reserved mussels in their shells, and serve.

900g/2lb fresh mussels

275g/10oz packet risotto

30ml/2 tbsp chopped fresh coriander (cilantro)

30ml/2 tbsp double (heavy) cream

FROM THE STORECUPBOARD

salt and ground black pepper

Crab Risotto

This simple risotto has a subtle flavour that makes the most of delicate crab. It makes a tempting main course or appetizer. It is important to use a good quality risotto rice, which will give a deliciously creamy result, but the cooked grains are still firm to the bite.

SERVES THREE TO FOUR

2 large cooked crabs

275g/10oz/1¹/₂ cups risotto rice

1.2 litres/2 pints/5 cups simmering fish stock

30ml/2 tbsp mixed finely chopped fresh herbs such as chives, tarragon and parsley

FROM THE STORECUPBOARD

salt and ground black pepper

1 One at a time, hold the crabs and hit the underside with the heel of your hand. This should loosen the shell from the body. Using your thumbs, push against the body and pull away from the shell. Remove and discard the intestines and the grey gills.

2 Break off the claws and legs, then use a hammer or crackers to break them open. Using a pick, remove the meat from the claws and legs. Place the meat on a plate.

3 Using a skewer, pick out the white meat from the body cavities and place with the claw and leg meat, reserving a little white meat to garnish. Scoop out the brown meat from the shell and add to the rest of the crab meat.

4 Place the rice in a pan and add one-quarter of the stock. Bring to the boil and cook, stirring, until the liquid has been absorbed. Adding a ladleful of stock at a time, cook, stirring, until about two-thirds of the stock has been absorbed. Stir in the crab meat and herbs, and continue cooking, adding the remaining stock.

5 When the rice is almost cooked, remove it from the heat and adjust the seasoning. Cover and leave to stand for 3 minutes. Serve garnished with the reserved white crab meat.

Coconut Rice

This rich dish is usually served with a tangy papaya salad to balance the sweetness of the coconut milk and sugar. It is one of those comforting treats that everyone enjoys.

SERVES FOUR TO SIX

1 Place the measured water, coconut milk, salt and sugar in a heavy pan. Wash the rice in cold water until it runs clear.

2 Add the jasmine rice, cover tightly with a lid and bring to the boil over a medium heat. Reduce the heat to low and simmer gently, without lifting the lid unnecessarily, for 15–20 minutes, until the rice is tender and cooked through. Test it by biting a grain.

3 Turn off the heat and leave the rice to rest in the pan, still covered with the lid, for a further 5–10 minutes.

4 Gently fluff up the rice grains with chopsticks or a fork before transferring it to a warmed dish and serving.

250ml/8fl oz/1 cup water

475ml/16fl oz/2 cups coconut milk

30ml/2 tbsp granulated sugar

450g/1lb/2²/₃ cups jasmine rice

FROM THE STORECUPBOARD

2.5ml/¹/₂ tsp salt

COOK'S TIP
For a special occasion serve in a halved papaya and garnish with thin shreds of fresh coconut.

Savoury Ground Rice

Savoury ground rice is often served as an accompaniment to soups and stews in West Africa.

SERVES FOUR

1 Place the water in a saucepan. Pour in the milk, bring to the boil and add the salt and parsley.

2 Add the butter or margarine and the ground rice, stirring with a wooden spoon to prevent the rice from becoming lumpy.

3 Cover the pan and cook over a low heat for about 15 minutes, beating the mixture every 2 minutes to prevent the formation of lumps.

4 To test if the rice is cooked, rub a pinch of the mixture between your fingers: if it feels smooth and fairly dry, it is ready. Serve hot.

300ml/¹/₂ pint/1¹/₄ cups water

300ml/¹/₂ pint/1¹/₄ cups milk

15ml/1 tbsp chopped fresh parsley

25g/1oz/2 tbsp butter or margarine

275g/10oz/1²/₃ cups ground rice

FROM THE STORECUPBOARD

salt

COOK'S TIP

Ground rice is a creamy white colour, with a grainy texture. Although often used in sweet dishes, it is a tasty grain to serve with savoury dishes too. The addition of milk gives a creamier flavour if preferred.

Vegetarian Dishes

FRESH-TASTING VEGETABLES, MILD EGGS,
RICH AND CREAMY CHEESES AND AROMATIC HERBS
AND SPICES ARE GREAT PARTNERS AND CAN BE COMBINED
TO MAKE A DELICIOUS ARRAY OF VEGETARIAN MAIN
MEALS. ENJOY WONDERFUL DISHES SUCH AS BAKED
STUFFED VEGETABLES, RICHLY FLAVOURED TARTS
AND LIGHT-AS-AIR SOUFFLÉS.

Aubergines with Cheese Sauce

This wonderfully simple dish of aubergines in cheese sauce is delicious hot and the perfect dish to assemble ahead of time ready for baking at the last minute. Kashkaval cheese is particularly good in this recipe – it is a hard yellow cheese made from sheep's milk and is originally from the Balkans. Serve with lots of crusty bread to mop up the delicious aubergine-flavoured cheese sauce.

SERVES FOUR TO SIX

1 Layer the aubergine slices in a bowl or colander, sprinkling each layer with salt, and leave to drain for at least 30 minutes. Rinse well, then pat dry with kitchen paper.

2 Heat the oil in a frying pan, then cook the aubergine slices until golden brown on both sides. Remove from the pan and set aside.

3 Preheat the oven to 180°C/350°F/Gas 4. Mix most of the grated cheese into the savoury white or béchamel sauce, reserving a little to sprinkle on top of the finished dish.

4 Arrange a layer of the aubergines in an ovenproof dish, then pour over some sauce. Repeat, ending with sauce. Sprinkle with the reserved cheese. Bake for 35–40 minutes until golden.

2 large aubergines (eggplants), cut into 5mm/¹/₄ in thick slices

400g/14oz/3¹/₂ cups grated cheese, such as kashkaval, Gruyère, or a mixture of Parmesan and Cheddar

600ml/1 pint/2¹/₂ cups savoury white sauce or béchamel sauce

FROM THE STORECUPBOARD

about 60ml/4 tbsp olive oil

salt and ground black pepper

Mushroom Stroganoff

This creamy mixed mushroom sauce is ideal for a dinner party. Serve it with toasted buckwheat, brown rice or a mixture of wild rices and garnish with snipped chives. For best results, choose a variety of different mushrooms – wild mushrooms such as chanterelles, ceps and morels add a delicious flavour and texture to the stroganoff, as well as adding colour and producing a decorative appearance.

SERVES FOUR

900g/2lb mixed mushrooms, cut into bitesize pieces, including ²/₃ button (white) mushrooms and ¹/₃ assorted wild or unusual mushrooms

350ml/12fl oz/1¹/₂ cups white wine sauce

250ml/8fl oz/1 cup sour cream

FROM THE STORECUPBOARD

25g/1oz/2 tbsp butter

salt and ground black pepper

1 Melt the butter in a pan and quickly cook the mushrooms, in batches, over a high heat, until brown. Transfer the mushrooms to a bowl after cooking each batch.

2 Add the sauce to the juices remaining in the pan and bring to the boil, stirring. Reduce the heat and replace the mushrooms with any juices from the bowl. Stir well and heat for a few seconds, then remove from the heat.

3 Stir the sour cream into the cooked mushroom mixture and season to taste with salt and lots of freshly ground black pepper. Heat through gently for a few seconds, if necessary, then transfer to warm plates and serve immediately.

Red Onion and Goat's Cheese Pastries

These attractive little tartlets couldn't be easier to make. Garnish them with fresh thyme sprigs and serve with a selection of salad leaves and a tomato and basil salad for a light lunch or quick supper. A wide variety of different types of goat's cheeses are available – the creamy log-shaped types without a rind are most suitable for these pastries. Ordinary onions can be used instead of red, if you prefer.

SERVES FOUR

1 Heat the oil in a large, heavy frying pan, add the onions and cook over a gentle heat for 10 minutes, or until softened, stirring occasionally to prevent them from browning. Add seasoning to taste and cook for a further 2 minutes. Remove the pan from the heat and leave to cool.

2 Preheat the oven to 220°C/425°F/Gas 7. Unroll the puff pastry and using a 15cm/6in plate as a guide, cut out four rounds. Place the pastry rounds on a dampened baking sheet and, using the point of a sharp knife, score a border, 2cm/¾in inside the edge of each pastry round.

3 Divide the onions among the pastry rounds and top with the goat's cheese. Bake for 25–30 minutes until golden brown.

450g/1lb red onions, sliced

425g/15oz packet ready-rolled puff pastry

115g/4oz/1 cup goat's cheese, cubed

FROM THE STORECUPBOARD

15ml/1 tbsp olive oil

salt and ground black pepper

EXTRAS

To make richer-flavoured pastries ring the changes by spreading the pastry base with red or green pesto or tapenade before you top with the goat's cheese and cooked onions.

Baked Leek and Potato Gratin

Potatoes baked in a creamy cheese sauce make the ultimate comfort dish, whether served as an accompaniment to pork or fish dishes or, as here, with plenty of leeks and melted cheese as a main course. When preparing leeks, separate the leaves and rinse them thoroughly under cold running water, as soil and grit often get caught between the layers.

SERVES FOUR TO SIX

1 Preheat the oven to 180°C/350°F/Gas 4. Cook the potatoes in plenty of lightly salted, boiling water for 3 minutes, until slightly softened, then drain. Cut the leeks into 1cm/½in lengths and blanch them in boiling water for 1 minute, until softened, then drain.

2 Turn half the potatoes into a shallow, ovenproof dish and spread them out to the edge. Cover with two-thirds of the leeks, then add the remaining potatoes. Tuck the slices of cheese and the remaining leeks in among the top layer of potatoes. Season and pour the cream over.

3 Bake for 1 hour, until tender and golden. Cover with foil if the top starts to overbrown before the potatoes are tender.

900g/2lb medium potatoes, thinly sliced

2 large leeks, trimmed

200g/7oz ripe Brie or Camembert cheese, sliced

450ml/³⁄₄ pint/scant 2 cups single (light) cream

FROM THE STORECUPBOARD

salt and ground black pepper

Mushroom Polenta

This simple recipe uses freshly made polenta, but for an even easier version you can substitute ready-made polenta and slice it straight into the dish, ready for baking. The cheesy mushroom topping is also delicious on toasted herb or sun-dried tomato bread as a light lunch or supper. Any combination of mushrooms will work – try a mixture of button (white) and wild mushrooms as an alternative.

SERVES FOUR

1 Line a 28 x 18cm/11 x 7in shallow baking tin (pan) with baking parchment. Bring 1 litre/1¾ pints/4 cups water with 5ml/1 tsp salt to the boil in a large pan. Add the polenta in a steady stream, stirring constantly. Bring back to the boil, stirring, and cook for 5 minutes, until thick and smooth. Turn the polenta into the prepared tin and spread it out into an even layer. Leave to cool.

2 Preheat the oven to 200°C/400°F/Gas 6. Melt the butter in a frying pan and cook the mushrooms for 3–5 minutes, until golden. Season with salt and lots of freshly ground black pepper.

3 Turn out the polenta on to a chopping board. Peel away the parchment and cut the polenta into large squares. Pile the squares into a shallow, ovenproof dish. Sprinkle with half the cheese, then pile the mushrooms on top and pour over their buttery juices. Sprinkle with the remaining cheese and bake for about 20 minutes, until the cheese is melting and pale golden.

250g/9oz/1¹/₂ cups quick-cook polenta

50g/2oz/¹/₄ cup butter

400g/14oz chestnut mushrooms, sliced

175g/6oz/1¹/₂ cups grated Gruyère cheese

FROM THE STORECUPBOARD

salt and ground black pepper

Tomato and Tapenade Tarts

These delicious individual tarts look and taste fantastic, despite the fact that they demand very little time or effort. The mascarpone cheese topping melts as it cooks to make a smooth, creamy sauce. Cherry tomatoes have a delicious sweet flavour with a low acidity, but plum tomatoes or vine-ripened tomatoes are also suitable for these tarts and will give delicious results. Red pesto can be used instead of the tapenade if you prefer a subtler flavour.

SERVES FOUR

1 Preheat the oven to 220°C/425°F/Gas 7. Lightly grease a large baking sheet and sprinkle it with water. Roll out the pastry on a lightly floured surface and cut out four 16cm/6½in rounds, using a bowl or small plate as a guide.

2 Transfer the pastry rounds to the prepared baking sheet. Using the tip of a sharp knife, mark a shallow cut 1cm/½in in from the edge of each round to form a rim.

3 Reserve half the tapenade and spread the rest over the pastry rounds, keeping the paste inside the marked rim. Cut half the tomatoes in half. Pile all the tomatoes, whole and halved, on the pastry, again keeping them inside the rim. Season lightly.

4 Bake for 20 minutes, until the pastry is well risen and golden. Dot with the remaining tapenade. Spoon a little mascarpone on the centre of the tomatoes and season with black pepper. Bake for a further 10 minutes, until the mascarpone has melted to make a sauce. Serve the tarts warm.

500g/1¼lb puff pastry, thawed if frozen

60ml/4 tbsp black or green olive tapenade

500g/1¼lb cherry tomatoes

90g/3½oz/scant ½ cup mascarpone cheese

FROM THE STORECUPBOARD

salt and ground black pepper

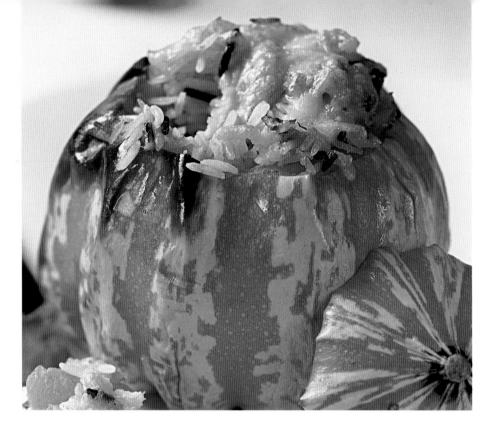

Stuffed Baby Squash

It is worth making the most of baby squash while they are in season. Use any varieties you can find and do not worry too much about choosing vegetables of uniform size, as an assortment of different types and sizes looks attractive. The baked vegetables can easily be shared out at the table. Serve with warm sun-dried tomato bread and a ready-made spicy tomato sauce for a hearty autumn supper.

SERVES FOUR

1 Preheat the oven to 190°C/375°F/Gas 5. Pierce the squash in with the tip of a knife. Bake for 30 minutes, until the squash are tender. Leave until cool enough to handle.

2 Meanwhile, cook the rice in salted, boiling water for 12 minutes, until tender, then drain. Slice a lid off the top of each squash and scoop out and discard the seeds. Scoop out and chop the flesh.

3 Heat the oil in a frying pan and cook the chopped squash for 5 minutes. Reserve 60ml/4 tbsp of the cheese, add the remainder to the pan with the rice and a little salt. Mix well.

4 Pile the mixture into the squash shells and place in a dish. Sprinkle with the remaining cheese and bake for 20 minutes.

4 small squash, each about 350g/12oz

200g/7oz/1 cup mixed wild and basmati rice

150g/5oz/1¼ cups grated Gruyère cheese

FROM THE STORECUPBOARD

60ml/4 tbsp chilli and garlic oil

salt and ground black pepper

Roasted Peppers with Halloumi and Pine Nuts

Halloumi cheese is creamy-tasting and has a firm texture and salty flavour that contrast well with the succulent sweet peppers. This is a good dish to assemble in advance. Halloumi is usually served cooked and lends itself well to barbecuing, frying or grilling (broiling). When heated the exterior hardens while the interior softens and is similar to mozzarella cheese.

SERVES FOUR

1 Preheat the oven to 220°C/425°F/Gas 7. Halve the red peppers, leaving the stalks intact, and discard the seeds. Seed and coarsely chop the orange or yellow peppers. Place the red pepper halves on a baking sheet and fill with the chopped peppers. Drizzle with half the garlic or herb olive oil and bake for 25 minutes, until the edges of the peppers are beginning to char.

2 Dice the cheese and tuck in among the chopped peppers. Sprinkle with the pine nuts and drizzle with the remaining oil. Bake for a further 15 minutes, until well browned. Serve warm.

4 red and 2 orange or yellow (bell) peppers

250g/9oz halloumi cheese

50g/2oz/¹/₂ cup pine nuts

FROM THE STORECUPBOARD

60ml/4 tbsp garlic or herb olive oil

salt and ground black pepper

Spicy Chickpea Samosas

A blend of crushed chickpeas and coriander sauce makes an interesting alternative to the more familiar meat or vegetable fillings in these little pastries. The samosas look pretty garnished with fresh coriander leaves and finely sliced onion and are delicious served with a simple dip made from Greek (US strained plain) yogurt and chopped fresh mint leaves.

MAKES EIGHTEEN

1 Preheat the oven to 220°C/425°F/Gas 7. Process half the chickpeas to a paste in a food processor. Tip the paste into a bowl and add the whole chickpeas, the hara masala or coriander sauce, and a little salt. Mix until well combined.

2 Lay a sheet of filo pastry on a work surface and cut into three strips. Brush the strips with a little of the oil. Place a dessertspoon of the filling at one end of a strip. Turn one corner diagonally over the filling to meet the long edge. Continue folding the filling and the pastry along the length of the strip, keeping the triangular shape. Transfer to a baking sheet and repeat with the remaining filling and pastry.

3 Brush the pastries with any remaining oil and bake for 15 minutes, until the pastry is golden. Cool before serving.

2 x 400g/14oz cans chickpeas, drained and rinsed

120ml/4fl oz/$\frac{1}{2}$ cup hara masala or coriander (cilantro) sauce

275g/10oz filo pastry

FROM THE STORECUPBOARD

60ml/4 tbsp chilli and garlic oil

salt and ground black pepper

Tofu and Pepper Kebabs

A simple coating of ground, dry-roasted peanuts pressed on to cubed tofu provides plenty of additional flavour along with the peppers. Use metal or bamboo skewers for the kebabs – if you use bamboo, then soak them in cold water for 30 minutes before using to prevent them from scorching during cooking. The kebabs can also be cooked on a barbecue, if you prefer.

SERVES FOUR

1 Pat the tofu dry on kitchen paper and then cut it into small cubes. Grind the peanuts in a blender or food processor and transfer to a plate. Turn the tofu cubes in the ground nuts to coat.

2 Preheat the grill (broiler) to moderate. Halve and seed the peppers, and cut them into large chunks. Thread the chunks of pepper on to four large skewers with the tofu cubes and place on a foil-lined grill rack.

3 Grill (broil) the kebabs, turning frequently, for 10–12 minutes, or until the peppers and peanuts are beginning to brown. Transfer the kebabs to plates and serve with the dipping sauce.

250g/9oz firm tofu

50g/2oz/¹/₂ cup dry-roasted peanuts

2 red and 2 green (bell) peppers

60ml/4 tbsp sweet chilli dipping sauce

FROM THE STORECUPBOARD

salt and ground black pepper

Mixed Bean and Tomato Chilli

Here, mixed beans, fiery red chilli and plenty of freshly chopped coriander are simmered in a tomato sauce to make a delicious vegetarian chilli. Always a popular dish, chilli can be served with a variety of accompaniments – choose from baked potatoes, baked rice, crusty bread or tortillas. Garnish with slices of tomato, chopped celery or sweet (bell) pepper and top with natural (plain) yogurt.

SERVES FOUR

1 Pour the tomato sauce and mixed beans into a pan. Seed and thinly slice the chilli, then add it to the pan. Reserve a little of the coriander, chop the remainder and add it to the pan.

2 Bring the mixture to the boil, reduce the heat, cover and simmer gently for 10 minutes. Stir the mixture occasionally and add a dash of water if the sauce starts to dry out.

3 Ladle the chilli into warmed individual serving bowls and top with a spoonful of yogurt to serve.

400g/14oz jar tomato and herb sauce

2 x 400g/14oz cans mixed beans, drained and rinsed

1 fresh red chilli

large handful of fresh coriander (cilantro)

FROM THE STORECUPBOARD

salt and ground black pepper

Cheese and Tomato Soufflés

Using a ready-made cheese sauce takes the effort out of soufflé making. The key to success when making soufflés is to whisk the egg whites thoroughly to incorporate as much air as possible. During the cooking time don't open the oven door – the cold draught could cause the delicate mixture to collapse.

SERVES SIX

1 Preheat the oven to 200°C/400°F/Gas 6. Turn the cheese sauce into a bowl. Thinly slice the sun-dried tomatoes and add to the bowl with 90g/3½oz/generous 1 cup of the Parmesan, the egg yolks and seasoning. Stir until well combined.

2 Brush the base and sides of six 200ml/7fl oz/scant 1 cup ramekins with the oil and then coat the insides of the dishes with half the remaining cheese, tilting them until evenly covered.

3 Whisk the egg whites in a clean bowl until stiff. Use a large metal spoon to stir one-quarter of the egg whites into the sauce, then fold in the remainder. Spoon the mixture into the prepared dishes and sprinkle with the remaining Parmesan cheese. Place on a baking sheet and bake for 15–18 minutes, until well risen and golden. Serve the soufflés as soon as you remove them from the oven.

350g/12oz tub fresh cheese sauce

50g/2oz sun-dried tomatoes in olive oil, drained, plus 10ml/ 2 tsp of the oil

130g/4¹⁄₂oz/1¹⁄₃ cups grated Parmesan cheese

4 large (US extra large) eggs, separated

FROM THE STORECUPBOARD

salt and ground black pepper

Classic Margherita Pizza

Bought pizza base mixes are a great storecupboard stand-by. A Margherita Pizza makes a lovely simple supper, but of course you can add any extra toppings you like. Prosciutto and rocket (arugula) make a great addition – just add them to the pizza after it is cooked.

SERVES TWO

half a 300g/11oz packet pizza base mix

45ml/3 tbsp ready-made tomato and basil sauce

150g/5oz mozzarella, sliced

FROM THE STORECUPBOARD

15ml/1 tbsp herb-infused olive oil

salt and ground black pepper

1 Make the pizza base mix according to the instructions on the packet. Brush the base with a little of the olive oil and spread over the tomato and basil sauce, not quite to the edges.

2 Arrange the slices of mozzarella on top of the pizza and bake for 25–30 minutes, or until golden.

3 Drizzle the remaining oil on top of the pizza, season with salt and black pepper and serve immediately, garnished with fresh basil leaves.

Cheesy Leek and Couscous Cake

The tangy flavour of sharp Cheddar cheese goes perfectly with the sweet taste of leeks. The cheese melts into the couscous and helps it stick together, making a firm cake that's easy to cut into wedges. Serve with a crisp green salad.

SERVES FOUR

300g/11oz couscous

2 leeks, sliced

200g/7oz mature Cheddar or Monterey Jack, grated

FROM THE STORECUPBOARD

45ml/3 tbsp olive oil

salt and ground black pepper

VARIATION
There are endless variations on this tangy, tasty cake but choose a cheese that melts well because it will help the cake to stick together. Try using caramelized onions and blue cheese in place of the leeks and Cheddar.

1 Put the couscous in a large heatproof bowl and pour over 450ml/³/₄ pint/scant 2 cups boiling water. Cover and set aside for about 15 minutes, or until all the water has been absorbed.

2 Heat 15ml/1 tbsp of the oil in a 23cm/9in non-stick frying pan. Add the leeks and cook over a medium heat for 4–5 minutes, stirring occasionally, until tender and golden.

3 Remove the leeks with a slotted spoon and stir them into the couscous. Add the grated cheese and some salt and pepper and stir through. Heat the remaining oil in the pan and tip in the couscous and leek mixture. Pat down firmly to form a cake and cook over a fairly gentle heat for 15 minutes, or until the underside is crisp and golden.

4 Slide the couscous cake onto a plate, then invert it back into the pan to cook the other side. Cook for a further 5–8 minutes, or until golden, then remove from the heat. Slide on to a board and serve cut into wedges.

Potato and Onion Tortilla

This deep-set omelette with sliced potatoes and onions is the best-known Spanish tortilla and makes a deliciously simple meal when served with a leafy salad and crusty bread. Tortilla are often made with a variety of ingredients – chopped red or yellow (bell) peppers, cooked peas, corn, or grated Cheddar or Gruyère cheese can all be added to the mixture in step 2, if you like.

SERVES FOUR TO SIX

800g/1³/₄lb medium potatoes

2 onions, thinly sliced

6 eggs

FROM THE STORECUPBOARD

100ml/3¹/₂fl oz/scant ¹/₂ cup extra virgin olive oil

salt and ground black pepper

1 Thinly slice the potatoes. Heat 75ml/5 tbsp of the oil in a frying pan and cook the potatoes, turning frequently, for 10 minutes. Add the onions and seasoning, and continue to cook for a further 10 minutes, until the vegetables are tender.

2 Meanwhile, beat the eggs in a large bowl with a little seasoning. Tip the potatoes and onions into the eggs and mix gently. Leave to stand for 10 minutes.

3 Wipe out the pan with kitchen paper and heat the remaining oil in it. Pour the egg mixture into the pan and spread it out in an even layer. Cover and cook over a very gentle heat for 20 minutes, until the eggs are just set. Serve cut into wedges.

Spiced Lentils

The combination of lentils, tomatoes and cheese is widely used in Mediterranean cooking. The tang of feta cheese complements the slightly earthy flavour of the attractive dark lentils. True Puy lentils come from the region of France, Le Puy, which has a unique climate and volcanic soil in which they thrive.

SERVES FOUR

250g/9oz/1¹/₂ cups Puy lentils

200g/7oz feta cheese

75ml/5 tbsp sun-dried tomato purée (paste)

small handful of fresh chervil or flat leaf parsley, chopped, plus extra to garnish

FROM THE STORECUPBOARD

salt and ground black pepper

1 Place the lentils in a heavy pan with 600ml/1 pint/2½ cups water. Bring to the boil, reduce the heat and cover the pan. Simmer gently for about 20 minutes, until the lentils are just tender and most of the water has been absorbed.

2 Crumble half the feta cheese into the pan. Add the sun-dried tomato purée, chopped chervil or flat leaf parsley and a little salt and freshly ground black pepper. Heat through for 1 minute.

3 Transfer the lentil mixture and juices to warmed plates or bowls. Crumble the remaining feta cheese on top and sprinkle with the fresh herbs to garnish. Serve hot.

Roast Acorn Squash with Spinach and Gorgonzola

Roasting squash brings out its sweetness, here offset by tangy cheese. Acorn squash has been used here, but any type of squash will give delicious results.

SERVES FOUR

4 acorn squash

250g/9oz baby spinach leaves, washed

200g/7oz Gorgonzola cheese, sliced

FROM THE STORECUPBOARD

45ml/3 tbsp garlic-infused olive oil

salt and ground black pepper

1 Preheat the oven to 190°C/375°F/Gas 5. Cut the tops off the squash, and scoop out and discard the seeds. Place the squash, cut side up, in a roasting pan and drizzle with 30ml/2 tbsp of the oil. Season with salt and pepper and bake for 30–40 minutes, or until tender.

2 Heat the remaining oil in a large frying pan and add the spinach leaves. Cook over a medium heat for 2–3 minutes, until the leaves are just wilted. Season with salt and pepper and divide between the squash halves.

3 Top with the Gorgonzola and return to the oven for 10 minutes, or until the cheese has melted. Season with ground black pepper and serve.

Creamy Red Lentil Dhal

This makes a tasty winter supper for vegetarians and meat eaters alike. Serve with naan bread, coconut cream and fresh coriander (cilantro) leaves. The coconut cream gives this dish a really rich taste.

SERVES FOUR

500g/1¹/₄lb/2 cups red lentils

15ml/1 tbsp hot curry paste

FROM THE STORECUPBOARD

15ml/1 tbsp sunflower oil

salt and ground black pepper

1 Heat the oil in a large pan and add the lentils. Fry for 1–2 minutes, stirring continuously, then stir in the curry paste and 600ml/1 pint/2¹/₂ cups boiling water.

2 Bring the mixture to the boil, then reduce the heat to a gentle simmer. Cover the pan and cook for 15 minutes, stirring occasionally, until the lentils are tender and the mixture has thickened.

3 Season the dhal with plenty of salt and ground black pepper to taste, and serve piping hot.

Wild Mushroom and Fontina Tart

Use any types of wild mushrooms you like in this tart – chanterelles, morels, horns of plenty and ceps all have wonderful flavours. It makes an impressive vegetarian main course, served with a green salad.

SERVES SIX

225g/8oz ready-made shortcrust pastry, thawed if frozen

350g/12oz/5 cups mixed wild mushrooms, sliced if large

150g/5oz Fontina cheese, sliced

FROM THE STORECUPBOARD

50g/2oz/¹/₄ cup butter

salt and ground black pepper

1 Preheat the oven to 190°C/375°F/Gas 5. Roll out the pastry and use to a line a 23cm/9in loose-bottomed flan tin (tart pan). Chill the pastry for 30 minutes, then bake blind for 15 minutes. Set aside.

2 Heat the butter in a large frying pan until foaming. Add the mushrooms and season with salt and ground black pepper. Cook over a medium heat for 4–5 minutes, moving the mushrooms about and turning them occasionally with a wooden spoon, until golden.

3 Arrange the mushrooms in the cooked pastry case with the Fontina. Return the tart to the oven for 10 minutes, or until the cheese is golden and bubbling. Serve hot.

Parmigiana di Melanzane

This flavoursome Italian dish can be served as a vegetarian main course, or as an accompaniment to meat or chicken dishes. For a delicious variation, layer a few artichoke hearts between the slices of aubergine.

SERVES EIGHT

900g/2lb aubergines (eggplants), sliced lengthways

600ml/1 pint/2¹⁄₂ cups garlic and herb passata (bottled strained tomatoes)

115g/4oz/1¹⁄₄ cups freshly grated Parmesan cheese

FROM THE STORECUPBOARD

60ml/4 tbsp olive oil

salt and ground black pepper

1 Preheat the grill (broiler) to high. Brush the aubergine slices with the oil and season with salt and pepper to taste. Arrange them in a single layer on a grill pan and grill (broil) for 4–5 minutes on each side, until golden and tender. (You will have to do this in batches.)

2 Preheat the oven to 190°C/375°F/Gas 5. Spoon a little passata into a large baking dish. Arrange a single layer of aubergine slices over the top and sprinkle with some grated Parmesan cheese. Repeat the layers of passata, aubergine and Parmesan until all the ingredients have been used up, finishing with a good sprinkling of Parmesan. Bake for 20–25 minutes, or until golden and bubbling.

Vegetables and Side Dishes

A FEW CAREFULLY CHOSEN INGREDIENTS CAN BE BROUGHT

TOGETHER TO CREATE MOUTHWATERING SIDE DISHES

AND ACCOMPANIMENTS THAT WILL COMPLEMENT AND

ENHANCE ANY MAIN DISH. THIS COLLECTION OF TASTY

AND COLOURFUL COMBINATIONS OF VEGETABLES MAKES

HEALTHY EATING A TEMPTING TREAT.

Japanese-style Spinach
with Toasted Sesame Seeds

This Japanese speciality, known as *O-hitashi*, has been served as a side dish on dining tables in Japan for centuries. Seasonal green vegetables are simply blanched and cooled and formed into little towers. With a little help from soy sauce and sesame seeds, they reveal their true flavour. Serve the spinach towers with simply cooked chicken, or fish such as salmon or tuna.

SERVES FOUR

1 Blanch the spinach leaves in boiling water for 15 seconds. For Japanese-type spinach, hold the leafy part and slip the stems into the pan. After 15 seconds, drop in the leaves and cook for 20 seconds.

2 Drain immediately and place the spinach under running water. Squeeze out all the excess water by hand. Now what looked like a large amount of spinach has become a ball, roughly the size of an orange. Mix the shoyu and water, then pour on to the spinach. Mix well and leave to cool.

3 Meanwhile, put the sesame seeds in a dry frying pan and stir or toss until they start to pop. Remove from the heat and leave to cool.

4 Drain the spinach and squeeze out the excess sauce with your hands. Form the spinach into a log shape of about 4cm/1½in in diameter on a chopping board. Squeeze again to make it firm. With a sharp knife, cut it across into four cylinders.

5 Place the spinach cylinders on a large plate or individual dishes. Sprinkle with the toasted sesame seeds and serve.

450g/1lb fresh young spinach

30ml/2 tbsp shoyu

30ml/2 tbsp water

15ml/1 tbsp sesame seeds

COOK'S TIP *Japanese spinach, the long-leaf type with the stalks and pink root intact, is best, but you can use ordinary young spinach leaves, or any soft and deep-green salad leaves – such as watercress, rocket (arugula) or lamb's lettuce.*

Braised Lettuce and Peas with Spring Onions

This light vegetable dish is based on the classic French method of braising peas with lettuce and spring onions in butter, and is delicious served with simply grilled fish or roast or grilled duck. A sprinkling of chopped fresh mint makes a fresh, flavoursome and extremely pretty garnish. Other legumes such as broad (fava) beans, mangetouts (snow peas) and sugar snap peas can be used instead of peas to create a delicious variation.

SERVES FOUR

1 Melt half the butter in a wide, heavy pan over a low heat. Add the lettuces and spring onions.

2 Turn the vegetables in the butter, then sprinkle in salt and plenty of freshly ground black pepper. Cover, and cook the vegetables very gently for 5 minutes, stirring once.

3 Add the peas and turn them in the buttery juices. Pour in 120ml/4fl oz/½ cup water, then cover and cook over a gentle heat for a further 5 minutes. Uncover and increase the heat to reduce the liquid to a few tablespoons.

4 Stir in the remaining butter and adjust the seasoning. Transfer to a warmed serving dish and serve immediately.

50g/2oz/¹/₄ cup butter

4 Little Gem (Bibb) lettuces, halved lengthways

2 bunches spring onions (scallions), trimmed

400g/14oz shelled peas (about 1kg/2¹/₄lb in pods)

FROM THE STORECUPBOARD

salt and ground black pepper

EXTRA — *Braise about 250g/9oz baby carrots with the lettuce.*

Asparagus with Lemon Sauce

Sometimes less is more: here a simple egg and lemon dressing brings out the best in asparagus. Serve the asparagus as an appetizer or side dish; alternatively, enjoy it for a light supper, with bread and butter to mop up the juices. When buying asparagus, look for bright coloured firm spears with tight buds – avoid those with tough woody stems. Choose roughly even-sized spears for uniform cooking.

SERVES FOUR

1 Cook the bundle of asparagus in a tall pan of lightly salted, boiling water for 7–10 minutes.

2 Drain well and arrange the asparagus in a serving dish. Reserve 200ml/7fl oz/scant 1 cup of the cooking liquid.

3 Blend the cornflour with the cooled, reserved cooking liquid and place in a pan. Bring to the boil, stirring constantly, and cook over a gentle heat until the sauce thickens slightly. Remove the pan from the heat and leave to cool.

4 Beat the egg yolks with the lemon juice and stir into the cooled sauce. Cook over a low heat, stirring constantly, until the sauce is thick. Be careful not to overheat the sauce or it may curdle. As soon as the sauce has thickened, remove the pan from the heat and continue stirring for 1 minute. Taste and season with salt. Leave the sauce to cool slightly.

5 Stir the cooled lemon sauce, then pour a little over the cooked asparagus. Cover and chill in the refrigerator for at least 2 hours before serving with the rest of the sauce.

675g/1¹/₂lb asparagus, tough ends removed, and tied in a bundle

15ml/1 tbsp cornflour (cornstarch)

2 egg yolks

juice of 1¹/₂ lemons

FROM THE STORECUPBOARD

salt and ground black pepper

COOK'S TIP *For a slightly less tangy sauce, add a little caster (superfine) sugar with the salt in step 4.*

Caramelized Shallots

Sweet, golden shallots are good with all sorts of main dishes, including poultry or meat. Shallots have a less distinctive aroma than common onions and a milder flavour; they are also considered to be easier to digest. These caramelized shallots are also excellent with braised or roasted chestnuts, carrots or chunks of butternut squash. You may like to garnish the shallots with sprigs of fresh thyme before serving.

SERVES FOUR TO SIX

1 Heat the butter or oil in a large frying pan and add the shallots or onions in a single layer. Cook gently, turning occasionally, until they are lightly browned.

2 Sprinkle the sugar over the shallots and cook gently, turning the shallots in the juices, until the sugar begins to caramelize. Add the wine or port and let the mixture bubble for 4–5 minutes.

3 Add 150ml/¼ pint/⅔ cup water and seasoning. Cover and cook for 5 minutes, then remove the lid and cook until the liquid evaporates and the shallots are tender and glazed. Adjust the seasoning before serving.

500g/1¼lb shallots or small onions, peeled with root ends intact

15ml/1 tbsp golden caster (superfine) sugar

30ml/2 tbsp red or white wine or port

FROM THE STORECUPBOARD

50g/2oz/¼ cup butter or 60ml/4 tbsp olive oil

salt and ground black pepper

Green Beans with Almond Butter and Lemon

The mild flavour of the almonds in this dish makes it a perfect accompaniment for baked or grilled oily fish such as trout or mackerel.

SERVES FOUR

350g/12oz green beans, trimmed

50g/2oz/¹⁄₃ cup whole blanched almonds

grated rind and juice of 1 unwaxed lemon

FROM THE STORECUPBOARD

50g/2oz/¹⁄₄ cup butter

salt and ground black pepper

1 Cook the beans in a pan of salted boiling water for about 3 minutes, or until just tender. Drain well. Meanwhile, melt the butter in a large frying pan until foamy.

2 Add the almonds to the pan and cook, stirring occasionally, for 2–3 minutes, or until golden. Remove from the heat and toss with the beans, lemon rind and juice, and season.

VARIATION This salad is delicious made with different types of nuts. Use the same quantity of roughly chopped shelled walnuts or blanched hazelnuts in place of the almonds.

Garlicky Green Salad with Raspberry Dressing

Adding a splash of raspberry vinegar to the dressing enlivens a simple green salad, turning it into a sophisticated side dish.

SERVES FOUR

2 garlic cloves, finely sliced

4 handfuls of green salad leaves

15ml/1 tbsp raspberry vinegar

FROM THE STORECUPBOARD

45ml/3 tbsp olive oil

salt and ground black pepper

1 Heat the oil in a small pan and add the garlic. Fry gently for 1–2 minutes, or until just golden, being careful not to burn the garlic. Remove the garlic with a slotted spoon and drain on kitchen paper. Pour the oil into a small bowl.

2 Arrange the salad leaves in a serving bowl. Whisk the raspberry vinegar into the reserved oil and season with salt and ground black pepper.

3 Pour the garlic dressing over the salad leaves and toss to combine. Sprinkle over the fried garlic slices and serve.

Cauliflower with Garlic Crumbs

This simple dish makes a great accompaniment to any meat or fish dish. When buying cauliflower look for creamy white coloured florets with the inner green leaves curled round the flower. Discard cauliflowers with discoloured patches or yellow leaves. As an alternative, try using broccoli florets instead of the cauliflower. Broccoli should have a fresh appearance: avoid yellowing specimens and those that feel soft or are wilting.

SERVES FOUR TO SIX

1 Steam or boil the cauliflower in salted water until just tender. Drain and leave to cool.

2 Heat 60–75ml/4–5 tbsp of the olive or vegetable oil in a pan, add the breadcrumbs and cook over a medium heat, tossing and turning, until browned and crisp. Add the garlic, turn once or twice, then remove from the pan and set aside.

3 Heat the remaining oil in the pan, then add the cauliflower, mashing and breaking it up a little as it lightly browns in the oil. (Do not overcook but just cook until lightly browned.)

4 Add the garlic breadcrumbs to the pan and cook, stirring, until well combined, with some of the cauliflower still holding its shape. Season and serve hot or warm.

1 large cauliflower, cut into bitesize florets

130g/4¹/₂oz/2¹/₄ cups dry white or wholemeal (whole-wheat) breadcrumbs

3–5 garlic cloves, thinly sliced or chopped

FROM THE STORECUPBOARD

90–120ml/6–8 tbsp olive or vegetable oil

salt and ground black pepper

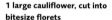

COOK'S TIP

Serve this garlicky cauliflower dish as they do in Italy, with cooked pasta, such as spaghetti.

Summer Squash and Baby New Potatoes in Warm Dill Sour Cream

Fresh vegetables and fragrant dill are delicious tossed in a simple sour cream or yogurt sauce. Choose small squash with bright skins that are free from blemishes and bruises. To make a simpler potato salad, pour the dill sour cream over warm cooked potatoes. Serve either version of the potato salad with poached salmon or chargrilled chicken.

SERVES FOUR

1 Cut the squash into pieces about the same size as the potatoes. Put the potatoes in a pan and add water to cover and a pinch of salt. Bring to the boil, then simmer for about 10 minutes, until almost tender. Add the squash and continue to cook until the vegetables are just tender, then drain.

2 Put the vegetables into a wide, shallow pan and gently stir in the finely chopped fresh dill and chives.

3 Remove the pan from the heat and stir in the sour cream or yogurt. Return to the heat and heat gently until warm. Season and serve.

400g/14oz mixed squash, such as yellow and green courgettes (zucchini), and green patty pan

400g/14oz baby new potatoes

1 large handful mixed fresh dill and chives, finely chopped

300ml/¹/₂ pint/1¹/₄ cups sour cream or Greek (US strained plain) yogurt

FROM THE STORECUPBOARD

salt and ground black pepper

Roast Asparagus with Crispy Prosciutto

Choose tender, fine asparagus for this recipe, as it cooks through quickly in the oven without losing its flavour or texture.

SERVES FOUR

350g/12oz fine asparagus spears, trimmed

1 small handful of fresh basil leaves

4 prosciutto slices

FROM THE STORECUPBOARD

30ml/2 tbsp olive oil

salt and ground black pepper

1 Preheat the oven to 190°C/375°F/Gas 5. Put the asparagus in a roasting pan and drizzle with the olive oil. Sprinkle over the basil and season with salt and ground black pepper. Gently stir to coat in the oil, then spread the asparagus in a single layer.

2 Lay the slices of prosciutto on top of the asparagus and cook for 10–15 minutes, or until the prosciutto is crisp and the asparagus is just tender. Serve immediately.

Garlicky Roasties

Potatoes roasted in their skins retain a deep, earthy taste (and, as a bonus, absorb less fat too) while the garlic mellows on cooking to give a pungent but not overly-strong taste to serve alongside or squeezed over as a garnish.

SERVES FOUR

1 Preheat the oven to 240°C/475°F/Gas 9. Place the potatoes in a pan of cold water and bring to the boil. Drain.

2 Combine the oils in a roasting tin and place in the oven to get really hot. Add the potatoes and garlic and coat in oil.

3 Sprinkle with salt and roast for 10 minutes. Reduce the heat to 200°C/400°F/Gas 6. Continue roasting, basting occasionally, for 30–40 minutes.

4 Serve each portion with several cloves of garlic.

1kg/2¹⁄₄lb small floury potatoes

10ml/2 tsp walnut oil

2 whole garlic bulbs, unpeeled

FROM THE STORECUPBOARD

60–75ml/4–5 tbsp sunflower oil

salt and ground black pepper

Leek Fritters

These crispy fried morsels are best served at room temperature, with a good squeeze of lemon juice and a sprinkling of salt and freshly grated nutmeg. Matzo meal, a traditional Jewish ingredient, is used in these fritters: it is made from crumbled matzo, an unleavened bread, similar to water biscuits. Matzo meal is used in a similar way to breadcrumbs, which can also be used to make these fritters.

SERVES FOUR

1 Cook the leeks in salted boiling water for 5 minutes, or until just tender and bright green. Drain well and leave to cool.

2 Chop the leeks coarsely. Put in a bowl and combine with the matzo meal, eggs and seasoning.

3 Heat 5mm/¼in oil in a frying pan. Using two tablespoons, carefully spoon the leek mixture into the hot oil. Cook over a medium-high heat until golden brown on the underside, then turn and cook the second side. Drain on kitchen paper. Add more oil if needed and heat before cooking more mixture.

4 large leeks, total weight about 1kg/2¹/₄lb, thickly sliced

120–175ml/4–6fl oz/¹/₂–³/₄ cup coarse matzo meal

2 eggs, lightly beaten

FROM THE STORECUPBOARD

olive or vegetable oil, for shallow frying

salt and ground black pepper

Deep-fried Artichokes

This is an Italian speciality, named *carciofi alla giudia*. The artichokes are baked, then pressed to open them and plunged into hot oil, where their leaves twist and brown, turning the artichokes into crispy flowers. Serve with lamb or pork steaks.

SERVES FOUR

2–3 lemons, halved

4–8 small young globe artichokes

olive or vegetable oil, for deep-frying

1 Fill a large bowl with cold water and stir in the juice of one or two of the lemons. Trim and discard the stems of the artichokes, then trim off their tough ends and remove all the tough outer leaves until you reach the pale pointed centre. Carefully open the leaves of one of the artichokes by pressing it against the table or poking them open. Trim the tops if they are sharp.

2 If there is any choke inside the artichoke, remove it with a melon baller or small pointed spoon. Put the artichoke in the acidulated water and prepare the remaining artichokes in the same way.

3 Put the artichokes in a large pan and pour over water to cover. Bring to the boil, reduce the heat and simmer for 10–15 minutes, or until partly cooked. If they are small, cook them for only 10 minutes. Drain the artichokes and leave upside down until cool enough to handle. Press them open gently, being careful not to break them apart.

4 Fill a pan with oil to a depth of 5–7.5cm/2–3in and heat. Add one or two artichokes at a time, with the leaves uppermost, and press down with a spoon to open up the leaves. Fry for 5–8 minutes, turning, until golden and crisp. Remove from the pan, and drain on kitchen paper. Serve immediately, with the remaining lemon cut into wedges.

COOK'S TIP *Select immature artichokes, before their chokes have formed. If you like, you can prepare and boil them ahead and deep-fry just before serving.*

Stir-fried Broccoli with Soy Sauce and Sesame Seeds

Purple sprouting broccoli has been used for this recipe, but when it is not available an ordinary variety of broccoli, such as calabrese, will also work very well.

SERVES TWO

225g/8oz purple sprouting broccoli

15ml/1 tbsp soy sauce

15ml/1 tbsp toasted sesame seeds

FROM THE STORECUPBOARD

15ml/1 tbsp olive oil

salt and ground black pepper

1 Using a sharp knife, cut off and discard any thick stems from the broccoli and cut the broccoli into long, thin florets.

2 Heat the olive oil in a wok or large frying pan and add the broccoli. Stir-fry for 3–4 minutes, or until tender, adding a splash of water if the pan becomes too dry.

3 Add the soy sauce to the broccoli, then season with salt and ground black pepper to taste. Add sesame seeds, toss to combine and serve immediately.

Stir-fried Brussels Sprouts with Bacon and Caraway Seeds

This is a great way of cooking Brussels sprouts, helping to retain their sweet flavour and crunchy texture. Stir-frying guarantees that there will not be a single soggy sprout in sight, which is often what puts people off these fabulous vegetables.

SERVES FOUR

1 Using a sharp knife, cut the Brussels sprouts into fine shreds and set aside. Heat the oil in a wok or large frying pan and add the bacon. Cook for 1–2 minutes, or until the bacon is beginning to turn golden.

2 Add the shredded sprouts to the wok or pan and stir-fry for 1–2 minutes, or until lightly cooked.

3 Season the sprouts with salt and ground black pepper to taste and stir in the caraway seeds. Cook for a further 30 seconds, then serve immediately.

450g/1lb Brussels sprouts, trimmed and washed

2 streaky (fatty) bacon rashers (strips), finely chopped

10ml/2 tsp caraway seeds, lightly crushed

FROM THE STORECUPBOARD

30ml/2 tbsp sunflower oil

salt and ground black pepper

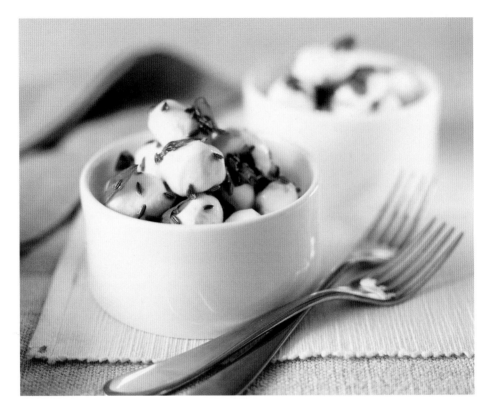

Bocconcini with Fennel and Basil

These tiny balls of mozzarella are best when they're perfectly fresh. They should be milky and soft when you cut into them. Buy them from an Italian delicatessen or a good cheese shop.

SERVES SIX

1 Drain the bocconcini well and place in a bowl. Stir in the olive oil, fennel seeds and basil, and season with salt and pepper. Cover and chill for 1 hour.

2 Remove the bowl from the refrigerator and leave to stand for about 30 minutes for the cheese to return to room temperature before serving.

COOK'S TIP

Bocconcini are mini mozzarella balls, each one hand-stretched and rolled, then preserved in brine. If you can't find bocconcini, use ordinary mozzarella cut into bitesize pieces.

450g/1lb bocconcini mozzarella

5ml/1 tsp fennel seeds, lightly crushed

a small bunch of fresh basil leaves, roughly torn

FROM THE STORECUPBOARD

45ml/3 tbsp extra virgin olive oil

salt and ground black pepper

Noodles with Sesame - roasted Spring Onions

You can use any kind of noodles for this Asian-style dish. Rice noodles look and taste particularly good, but egg noodles work very well too. Serve with fish and chicken dishes.

SERVES FOUR

1 bunch of spring onions (scallions), trimmed

225g/8oz flat rice noodles

30ml/2 tbsp oyster sauce

FROM THE STORECUPBOARD

30ml/2 tbsp sesame oil

salt and ground black pepper

1 Preheat the oven to 200°C/400°F/Gas 6. Cut the spring onions into three pieces, then put them in a small roasting pan and season with salt and pepper.

2 Drizzle the sesame oil over the spring onions and roast for 10 minutes, until they are slightly charred and tender. Set aside.

3 Cook the noodles according to the instructions on the packet and drain thoroughly. Toss with the spring onions and oyster sauce, and season with ground black pepper. Serve immediately.

Spicy Potato Wedges

These wedges are easy to make and can be served on their own with a garlic mayonnaise dip or as an accompaniment to meat or fish dishes. To make extra-hot potato wedges, use chilli powder instead of paprika.

SERVES FOUR

675g/1½lb floury potatoes, such as Maris Piper

10ml/2 tsp paprika

5ml/1 tsp ground cumin

FROM THE STORECUPBOARD

45ml/3 tbsp olive oil

salt and ground black pepper

1 Preheat the oven to 190°C/375°F/Gas 5. Using a sharp knife, cut the potatoes into chunky wedges and place in a roasting pan.

2 In a small bowl, combine the olive oil with the paprika and cumin and season with plenty of salt and ground black pepper. Pour the mixture over the potatoes and toss well to coat thoroughly.

3 Spread the potatoes in a single layer in the roasting pan and bake for 30–40 minutes, or until golden brown and tender. Serve immediately.

Crisp and Golden Roast Potatoes with Goose Fat and Garlic

Goose fat gives the best flavour to roast potatoes and is now widely available in cans in supermarkets. However, if you can't find goose fat, or you want to make a vegetarian version of these potatoes, use a large knob (pat) of butter or 15ml/1 tbsp olive oil instead. If you like, add a couple of bay leaves to the potatoes before roasting; they impart a lovely flavour.

SERVES FOUR

675g/1½lb floury potatoes, such as Maris Piper, peeled

30ml/2 tbsp goose fat

12 garlic cloves, unpeeled

FROM THE STORECUPBOARD

salt and ground black pepper

1 Preheat the oven to 190°C/375°F/Gas 5. Cut the potatoes into large chunks and cook in a pan of salted, boiling water for 5 minutes. Drain well and give the colander a good shake to fluff up the edges of the potatoes. Return the potatoes to the pan and place it over a low heat for 1 minute to steam off any excess water.

2 Meanwhile, spoon the goose fat into a roasting pan and place in the oven until hot, about 5 minutes. Add the potatoes to the pan with the garlic and turn to coat in the fat. Season well with salt and ground black pepper and roast for 40–50 minutes, turning occasionally, until the potatoes are golden and tender.

Tomato and Aubergine Gratin

This colourful, Mediterranean dish makes the perfect partner to grilled, pan-fried or baked meat or poultry. If you prefer, thinly sliced courgettes (zucchini) can be used in this dish instead of the aubergines. Grill the courgettes for 10–15 minutes. Choose plum tomatoes if you can – they have fewer seeds than most round tomatoes, so are less watery and are ideal for cooking.

SERVES FOUR TO SIX

1 Preheat the grill (broiler). Thinly slice the aubergines and arrange them in a single layer on a foil-lined grill rack. Brush the aubergine slices with some of the oil and grill (broil) for 15–20 minutes, turning once, until golden on both sides. Brush the second side with more oil after turning the slices.

2 Preheat the oven to 200°C/400°F/Gas 6. Toss the aubergine and tomato slices together in a bowl with a little seasoning, then pile them into a shallow, ovenproof dish. Drizzle with any remaining olive oil and sprinkle with the grated Parmesan cheese. Bake for 20 minutes, until the cheese is golden and the vegetables are hot. Serve the gratin immediately.

2 medium aubergines (eggplants), about 500g/1^1/$_4$lb

400g/14oz ripe tomatoes, sliced

40g/1^1/$_2$oz/^{1}/$_2$cup freshly grated Parmesan cheese

FROM THE STORECUPBOARD

90ml/6 tbsp olive oil

salt and ground black pepper

Bubble and Squeak

Whether you have leftovers or cook this old-fashioned classic from fresh, be sure to give it a really good "squeak" in the pan so it turns a rich honey brown. Serve as an accompaniment to grilled pork chops or fried eggs, or simply serve with warm bread for a quick supper. If you prefer, cook the bubble and squeak in individual-sized portions – divide into four and form into patties before cooking.

SERVES FOUR

1 Heat 30ml/2 tbsp of the bacon fat or oil in a heavy frying pan. Add the onion and cook over a medium heat, stirring frequently, until softened but not browned.

2 In a bowl, mix together the potatoes and cooked cabbage or sprouts and season with salt and plenty of pepper to taste.

3 Add the vegetables to the pan with the cooked onions, stir well, then press the vegetable mixture into a large, even cake.

4 Cook over a medium heat for about 15 minutes, until the cake is browned underneath.

5 Invert a large plate over the pan, and, holding it tightly against the pan, turn them both over together. Lift off the frying pan, return it to the heat and add the remaining bacon fat or oil. When hot, slide the cake back into the pan, browned side uppermost.

6 Cook over a medium heat for 10 minutes, or until the underside is golden brown. Serve hot, in wedges.

60ml/4 tbsp bacon fat or vegetable oil

1 medium onion, chopped

450g/1lb floury potatoes, cooked and mashed

225g/8oz cooked cabbage or Brussels sprouts, chopped

FROM THE STORECUPBOARD

salt and ground black pepper

Cheesy Creamy Leeks

This is quite a rich accompaniment that could easily be served as a meal in itself with brown rice or couscous. Cheddar cheese has been used here for a slightly stronger flavour, but you could use a milder Swiss cheese, such as Gruyère, if you like.

SERVES FOUR

4 large leeks or 12 baby leeks, trimmed and washed

150ml/^{1}/$_4$ pint/^{2}/$_3$ cup double (heavy) cream

75g/3oz mature Cheddar or Monterey Jack cheese, grated

FROM THE STORECUPBOARD

15ml/1 tbsp olive oil

salt and ground black pepper

1 Preheat the grill (broiler) to high. If using large leeks, slice them lengthways. Heat the oil in a large frying pan and add the leeks. Season with salt and pepper and cook for about 4 minutes, stirring occasionally, until starting to turn golden.

2 Pour the cream into the pan and stir until well combined. Allow to bubble gently for a few minutes.

3 Preheat the grill (broiler). Transfer the creamy leeks to a shallow ovenproof dish and sprinkle with the cheese. Grill for 4–5 minutes, or until the cheese is golden brown and bubbling and serve immediately.

Creamy Polenta with Dolcelatte

Soft-cooked polenta is a tasty accompaniment to meat dishes and makes a delicious change from the usual potatoes or rice. It can also be enjoyed on its own as a hearty snack.

SERVES FOUR TO SIX

900ml/1¹/₂ pints/3³/₄ cups milk

115g/4oz/1 cup instant polenta

115g/4oz Dolcelatte cheese

FROM THE STORECUPBOARD

60ml/4 tbsp extra virgin olive oil

salt and ground black pepper

1 Pour the milk into a large pan and bring to the boil, then add a good pinch of salt. Remove the pan from the heat and pour in the polenta in a slow, steady stream, stirring constantly to combine.

2 Return the pan to a low heat and simmer gently, stirring constantly, for 5 minutes. Remove the pan from the heat and stir in the olive oil.

3 Spoon the polenta into a serving dish and crumble the cheese over the top. Season with more ground black pepper and serve immediately.

Fennel, Potato and Garlic Mash

This flavoursome mash of potato, fennel and garlic goes well with practically all main dishes, whether fish, poultry or meat. Floury varieties of potato such as Pentland Squire, King Edward or Marfona are best for mashing as they produce a light fluffy result. Waxy potatoes are more suitable for baking, or for salads, as they produce a dense, rather starchy mash.

SERVES FOUR

1 Boil the potatoes in water for 20 minutes, until tender.

2 Meanwhile, trim and chop the fennel, reserving any feathery tops. Chop the tops and set them aside. Heat 30ml/ 2 tbsp of the oil in a pan. Add the fennel, cover and cook over a low heat for 20–30 minutes, until soft but not browned.

3 Drain and mash the potatoes. Purée the fennel in a food mill or blender and beat it into the potato with the remaining oil.

4 Warm the milk or cream and beat sufficient into the potato and fennel to make a creamy, light mixture. Season to taste and reheat gently, then beat in any chopped fennel tops. Serve immediately.

800g/1³/₄lb potatoes, cut into chunks

2 large fennel bulbs

120–150ml/4–5fl oz/ ¹/₂–²/₃ cup milk or single (light) cream

FROM THE STORECUPBOARD

90ml/6 tbsp garlic-flavoured olive oil

salt and ground black pepper

Champ

This traditional Irish dish of potatoes and green or spring onions is enriched with a wickedly indulgent amount of butter – for complete indulgence, replace 60ml/4 tbsp of the milk with crème fraîche or buttermilk. Serve the champ as an accompaniment to beef or lamb stew for a warming and hearty winter meal.

SERVES FOUR

1kg/2¼lb potatoes, cut into chunks

300ml/½ pint/1¼ cups milk

1 bunch spring onions (scallions), thinly sliced, plus extra to garnish

115g/4oz/½ cup salted butter

FROM THE STORECUPBOARD

salt and ground black pepper

1 Boil the potatoes in lightly salted water for 20–25 minutes, or until they are tender. Drain and mash the potatoes with a fork until smooth.

2 Place the milk, spring onions and half the butter in a small pan and set over a low heat until just simmering. Cook for 2–3 minutes, until the butter has melted and the spring onions have softened.

3 Beat the milk mixture into the mashed potato using a wooden spoon until the mixture is light and fluffy. Reheat gently, adding seasoning to taste.

4 Turn the potato into a warmed serving dish and make a well in the centre with a spoon. Place the remaining butter in the well and let it melt. Serve immediately, sprinkled with extra spring onion.

EXTRAS *To make colcannon, another Irish speciality, follow the main recipe, using half the butter. Cook about 500g/1¼lb finely shredded green cabbage or kale in a little water until just tender, drain thoroughly and then beat into the creamed potato. This is delicious served with sausages and grilled (broiled) ham or bacon. The colcannon may also be fried in butter and then browned under the grill (broiler).*

Salads

WHETHER SERVED AS A MAIN COURSE OR AN
ACCOMPANIMENT, SALADS ARE ALWAYS A REFRESHING
AND WELCOME CHANGE. THE MOST SUCCESSFUL ARE
COMPOSED OF ONLY A FEW INGREDIENTS – COOKED OR
RAW – WHOSE COLOURS, TEXTURES AND FLAVOURS
COMPLEMENT AND BALANCE PERFECTLY.

Sour Cucumber with Fresh Dill

This is half pickle, half salad, and totally delicious served with pumpernickel or other coarse, dark, full-flavoured bread, as a light meal or an appetizer. Choose smooth-skinned, smallish cucumbers for this recipe as larger ones tend to be less tender, with tough skins and bitter indigestible seeds. If you can only buy a large cucumber, peel it before slicing.

SERVES FOUR

1 In a large mixing bowl, combine together the thinly sliced cucumbers and the thinly sliced onion. Season the vegetables with salt and toss together until they are thoroughly combined. Leave the mixture to stand in a cool place for 5–10 minutes.

2 Add the cider vinegar, 30–45ml/2–3 tbsp water and the chopped fresh dill to the cucumber and onion mixture. Toss all the ingredients together until well combined, then chill in the refrigerator for a few hours, or until ready to serve.

2 small cucumbers, thinly sliced

3 onions, thinly sliced

75–90ml/5–6 tbsp cider vinegar

30–45ml/2–3 tbsp chopped fresh dill

FROM THE STORECUPBOARD

salt and ground black pepper

Beetroot with Fresh Mint

This simple and decorative beetroot salad can be served as part of a selection of salads, as an appetizer, or as an accompaniment to grilled or roasted pork or lamb. Balsamic vinegar is a rich, dark vinegar with a mellow, deep flavour. It can be used to dress a variety of salad ingredients and is particularly good drizzled over a tomato and basil salad.

SERVES FOUR

1 Slice the beetroot or cut into even-size dice with a sharp knife. Put the beetroot in a bowl. Add the balsamic vinegar, olive oil and a pinch of salt and toss together to combine.

2 Add half the thinly shredded fresh mint to the salad and toss lightly until thoroughly combined. Place the salad in the refrigerator and chill for about 1 hour. Serve garnished with the remaining thinly shredded mint leaves.

EXTRAS
To make Tunisian beetroot, add a little harissa to taste and substitute chopped fresh coriander (cilantro) for the shredded mint.

4–6 cooked beetroot (beet)

15–30ml/1–2 tbsp balsamic vinegar

1 bunch fresh mint, leaves stripped and thinly shredded

FROM THE STORECUPBOARD

30ml/2 tbsp olive oil

salt and ground black pepper

Globe Artichokes with Green Beans and Garlic Dressing

Piquant garlic dressing or creamy aioli go perfectly with these lightly-cooked vegetables. Serve lemon wedges with the artichokes so that their juice may be squeezed over to taste. The vegetables can also be garnished with finely shredded lemon rind. Artichokes should feel heavy for their size – make sure that the inner leaves are wrapped tightly round the choke and the heart inside.

SERVES FOUR TO SIX

225g/8oz green beans

3 small globe artichokes

250ml/8fl oz/1 cup garlic dressing or aioli

FROM THE STORECUPBOARD

15ml/1 tbsp lemon-flavoured olive oil

salt and ground black pepper

1 Cook the beans in boiling water for 1–2 minutes, until slightly softened. Drain well.

2 Trim the artichoke stalks close to the base. Cook them in a large pan of salted water for about 30 minutes, or until you can easily pull away a leaf from the base. Drain well.

3 Using a sharp knife, halve them lengthways and ease out their chokes using a teaspoon.

4 Arrange the artichokes and beans on serving plates and drizzle with the oil. Season with coarse salt and a little pepper. Spoon the garlic dressing or aioli into the hearts and serve warm.

5 To eat the artichokes, pull the leaves from the base one at a time and use to scoop a little of the dressing. It is only the fleshy end of each leaf that is eaten as well as the base, bottom or "fond".

Halloumi and Grape Salad

Firm and salty halloumi cheese is a great standby ingredient for turning a simple salad into a special dish. In this recipe it is tossed with sweet, juicy grapes, which complement its flavour and texture. Fresh young thyme leaves and dill taste especially good mixed with the salad. Serve with a crusty walnut or sun-dried tomato bread for a light lunch.

SERVES FOUR

1 Toss together the salad leaves and fresh herb sprigs and the green and black grapes, then transfer to a large serving plate.

2 Thinly slice the halloumi cheese. Heat a large non-stick frying pan. Add the sliced halloumi cheese and cook briefly until it just starts to turn golden brown on the underside. Turn the cheese with a fish slice or metal spatula and cook the other side until it is golden brown.

3 Arrange the fried cheese over the salad on the plate. Pour over the oil and lemon juice or vinegar dressing and serve immediately while the cheese is still hot.

150g/5oz mixed salad leaves and tender fresh herb sprigs

175g/6oz mixed seedless green and black grapes

250g/9oz halloumi cheese

75ml/5 tbsp oil and lemon juice or vinegar dressing

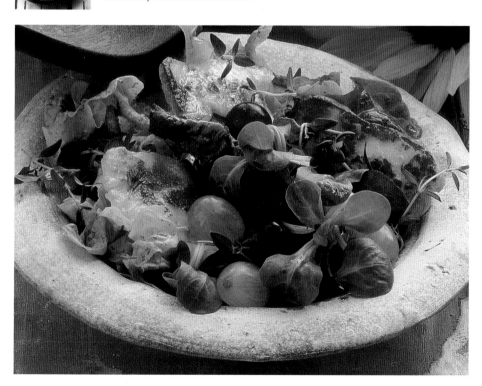

Watermelon and Feta Salad

The combination of sweet watermelon with salty feta cheese is inspired by Turkish tradition. The salad may be served plain and light, on a leafy base, or with a herbed vinaigrette dressing drizzled over. It is perfect served as an appetizer. Feta cheese is salty because it is preserved in brine – but the salt is not supposed to overpower the taste of the cheese.

SERVES FOUR

4 slices watermelon, chilled

130g/4¹/₂oz feta cheese, preferably sheep's milk feta, cut into bitesize pieces

handful of mixed seeds, such as lightly toasted pumpkin seeds and sunflower seeds

10–15 black olives

1 Cut the rind off the watermelon and remove as many seeds as possible. Cut the flesh into triangular-shaped chunks.

2 Mix the watermelon, feta cheese, mixed seeds and black olives. Cover and chill the salad for 30 minutes before serving.

COOK'S TIP *The best choice of olives for this recipe are plump black Mediterranean ones, such as kalamata, other shiny, brined varieties or dry-cured black olives.*

Tomato, Bean and Fried Basil Salad

Infusing basil in hot oil brings out its wonderful, aromatic flavour, which works so well in almost any tomato dish. Various canned beans or chickpeas can be used instead of mixed beans in this simple dish, as they all taste good and make a wholesome salad to serve as an accompaniment or a satisfying snack with some warm, grainy bread.

SERVES FOUR

1 Reserve one-third of the basil leaves for garnish, then tear the remainder into pieces. Pour the olive oil into a small pan. Add the torn basil and heat gently for 1 minute, until the basil sizzles and begins to colour.

2 Place the halved cherry tomatoes and beans in a bowl. Pour in the basil oil and add a little salt and plenty of freshly ground black pepper. Toss the ingredients together gently, cover and leave to marinate at room temperature for at least 30 minutes. Serve the salad sprinkled with the remaining basil leaves.

15g/¹/₂oz/¹/₂ cup fresh basil leaves

300g/11oz cherry tomatoes, halved

400g/14oz can mixed beans, drained and rinsed

FROM THE STORECUPBOARD

75ml/5 tbsp extra virgin olive oil

salt and ground black pepper

Moroccan Date, Orange and Carrot Salad

Take exotic fresh dates and marry them with everyday ingredients, such as carrots and oranges, to make this deliciously different salad. The salad looks really pretty arranged on a base of sweet Little Gem (Bibb) lettuce leaves. This fruity salad is excellent served with chargrilled lamb steaks, or with skewered lamb.

SERVES FOUR

3 carrots

3 oranges

115g/4oz fresh dates, stoned (pitted) and cut lengthways into eighths

25g/1oz/¹/₄ cup toasted whole almonds, chopped

FROM THE STORECUPBOARD

salt and ground black pepper

1 Grate the carrots and place in a mound in a serving dish, or on four individual plates.

2 Peel and segment two of the oranges and arrange the orange segments around the carrot. Season with salt and freshly ground black pepper. Pile the dates on top, then sprinkle with the chopped, toasted almonds.

3 Squeeze the juice from the remaining orange and sprinkle it over the salad. Chill in the refrigerator for an hour before serving.

Pink Grapefruit and Avocado Salad

Smooth, creamy avocado and zesty citrus fruit are perfect partners in an attractive, refreshing salad. Pink grapefruit are tangy but not too sharp, or try large oranges for a sweeter flavour. Avocados turn brown quickly when exposed to the air: the acidic grapefruit juice will prevent this from occurring, so combine the ingredients as soon as the avocados have been sliced.

SERVES FOUR

1 Slice the top and bottom off a grapefruit, then cut off all the peel and pith from around the side. Working over a small bowl to catch the juices, cut out the segments from between the membranes and place them in a separate bowl. Squeeze any juices remaining in the membranes into the bowl, then discard them. Repeat with the remaining grapefruit.

2 Halve, stone (pit) and peel the avocados. Slice the flesh and add it to the grapefruit segments. Whisk a little salt and then the chilli oil into the grapefruit juice.

3 Pile the rocket leaves on to four serving plates and top with the grapefruit segments and avocado. Pour over the dressing and serve.

2 pink grapefruit

2 ripe avocados

90g/3¹/₂oz rocket (arugula)

FROM THE STORECUPBOARD

30ml/2 tbsp chilli oil

salt and ground black pepper

Turnip Salad in Sour Cream

Usually served cooked, raw young tender turnips have a tangy, slightly peppery flavour. Serve this as an accompaniment for grilled poultry or meat. It is also delicious as a light appetizer, garnished with parsley and paprika, and served with warmed flat breads such as pitta or naan. Garnish the salad with fresh flat leaf parsley and paprika, if you like.

SERVES FOUR

1 Thinly slice or coarsely grate the turnips. Alternatively, thinly slice half the turnips and grate the remaining half. Put in a bowl.

2 Add the onion and vinegar and season to taste with salt and plenty of freshly ground black pepper. Toss together, then stir in the sour cream. Chill well before serving.

VARIATIONS Large white radishes can be used instead of turnips and crème fraîche can be substituted for the sour cream. The salad is good with a selection of salads and cold dishes for a light lunch or long and leisurely supper.

2–4 young, tender turnips, peeled

¹/₄–¹/₂ onion, finely chopped

2–3 drops white wine vinegar, or to taste

60–90ml/4–6 tbsp sour cream

FROM THE STORECUPBOARD

salt and ground black pepper

Moroccan Carrot Salad

In this intriguing salad from North Africa, the carrots are lightly cooked before being tossed in a cumin and coriander vinaigrette. Cumin is widely used in Indian and Mexican cooking, as well as North African cuisines. It has a strong and spicy aroma and a warm pungent flavour that goes particularly well with root vegetables. This salad is a perfect accompaniment for both everyday or special meals.

SERVES FOUR TO SIX

3–4 carrots, thinly sliced

1.5ml/¹/₄ tsp ground cumin, or to taste

60ml/4 tbsp garlic-flavoured oil and vinegar dressing

30ml/2 tbsp chopped fresh coriander (cilantro) leaves or a mixture of coriander and parsley

FROM THE STORECUPBOARD

salt and ground black pepper

1 Cook the thinly sliced carrots by either steaming or boiling in lightly salted water until they are just tender but not soft. Drain the carrots, leave for a few minutes to dry and cool, then put into a mixing bowl.

2 Add the cumin, garlic dressing and herbs. Season to taste and chill well before serving. Check the seasoning just before serving and add more ground cumin, salt or black pepper, if required.

Warm Chorizo and Spinach Salad

Spanish chorizo sausage contributes an intense spiciness to any ingredient with which it is cooked. In this hearty warm salad, spinach has sufficient flavour to compete with the chorizo. Watercress or rocket (arugula) could be used instead of the spinach, if you prefer. For an added dimension use a flavoured olive oil – rosemary, garlic or chilli oil would work perfectly. Serve the salad with warm crusty bread to soak up all the delicious cooking juices.

SERVES FOUR

1 Discard any tough stalks from the spinach. Pour the oil into a large frying pan and add the sausage. Cook gently for 3 minutes, until the sausage slices start to shrivel slightly and colour.

2 Add the spinach leaves and remove the pan from the heat. Toss the spinach in the warm oil until it just starts to wilt. Add the sherry vinegar and a little seasoning. Toss the ingredients briefly, then serve immediately, while still warm.

225g/8oz baby spinach leaves

150g/5oz chorizo sausage, very thinly sliced

30ml/2 tbsp sherry vinegar

FROM THE STORECUPBOARD

90ml/6 tbsp olive oil

salt and ground black pepper

Potato and Olive Salad

This delicious salad is simple and zesty – the perfect choice for lunch, as an accompaniment, or as an appetizer. Similar in appearance to flat leaf parsley, fresh coriander has a distinctive pungent, almost spicy flavour. It is widely used in India, the Middle and Far East and in eastern Mediterranean countries. This potato salad is particularly good served as part of a brunch.

SERVES FOUR

8 large new potatoes

45–60ml/3–4 tbsp garlic-flavoured oil and vinegar dressing

60–90ml/4–6 tbsp chopped fresh herbs, such as coriander (cilantro) and chives

10–15 dry-fleshed black Mediterranean olives

FROM THE STORECUPBOARD

salt and ground black pepper

1 Cut the new potatoes into chunks. Put them in a pan, pour in water to cover and add a pinch of salt. Bring to the boil, then reduce the heat and cook gently for about 10 minutes, or until the potatoes are just tender. Drain well and leave in a colander to dry thoroughly and cool slightly.

2 When they are cool enough to handle, chop the potatoes and put them in a serving bowl.

3 Drizzle the garlic dressing over the potatoes. Toss well and sprinkle with the coriander and chives, and black olives. Chill in the refrigerator for at least 1 hour before serving.

EXTRAS *Add a pinch of ground cumin or a sprinkling of roasted whole cumin seeds to spice up the salad.*

Asparagus, Bacon and Leaf Salad

This excellent salad turns a plain roast chicken or simple grilled fish into an interesting meal, especially when served with buttered new potatoes. It also makes an appetizing first course or light lunch. A wide range of different salad leaves are readily available – frisée has feathery, curly, slightly bitter tasting leaves and is a member of the chicory family. Frisée leaves range in colour from yellow-white to yellow-green.

SERVES FOUR

1 Trim off any tough stalk ends from the asparagus and cut the spears into three, setting the tender tips aside. Heat a 1cm/½in depth of water in a frying pan until simmering. Reserve the asparagus tips and cook the remainder of the spears in the water for about 3 minutes, until almost tender. Add the tips and cook for 1 minute more. Drain and refresh under cold, running water.

2 Dry-fry the bacon until crisp and then set it aside to cool. Use kitchen scissors to snip it into bitesize pieces. Place the frisée or mixed leaf salad in a bowl and add the bacon.

3 Add the asparagus and a little black pepper to the salad. Pour the dressing over and toss the salad lightly, then serve.

500g/1¼lb medium asparagus spears

130g/4½oz thin-cut smoked back (lean) bacon

250g/9oz frisée lettuce leaves or mixed leaf salad

100ml/3½fl oz/scant ½ cup French dressing

FROM THE STORECUPBOARD

salt and ground black pepper

Anchovy and Roasted Pepper Salad

Sweet peppers, salty anchovies and plenty of garlic make an intensely flavoured salad that is delicious with meat, poultry or cheese. It also makes a tasty snack with olive bread. If you find that canned anchovies are too salty for your liking, you can reduce their saltiness by soaking them in milk for 20 minutes. Drain off the oil first and after soaking drain and rinse them in cold water.

SERVES FOUR

2 red, 2 orange and 2 yellow (bell) peppers, halved and seeded

50g/2oz can anchovies in olive oil

2 garlic cloves

45ml/3 tbsp balsamic vinegar

FROM THE STORECUPBOARD

salt and ground black pepper

1 Preheat the oven to 200°C/400°F/Gas 6. Place the peppers, cut side down, in a roasting pan. Roast for 30-40 minutes, until the skins are charred. Transfer the peppers to a bowl, cover with clear film (plastic wrap) and leave for 15 minutes.

2 Peel the peppers, then cut them into chunky strips. Drain the anchovies and halve the fillets lengthways.

3 Slice the garlic as thinly as possible and place it in a large bowl. Stir in the olive oil, vinegar and a little pepper. Add the peppers and anchovies and use a spoon and fork to fold the ingredients together. Cover and chill until ready to serve.

Hot Desserts

A HOT DESSERT MAKES THE PERFECT END TO A MEAL
AND CAN TAKE VERY LITTLE TIME TO PREPARE. A FEW
WELL-CHOSEN INGREDIENTS CAN BE TURNED INTO A
SUMPTUOUS, MOUTHWATERING TREAT WITH THE MINIMUM
OF EFFORT. MANY OF THE RECIPES IN THIS CHAPTER CAN
BE PREPARED IN ADVANCE AND SIMPLY POPPED IN THE
OVEN TO COOK WHILE YOU SERVE THE MAIN COURSE.

Plum and Almond Tart

To transform this tart into an extravagant dessert, dust with a little icing (confectioners') sugar and serve with a dollop of crème fraîche.

SERVES FOUR

1 Preheat the oven to 190°C/375°F/Gas 5. Unroll the pastry on to a large baking sheet. Using a small, sharp knife, score a border 5cm/2in from the edge of the pastry, without cutting all the way through.

2 Roll out the marzipan into a rectangle, to fit just within the pastry border, then lay it on top of the pastry, pressing down lightly with the tips of your fingers.

3 Scatter the sliced plums on top of the marzipan in an even layer and bake for 20–25 minutes, or until the pastry is risen and golden brown.

4 Carefully transfer the tart to a wire rack to cool slightly, then cut into squares or wedges and serve.

375g/13oz ready-rolled puff pastry, thawed if frozen

115g/4oz marzipan

6–8 plums, stoned and sliced

Baked Apples with Marsala

The Marsala cooks down with the juice from the apples and the butter to make a rich, sticky sauce. Serve these delicious apples with a spoonful of extra-thick cream.

SERVES SIX

1 Preheat the oven to 180°C/350°F/Gas 4. Using an apple corer, remove the cores from the apples and discard.

2 Place the apples in a small, shallow baking pan and stuff the figs into the holes in the centre of each apple.

3 Top each apple with a quarter of the butter and pour over the Marsala. Cover the pan tightly with foil and bake for about 30 minutes.

4 Remove the foil from the apples and bake for a further 10 minutes, or until the apples are tender and the juices have reduced slightly. Serve immediately with any remaining pan juices drizzled over the top.

4 medium cooking apples

50g/2oz/¹/₃ cup ready-to-eat dried figs

150ml/¹/₄ pint/²/₃ cup Marsala

FROM THE STORECUPBOARD

50g/2oz/¹/₄ cup butter, softened

Grilled Peaches with Meringues

Ripe peaches take on a fabulous scented fruitiness when grilled with brown sugar, and mini meringues are the perfect accompaniment. Serve with crème fraîche flavoured with a little grated orange rind. When buying peaches or nectarines, choose fruit with an attractive rosy bloom, avoiding any that have a green-tinged skin or feel hard. Nectarines have a smoother skin than peaches and are actually a type of peach native to China.

SERVES SIX

2 egg whites

115g/4oz/¹/₂ cup soft light brown sugar, reserving 5ml/1 tsp for the peaches

pinch of ground cinnamon

6 ripe peaches, or nectarines

1 Preheat the oven to 140°C/275°F/Gas 1. Line two large baking sheets with baking parchment.

2 Whisk the egg whites until they form stiff peaks. Gradually whisk in the sugar and ground cinnamon until the mixture is stiff and glossy. Pipe 18 very small meringues on to the trays and bake for 40 minutes. Leave in the oven to cool.

3 Meanwhile, halve and stone (pit) the peaches or nectarines, sprinkling each half with a little sugar as it is cut. Grill (broil) for 4–5 minutes, until just beginning to caramelize.

4 Arrange the grilled peaches on serving plates with the meringues and serve immediately.

COOK'S TIP

Use leftover egg whites to make these little cinnamon-flavoured meringues. The meringues can be stored in an airtight container for about 2 weeks. Serve them after dinner with coffee or with desserts in place of biscuits (cookies).

Summer Berries in Sabayon Glaze

This luxurious combination of summer berries under a light and fluffy liqueur sauce is lightly grilled to form a crisp, caramelized topping. Fresh or frozen berries can be used in this dessert. If you use frozen berries, defrost them in a sieve over a bowl to allow the juices to drip. Stir a little juice into the fruit before dividing among the dishes.

SERVES FOUR

1 Arrange the mixed summer berries or soft fruit in four individual flameproof dishes. Preheat the grill (broiler).

2 Whisk the yolks in a large bowl with the sugar and liqueur or wine. Place over a pan of hot water and whisk constantly until the mixture is thick, fluffy and pale.

3 Pour equal quantities of the yolk mixture into each dish. Place under the grill for 1–2 minutes, until just turning brown. Add an extra splash of liqueur, if you like, and serve immediately.

450g/1lb/4 cups mixed summer berries, or soft fruit

4 egg yolks

50g/2oz/¼ cup vanilla sugar or caster (superfine) sugar

120ml/4fl oz/½ cup liqueur, such as Cointreau or Kirsch, or a white dessert wine

Baked Ricotta Cakes with Red Sauce

These honey-flavoured desserts take only minutes to make from a few ingredients. The fragrant fruity sauce provides a contrast of both colour and flavour. The red berry sauce can be made a day in advance and chilled until ready to use. Frozen fruit doesn't need extra water, as it usually yields its juice easily on thawing.

SERVES FOUR

250g/9oz/generous 1 cup ricotta cheese

2 egg whites, beaten

60ml/4 tbsp scented honey, plus extra to taste

450g/1lb/4 cups mixed fresh or frozen fruit, such as strawberries, raspberries, blackberries and cherries

1 Preheat the oven to 180°C/350°F/Gas 4. Place the ricotta cheese in a bowl and break it up with a wooden spoon. Add the beaten egg whites and honey, and mix thoroughly until smooth and well combined.

2 Lightly grease four ramekins. Spoon the ricotta mixture into the prepared ramekins and level the tops. Bake for 20 minutes, or until the ricotta cakes are risen and golden.

3 Meanwhile, make the fruit sauce. Reserve about one-quarter of the fruit for decoration. Place the rest of the fruit in a pan, with a little water if the fruit is fresh, and heat gently until softened. Leave to cool slightly and remove any stones (pits) if using cherries.

4 Press the fruit through a sieve, then taste and sweeten with honey if it is too tart. Serve the sauce, warm or cold, with the ricotta cakes. Decorate with the reserved berries.

Apricot and Ginger Gratin

Made with tangy fresh apricots, this quick and easy dessert has a comforting, baked cheesecake-like flavour. For an even easier version of this delicious gratin, use 400g/14oz canned apricots in juice. Use juice from the can to beat into the cream cheese.

SERVES FOUR

1 Put the apricots in a pan with the sugar. Pour in 75ml/5 tbsp water and heat until barely simmering. Cover and cook very gently for 8–10 minutes, until they are tender but still holding their shape.

2 Preheat the oven to 200°C/400°F/Gas 6. Drain the apricots, reserving the syrup, and place in a large dish or divide among four individual ovenproof dishes. Set aside 90ml/6 tbsp of the syrup and spoon the remainder over the fruit.

3 Beat the cream cheese until softened, then gradually beat in the reserved syrup until smooth. Spoon the cheese mixture over the apricots. Sprinkle the biscuit crumbs over the cream cheese and juice mixture. Bake for 10 minutes, until the crumb topping is beginning to darken and the filling has warmed through. Serve immediately.

500g/1¼ lb apricots, halved and stoned (pitted)

75g/3oz/scant ½ cup caster (superfine) sugar

200g/7oz/scant 1 cup cream cheese

75g/3oz gingernut biscuits (gingersnaps), crushed to crumbs

Deep-fried Cherries

Fresh fruit coated with a simple batter and then deep-fried is delicious and makes an unusual dessert. These succulent cherries are perfect sprinkled with sugar and cinnamon and served with a classic vanilla ice cream.

SERVES FOUR TO SIX

450g/1lb ripe red cherries, on their stalks

225g/8oz batter mix

1 egg

FROM THE STORECUPBOARD

vegetable oil, for deep-frying

1 Gently wash the cherries and pat dry with kitchen paper. Tie the stalks together with fine string to form clusters of four or five cherries.

2 Make up the batter mix according to the instructions on the packet, beating in the egg. Pour the vegetable oil into a deep-fat fryer or large, heavy pan and heat to 190°C/375°F.

3 Working in batches, half-dip each cherry cluster into the batter and then carefully drop the cluster into the hot oil. Fry for 3–4 minutes, or until golden. Remove the deep-fried cherries with a wire-mesh skimmer or slotted spoon and drain on a wire rack placed over crumpled kitchen paper, and serve immediately.

Hot Blackberry and Apple Soufflé

The deliciously tart flavours of blackberry and apple complement each other perfectly to make a light, mouthwatering and surprisingly low-fat, hot dessert. Running a table knife around the inside edge of the soufflé dishes before baking helps the soufflés to rise evenly without sticking to the rim of the dish. Make this dish in early autumn, when there are plentiful supplies of blackberries.

MAKES SIX

1 Preheat the oven to 200°C/400°F/Gas 6. Put a baking sheet in the oven to heat. Cook the blackberries and apple in a pan for 10 minutes, or until the juice runs from the blackberries and the apple has pulped down well. Press through a sieve into a bowl. Stir in 50g/2oz/¼ cup caster sugar. Set aside to cool.

2 Put a spoonful of the fruit purée into each of six 150ml/¼ pint/ ⅔ cup greased and sugared individual soufflé dishes and smooth the surface. Set the dishes aside.

3 Whisk the egg whites in a large bowl until they form stiff peaks. Gradually whisk in the remaining caster sugar. Fold in the remaining fruit purée and spoon the flavoured meringue into the prepared dishes. Level the tops with a palette knife (metal spatula) and run a table knife around the edge of each dish.

4 Place the dishes on the hot baking sheet and bake for 10–15 minutes, until the soufflés have risen well and are lightly browned. Dust the tops with a little sugar and serve immediately.

350g/12oz/3 cups blackberries

1 large cooking apple, peeled and finely diced

3 egg whites

150g/5oz/³/₄ cup caster (superfine) sugar, plus extra caster or icing (confectioners') sugar for dusting

Caramelized Upside-down Pear Pie

In this gloriously sticky dessert, which is almost like the French classic *tarte tatin*, the pastry is baked on top of the fruit, which gives it a crisp and flaky texture. When inverted, the pie looks wonderful. Look for good-quality chilled pastry that you can freeze for future use. Serve with whipped cream, ice cream or just plain for a gloriously sticky dessert.

SERVES EIGHT

1 Peel, quarter and core the pears. Toss with some of the sugar in a bowl.

2 Melt the butter in a 27cm/10½in heavy, ovenproof omelette pan. Add the remaining sugar. When it changes colour, arrange the pears in the pan.

3 Continue cooking, uncovered, for 20 minutes, or until the fruit has completely caramelized.

4 Leave the fruit to cool in the pan. Preheat the oven to 200°C/400°F/Gas 6. Meanwhile, on a lightly floured surface, roll out the pastry to a round that is slightly larger than the diameter of the pan. Lay the pastry on top of the pears and then carefully tuck it in around the edge.

5 Bake for 15 minutes, then lower the oven temperature to 180°C/350°F/Gas 4. Bake for a further 15 minutes, or until the pastry is golden.

6 Let the pie cool in the pan for a few minutes. To unmould, run a knife around the pan's edge, then, using oven gloves, invert a plate over the pan and quickly turn the two over together.

7 If any pears stick to the pan, remove them gently with a palette knife (metal spatula) and replace them on the pie. The pie is best served warm.

5–6 firm, ripe pears

175g/6oz/scant 1 cup caster (superfine) sugar

225g/8oz (unsweetened) shortcrust pastry

FROM THE STORECUPBOARD

115g/4oz/¹/₂ cup butter

VARIATIONS

To make caramelized upside-down apple pie, replace the pears with eight or nine firm, full-flavoured eating apples – Cox's Orange Pippins would be a good choice. You will need more apples than pears, as they shrink during cooking.

Nectarines or peaches also work well, as does rhubarb. Rhubarb is tart, so you may need to add more sugar.

Blueberry and Almond Tart

This is a cheat's version of a sweet almond tart and the result is superb. Whisked egg whites and grated marzipan cook to form a light sponge under a tangy topping of contrasting blueberries. When whisking the egg whites for the filling, ensure all traces of yolk are removed – otherwise you won't be able to whisk them to their maximum volume.

SERVES SIX

250g/9oz (unsweetened) shortcrust pastry

175g/6oz/generous 1 cup white marzipan

4 large (US extra large) egg whites

130g/4¹/₂oz/ generous 1 cup blueberries

1 Preheat the oven to 200°C/400°F/Gas 6. Roll out the pastry and use to line a 23cm/9in round, loose-based flan tin (quiche pan). Line with greaseproof (waxed) paper and fill with baking beans, then bake for 15 minutes. Remove the beans and greaseproof paper and bake for a further 5 minutes. Reduce the oven temperature to 180°C/350°F/Gas 4.

2 Grate the marzipan. Whisk the egg whites until stiff. Sprinkle half the marzipan over them and fold in. Then fold in the rest.

3 Turn the mixture into the pastry case (pie shell) and spread it evenly. Sprinkle the blueberries over the top and bake for 20–25 minutes, until golden and just set. Leave to cool for 10 minutes before serving.

Baked Bananas with Ice Cream and Toffee Sauce

Bananas make one of the easiest of all desserts, just as welcome as a comforting winter treat as they are to follow a barbecue. For an extra sweet finishing touch, grate some plain (semisweet) chocolate on the bananas, over the sauce, just before serving. If baking on a barbecue, turn the bananas occasionally to ensure even cooking.

SERVES FOUR

4 large bananas

75g/3oz/scant $^1/_2$ cup light muscovado (brown) sugar

75ml/5 tbsp double (heavy) cream

4 scoops good-quality vanilla ice cream

1 Preheat the oven to 180°C/350°F/Gas 4. Put the unpeeled bananas in an ovenproof dish and bake for 15–20 minutes, until the skins are very dark and the flesh feels soft when squeezed.

2 Meanwhile, heat the light muscovado sugar in a small, heavy pan with 75ml/5 tbsp water until dissolved. Bring to the boil and add the double cream. Cook for 5 minutes, until the sauce has thickened and is toffee coloured. Remove from the heat.

3 Transfer the baked bananas in their skins to serving plates and split them lengthways to reveal the flesh. Pour some of the sauce over the bananas and top with scoops of vanilla ice cream. Serve any remaining sauce separately.

Roast Peaches with Amaretto

This is an excellent dessert to serve in summer, when peaches are at their juiciest and most fragrant. The apricot and almond flavour of the amaretto liqueur subtly enhances the sweet, fruity taste of ripe peaches. Serve with a spoonful of crème fraîche or whipped cream.

SERVES FOUR

1 Preheat the oven 190°C/375°F/Gas 5. Cut the peaches in half and prise out the stones (pits) with the point of the knife.

2 Place the peaches cut side up in a roasting pan. In a small bowl, mix the amaretto liqueur with the honey, and drizzle over the halved peaches, covering them evenly.

3 Bake the peaches for 20–25 minutes, or until tender. Place two peach halves on each serving plate and drizzle with the pan juices. Serve immediately.

4 ripe peaches

45ml/3 tbsp Amaretto di Sarone liqueur

45ml/3 tbsp clear honey

COOK'S TIP
You can cook these peaches over a barbecue. Place them on sheets of foil, drizzle over liqueur, then scrunch the foil around them to seal. Cook for 15–20 minutes.

Passion Fruit Soufflés

These simplified soufflés are so easy and work beautifully. The passion fruit adds a tropical note to a favourite classic. The soufflés look very pretty sprinkled with icing (confectioners') sugar.

SERVES FOUR

**200ml/7fl oz/scant 1 cup
ready-made fresh custard**

3 passion fruits, halved

2 egg whites

FROM THE STORECUPBOARD

**knob (pat) of softened butter,
for greasing**

1 Preheat the oven to 200°C/400°F/Gas 6. Grease four 200ml/7fl oz/scant 1 cup ramekin dishes with the butter.

2 Pour the custard into a large mixing bowl. Scrape out the seeds and juice from the halved passion fruit and stir into the custard until well combined.

3 Whisk the egg whites until stiff, and fold a quarter of them into the custard. Carefully fold in the remaining egg whites, then spoon the mixture into the ramekin dishes.

4 Place the dishes on a baking sheet and bake for 8–10 minutes, or until the soufflés are well risen. Serve immediately.

Zabaglione

Light as air and wonderfully heady, this warm, wine egg custard is a much-loved Italian dessert. Traditionally made with Sicilian Marsala, other fortified wines such as Madeira or sweet sherry can be used.

SERVES FOUR

1 Place the egg yolks and sugar in a large heatproof bowl and whisk with an electric beater until the mixture is pale and thick.

2 Gradually add the Marsala, Madeira or sweet sherry to the egg mixture, 15ml/1 tbsp at a time, whisking well after each addition.

3 Place the bowl over a pan of gently simmering water and whisk for 5–7 minutes, until thick: when the beaters are lifted, they should leave a thick trail on the surface of the mixture. Do not be tempted to give up when beating the mixture, as the zabaglione will be too runny and will be likely to separate if it is underbeaten.

4 Pour into four warmed, stemmed glasses and serve immediately, with amaretti for dipping.

4 egg yolks

50g/2oz/¹/₄ cup caster (superfine) sugar

60ml/4 tbsp Marsala, Madeira or sweet sherry

amaretti biscuits, to serve

EXTRAS

Marinate chopped strawberries in a little extra Marsala, Madeira or sweet sherry for an hour or so. Sweeten with sugar, if you like, and spoon into glasses before you add the zabaglione.

Grilled Pineapple and Rum Cream

The sweeter and juicier the pineapple, the more delicious the pan juices will be in this tropical dessert. To test whether the pineapple is ripe, gently pull the green spiky leaves at the top of the fruit. If they come away easily, the fruit is ripe and ready to use.

SERVES FOUR

1 Heat the butter in a frying pan and add the pineapple. Cook over a moderate to high heat until the pineapple is starting to turn golden. Add the rum and allow to bubble for 1–2 minutes. Remove the pan from the heat and set aside to cool completely.

2 Whip the cream until it is soft but not stiff. Fold the pineapple and rum mixture evenly through the cream, then divide it between four glasses and serve.

115g/4oz pineapple, roughly chopped

45ml/3 tbsp dark rum

300ml/¹/₂ pint/1¹/₄ cups double (heavy) cream

FROM THE STORECUPBOARD

25g/1oz/2 tbsp butter

Cold Desserts

BECAUSE THEY CAN BE MADE IN ADVANCE, COLD DESSERTS

ARE THE PERFECT CHOICE FOR ENTERTAINING. ALL THE

RECIPES IN THIS CHAPTER HAVE AN ELEGANT SIMPLICITY

THAT GUARANTEES SUCCESS WITH EVEN THE MOST

SOPHISTICATED DINNER GUESTS. HOWEVER, THESE

DESSERTS ARE SO EASY TO PREPARE THAT YOU WILL WANT

TO SERVE THEM FOR EVERYDAY MEALS TOO.

Oranges in Syrup

This recipe works well with most citrus fruits – for example, try pink grapefruit or sweet, perfumed clementines, which have been peeled but left whole. Serve the oranges with 300ml/½ pint/1¼ cups whipped cream flavoured with 5ml/1 tsp ground cinnamon, or 5ml/1 tsp ground nutmeg or with Greek (US strained plain) yogurt.

SERVES SIX

6 medium oranges

200g/7oz/1 cup sugar

**100ml/3¹/₂ fl oz/
scant ¹/₂ cup fresh
strong brewed coffee**

**50g/2oz/¹/₂ cup
pistachio nuts,
chopped (optional)**

1 Finely pare, shred and reserve the rind from one orange. Peel the remaining oranges. Cut each one crossways into slices, then re-form them, with a cocktail stick (toothpick) through the centre.

2 Put the sugar in a heavy pan and add 50ml/2fl oz/¼ cup water. Heat gently until the sugar dissolves, then bring to the boil and cook until the syrup turns pale gold.

3 Remove from the heat and carefully pour 100ml/3½fl oz/ scant ½ cup freshly boiling water into the pan. Return to the heat until the syrup has dissolved in the water. Stir in the coffee.

4 Add the oranges and the rind to the coffee syrup. Simmer for 15–20 minutes, turning the oranges once during cooking. Leave to cool, then chill. Serve sprinkled with pistachio nuts, if using.

COOK'S TIP *Choose a pan in which the oranges will just fit in a single layer – use a deep frying pan if you don't have a pan that is large enough.*

Fresh Fig Compote

A vanilla and coffee syrup brings out the wonderful flavour of figs – serve Greek (US strained plain) yogurt or vanilla ice cream with the poached fruit. A good selection of different honey is available – its aroma and flavour will be subtly scented by the plants surrounding the hives. Orange blossom honey works particularly well in this recipe, although any clear variety is suitable.

SERVES FOUR TO SIX

**400ml/14fl oz/
1²/₃ cups fresh
brewed coffee**

**115g/4oz/¹/₂ cup
clear honey**

1 vanilla pod (bean)

**12 slightly under-ripe
fresh figs**

1 Choose a frying pan with a lid, large enough to hold the figs in a single layer. Pour in the coffee and add the honey.

2 Split the vanilla pod lengthways and scrape the seeds into the pan. Add the vanilla pod, then bring to a rapid boil and cook until reduced to about 175ml/6fl oz/¾ cup.

3 Wash the figs and pierce the skins several times with a sharp skewer. Cut in half and add to the syrup. Reduce the heat, cover and simmer for 5 minutes. Remove the figs from the syrup with a slotted spoon and set aside to cool.

4 Strain the syrup over the figs. Allow to stand at room temperature for 1 hour before serving.

COOK'S TIP *Figs come in three main varieties – red, white and black – and all three are suitable for cooking. They are sweet and succulent, and complement the stronger, more pervasive flavours of coffee and vanilla very well.*

Pistachio and Rose Water Oranges

This light and citrusy dessert is perfect to serve after a heavy main course, such as a hearty meat stew or a leg of roast lamb. Combining three favourite Middle Eastern ingredients, it is delightfully fragrant and refreshing. If you don't have pistachio nuts, use hazelnuts instead.

SERVES FOUR

1 Slice the top and bottom off one of the oranges to expose the flesh. Using a small serrated knife, slice down between the pith and the flesh, working round the orange, to remove all the peel and pith. Slice the orange into six rounds, reserving any juice. Repeat with the remaining oranges.

2 Arrange the orange rounds on a serving dish. Mix the reserved juice with the rose water and drizzle over the oranges. Cover the dish with clear film (plastic wrap) and chill for about 30 minutes. Sprinkle the chopped pistachio nuts over the oranges to serve.

4 large oranges

30ml/2 tbsp rose water

30ml/2 tbsp shelled pistachio nuts, roughly chopped

COOK'S TIP

Rose-scented sugar is delicious sprinkled over fresh fruit salads. Wash and thoroughly dry a handful of rose petals and place in a sealed container filled with caster (superfine) sugar for 2–3 days. Remove the petals before using the sugar.

Lychee and Elderflower Sorbet

The flavour of elderflowers is famous for bringing out the essence of gooseberries, but what is less well known is how wonderfully it complements lychees.

SERVES FOUR

175g/6oz/³/₄ cup caster sugar

400ml/14fl oz/1²/₃ cups water

500g/1¹/₄lb fresh lychees, peeled and stoned

15ml/1 tbsp elderflower cordial

dessert biscuits, to serve

COOK'S TIP Switch the freezer to the coldest setting before making the sorbet – the faster the mixture freezes, the smaller the ice crystals that form and the better the final texture will be.

1 Place the sugar and water in a saucepan and heat gently until the sugar has dissolved. Increase the heat and boil for 5 minutes, then add the lychees. Lower the heat and simmer for 7 minutes. Remove from the heat and allow to cool.

2 Purée the fruit and syrup in a blender or food processor. Place a sieve over a bowl and pour the purée into it. Press through as much of the purée as possible with a spoon.

3 Stir the elderflower cordial into the strained purée, then pour the mixture into a freezerproof container. Freeze for 2 hours, until ice crystals start to form around the edges.

4 Remove the sorbet from the freezer and process briefly in a food processor or blender to break up the crystals. Repeat this process twice more, then freeze until firm. Transfer to the fridge for 10 minutes to soften slightly before serving in scoops, with biscuits.

Papayas in Jasmine Flower Syrup

The fragrant syrup can be prepared in advance, using fresh jasmine flowers from a house plant or the garden. You can also use fresh flowers as a garnish. The syrup tastes fabulous with papayas, but it is also good with all sorts of desserts. Try it with ice cream or spooned over lychees or mangoes.

SERVES FOUR

45ml/3 tbsp palm sugar or light muscovado (brown) sugar

20–30 jasmine flowers

2 ripe papayas

juice of 1 lime

1 Place 105ml/7 tbsp water in a small pan and add the sugar. Heat gently, stirring occasionally, until the sugar has dissolved, then simmer, without stirring, over a low heat for 4 minutes.

2 Pour into a bowl, leave to cool slightly, then add the jasmine flowers. Leave to steep for at least 20 minutes.

3 Peel the papayas and slice in half lengthways. Scoop out and discard the seeds. Place the papayas on serving plates and squeeze over the lime.

4 Strain the syrup into a clean bowl, discarding the flowers. Spoon the syrup over the papayas. If you like, decorate with a few fresh jasmine flowers.

Mango and Lime Fool

Canned mangoes are used here for convenience, but this zesty, tropical fruit fool tastes even better if made with fresh ones. Choose a variety with a good flavour, such as the fragrant Alphonso mango.

SERVES FOUR

400g/14oz can sliced mango, plus extra to garnish (optional)

grated rind of 1 lime, plus juice of ¹/₂ lime

150ml/¹/₄ pint/²/₃ cup double (heavy) cream

90ml/6 tbsp Greek (US strained plain) yogurt

1 Drain the canned mango slices and put them in a food processor, then add the grated lime rind and lime juice. Process until the mixture forms a smooth purée.

2 Alternatively, place the mango slices in a bowl and mash with a potato masher, then press through a sieve (strainer) into a bowl with the back of a wooden spoon. Stir in the lime rind and juice.

3 Pour the cream into a bowl and add the yogurt. Whisk until the mixture is thick and then quickly whisk in the mango mixture.

4 Spoon the fool into four tall cups or glasses and chill for at least 1 hour. Just before serving, decorate each glass with fresh mango slices, if you like.

Tangy Raspberry and Lemon Tartlets

You can make the pastry cases for these little tartlets in advance and store them in an airtight container until ready to serve.

SERVES FOUR

1 Preheat the oven to 190°C/375°F/Gas 5. Roll out the pastry and use to line four 9cm/3¹/₂in tartlet tins (muffin pans). Line each tin with a circle of baking parchment and fill with baking beans or uncooked rice.

2 Bake for 15–20 minutes, or until golden and cooked through. Remove the baking beans or rice and paper and take the pastry cases out of the tins. Leave to cool completely on a wire rack.

3 Set aside 12 raspberries for decoration and fold the remaining ones into the lemon curd. Spoon the mixture into the pastry cases and top with the reserved raspberries. Serve immediately.

175g/6oz ready-made short-crust pastry, thawed if frozen

120ml/8 tbsp good quality lemon curd

115g/4oz/²/₃ cup fresh raspberries

Crispy Mango Stacks with Raspberry Coulis

This makes a very healthy yet stunning dessert – it is low in fat and contains no added sugar. However, if the raspberries are a little sharp, you may prefer to add a pinch of sugar to the purée.

SERVES FOUR

3 filo pastry sheets, thawed if frozen

2 small ripe mangoes

115g/4oz/²/₃ raspberries, thawed if frozen

FROM THE STORECUPBOARD

50g/2oz/¹/₄ cup butter, melted

1 Preheat the oven to 200°C/400°F/Gas 6. Lay the filo sheets on a clean work surface and cut out four 10cm/4in rounds from each. Brush each round with the melted butter and lay the rounds on two baking sheets. Bake for 5 minutes, or until crisp and golden. Place on wire racks to cool.

2 Peel the mangoes, remove the stones and cut the flesh into thin slices. Put the raspberries in a food processor with 45ml/3 tbsp water and process to a purée. Place a pastry round on each of four serving plates. Top with a quarter of the mango and drizzle with a little of the raspberry purée. Repeat until all the ingredients have been used, finishing with a layer of mango and a drizzle of raspberry purée.

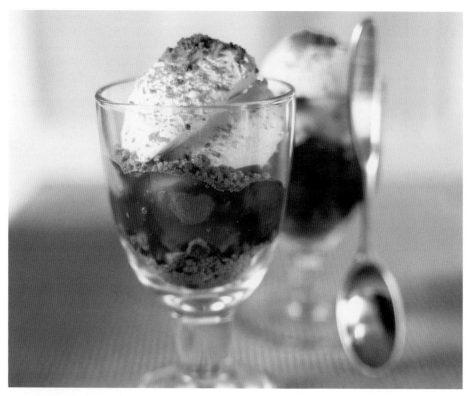

Rhubarb and Ginger Trifles

Choose a good quality jar of rhubarb compote for this recipe; try to find one with large, chunky pieces of fruit.

SERVES FOUR

12 gingernut biscuits (gingersnaps)

50ml/2fl oz/¼ cup rhubarb compote

450ml/¾ pint/scant 2 cups extra thick double (heavy) cream

1 Put the ginger biscuits in a plastic bag and seal. Bash the biscuits with a rolling pin until roughly crushed.

2 Set aside two tablespoons of crushed biscuits and divide the rest among four glasses.

3 Spoon the rhubarb compote on top of the crushed biscuits, then top with the cream. Place in the refrigerator and chill for about 30 minutes.

4 To serve, sprinkle the reserved crushed biscuits over the trifles and serve immediately.

Strawberry Cream Shortbreads

These pretty desserts are always popular. Serve them as soon as they are ready because the shortbread cookies will lose their lovely crisp texture if left to stand.

SERVES THREE

150g/5oz strawberries

450ml/³/₄ pint/scant 2 cups double (heavy) cream

6 round shortbread biscuits (cookies)

VARIATION *You can use any other berry you like for this dessert – try raspberries or blueberries. Two ripe, peeled peaches will also give great results.*

1 Reserve three strawberries for decoration. Hull the remaining strawberries and cut them in half.

2 Put the halved strawberries in a bowl and gently crush using the back of a fork. (Only crush the berries lightly; they should not be reduced to a purée.)

3 Put the cream in a large, clean bowl and whip to form soft peaks. Add the crushed strawberries and gently fold in to combine. (Do not overmix.)

4 Halve the reserved strawberries, then spoon the strawberry and cream mixture on top of the shortbread cookies. Decorate each one with half a strawberry and serve immediately.

Blackberries in Port

Pour this rich fruit compote over ice cream or serve it with a spoonful of clotted cream to create an attractive, rich dessert. It's unbelievably quick and easy to make and is the perfect end to a dinner party. Blackberries can be found growing wild on hedgerows in late summer and there's nothing better than picking them yourself for this lovely dessert.

SERVES FOUR

300ml/¹/₂ pint/1¹/₄ cups ruby port

75g/3oz/6 tbsp caster (superfine) sugar

450g/1lb/4 cups blackberries

1 Pour the port into a pan and add the sugar and 150ml/¹/₄ pint/²/₃ cup water. Stir over a gentle heat with a wooden spoon until the sugar has dissolved.

2 Remove the pan from the heat and stir in the blackberries. Set aside to cool, then pour into a bowl and cover with clear film (plastic wrap). Chill until ready to serve.

Baby Summer Puddings

This classic English dessert is always a favourite, and serving it in individual portions with spoonfuls of clotted cream makes it extra special. White bread that is more than a day old actually works better than fresh bread. Slices of brioche make a wonderful alternative to white bread.

SERVES FOUR

6 white bread slices, crusts removed

450g/1lb/4 cups summer fruits

75g/3oz/6 tbsp caster (superfine) sugar

COOK'S TIP *You can enjoy this lovely dessert even in the winter. Use frozen summer fruits, which are available in supermarkets all year round. Simply thaw the fruits, then cook as if using fresh fruits.*

1 Cut out four rounds from the bread slices, large enough to fit in the bottom of four 175ml/6fl oz/³/₄ cup dariole moulds.

2 Line the moulds with clear film (plastic wrap) and place a bread round in the base of each mould. Reserve two slices of bread and cut the remaining bread into slices and use to line the sides of the moulds, pressing to fit.

3 Put the summer fruits in a pan with the sugar and heat gently until the sugar has dissolved. Bring to the boil, then simmer gently for 2–3 minutes. Remove from the heat and leave to cool slightly, then spoon into the moulds.

4 Cut four rounds out of the remaining slices of bread to fit the top of the dariole moulds. Place the bread rounds on the fruit and push down to fit. Cover each dariole mould loosely with clear film and place a small weight on top.

5 Chill the desserts overnight, then turn out on to serving plates. Remove the clear film lining and serve immediately.

Raspberry Brûlée

Cracking through the caramelized sugary top of a crème brûlée to reveal the creamy custard underneath is always so satisfying. These ones have the added bonus of a deliciously rich, fruity custard packed with crushed raspberries.

SERVES FOUR

1 Tip the raspberries into a large bowl and crush with a fork. Add the custard and gently fold in until combined.

2 Divide the mixture between four 120ml/4fl oz/¹/₂ cup ramekin dishes. Cover each one with clear film (plastic wrap) and chill in the refrigerator for 2–3 hours.

3 Preheat the grill (broiler) to high. Remove the clear film from the ramekin dishes and place them on a baking sheet. Sprinkle the sugar over the custards and grill (broil) for 3–4 minutes, or until the sugar has caramelized.

4 Remove the custards from the grill and set aside for a few minutes to allow the sugar to harden, then serve.

115g/4oz fresh raspberries

300ml/¹/₂ pint/1¹/₄ cups ready-made fresh custard

75g/3oz caster (superfine) sugar

COOK'S TIP *You can now buy little gas blow torches for use in the kitchen. They make quick work of caramelizing the sugar on top of the brûlées – and are also fun to use!*

Portuguese Custard Tarts

Called *pastéis de nata* in Portugal, these tarts are traditionally served with a small strong coffee as a sweet breakfast dish, but they are equally delicious served as a pastry or dessert.

MAKES TWELVE

1 Preheat the oven to 200°C/400°F/Gas 6. Roll out the pastry and cut out twelve 13cm/5in rounds. Line a 12-hole muffin tin (pan) with the pastry rounds. Line each pastry round with a circle of baking parchment and some baking beans or uncooked rice.

2 Bake the tarts for 10–15 minutes, or until the pastry is cooked through and golden. Remove the paper and baking beans or rice and set aside to cool.

3 Spoon the custard into the pastry cases and dust with the icing sugar. Place the tarts under a preheated hot grill (broiler) and cook until the sugar caramelizes. Remove from the heat and leave to cool before serving.

225g/8oz ready-made puff pastry, thawed if frozen

175ml/6fl oz/³⁄₄ cup fresh ready-made custard

30ml/2 tbsp icing (confectioners') sugar

Chocolate Banana Fools

This de luxe version of banana custard looks great served in glasses. It can be made a few hours in advance and chilled until ready to serve.

SERVES FOUR

1 Put the chocolate in a heatproof bowl and melt in the microwave on high power for 1–2 minutes. Stir, then set aside to cool. (Alternatively, put the chocolate in a heatproof bowl and place it over a pan of gently simmering water and leave until melted, stirring frequently.)

115g/4oz plain (semisweet) chocolate, chopped

300ml/¹/₂ pint/1¹/₄ cups fresh custard

2 bananas

2 Pour the custard into a bowl and gently fold in the melted chocolate to make a rippled effect.

3 Peel and slice the bananas and stir these into the chocolate and custard mixture. Spoon into four glasses and chill for 30 minutes–1 hour before serving.

Lemon Posset

This simple creamy dessert has distant origins, dating back to the Middle Ages. It is perfect for warm summer evenings and is particularly good served with crisp shortbread cookies.

SERVES FOUR

1 Gently heat the cream and sugar together until the sugar has dissolved, then bring to the boil, stirring constantly. Add the lemon juice and rind and stir until the mixture thickens.

2 Pour the mixture into four heatproof serving glasses and chill until just set, then serve.

600ml/1 pint/2¹/₂ cups double (heavy) cream

175g/6oz/scant 1 cup caster (superfine) sugar

grated rind and juice of 2 unwaxed lemons

COOK'S TIP *To make shortbread cookies, put 225g/8oz/1 cup chilled butter in a food processor and add 115g/4oz/²/₃ cup caster (superfine) sugar, 225g/8oz/2 cups plain (all-purpose) flour and 115g/4oz/²/₃ cup ground rice. Process to form a dough, then shape into a log 5cm/2in wide and wrap in clear film (plastic wrap). Chill for 30 minutes. Preheat the oven to 190°C/375°F/Gas 5. Cut the dough into thin slices, and bake for 15–20 minutes.*

Chilled Chocolate and Espresso Mousse

Heady, aromatic espresso coffee adds a distinctive flavour to this smooth, rich mousse. For a special occasion, serve the mousse in stylish chocolate cups decorated with sprigs of mint, with mascarpone or clotted cream on the side.

SERVES FOUR

450g/1lb plain (semisweet) chocolate

45ml/3 tbsp freshly brewed espresso

4 eggs, separated

FROM THE STORECUPBOARD

25g/1oz/2 tbsp unsalted (sweet) butter

1 For each chocolate cup, cut a double thickness 15cm/6in square of foil. Mould it around a small orange, leaving the edges and corners loose to make a cup shape. Remove the orange and press the bottom of the foil case gently on a surface to make a flat base. Repeat to make four foil cups.

2 Break half the chocolate into small pieces and place in a bowl set over a pan of very hot water. Stir occasionally until the chocolate has completely melted.

3 Spoon the chocolate into the foil cups, spreading it up the sides with the back of a spoon to give a ragged edge. Chill for 30 minutes in the refrigerator, or until set hard. Gently peel away the foil, starting at the top edge.

4 To make the chocolate mousse, put the remaining chocolate and espresso into a bowl set over a pan of hot water and melt as before, until smooth and liquid. Stir in the butter, a little at a time. Remove the pan from the heat and then stir in the egg yolks.

5 Whisk the egg whites in a bowl until stiff, but not dry, then fold them into the chocolate mixture. Pour into a bowl and chill for at least 3 hours, or until the mousse is set. Scoop the chilled mousse into the chocolate cups just before serving.

Meringue Pyramid with Chocolate Mascarpone

This impressive cake makes a perfect centrepiece for a celebration buffet. Dust the pyramid with a little sieved icing (confectioners') sugar and sprinkle with just a few rose petals for simple but stunning presentation.

SERVES ABOUT TEN

200g/7oz plain (semisweet) chocolate

4 egg whites

150g/5oz/³⁄₄ cup caster (superfine) sugar

115g/4oz/³⁄₄ cup mascarpone cheese

1 Preheat the oven to 150°C/300°F/Gas 2. Line two large baking sheets with baking parchment or greaseproof (waxed) paper. Grate 75g/3oz of the chocolate.

2 Whisk the egg whites in a clean, grease-free bowl until they form stiff peaks. Gradually whisk in half the sugar, then add the rest and whisk until the meringue is very stiff and glossy. Add the grated chocolate and whisk lightly to mix.

3 Draw a 20cm/8in circle on the lining paper on one of the baking sheets, turn it upside down, and spread the marked circle evenly with about half the meringue. Spoon the remaining meringue in 28–30 teaspoonfuls on both baking sheets. Bake the meringue for 1–1½ hours, or until crisp and completely dried out.

4 Make the filling. Melt the remaining chocolate in a heatproof bowl over hot water. Cool slightly, then stir in the mascarpone. Cool the mixture until firm.

5 Spoon the chocolate mixture into a large piping (pastry) bag and use to sandwich the meringues together in pairs, reserving a small amount of filling for the pyramid.

6 Arrange the filled meringues on a serving platter, piling them up in a pyramid and keeping them in position with a few well-placed dabs of the reserved filling.

Classic Chocolate Roulade

This rich, squidgy chocolate roll should be made at least eight hours before serving to allow it to soften. Expect the roulade to crack a little when you roll it up, and sprinkle with a little grated chocolate, if you like, as a final decoration. When melting chocolate, break it into even-sized pieces and place in a dry heatproof bowl over hot water. If the water is too hot the chocolate will turn grainy and scorch; if the chocolate is splashed with water it will harden and acquire a dull finish.

SERVES EIGHT

1 Preheat the oven to 180°C/350°F/Gas 4. Grease and line a 33 x 23cm/13 x 9in Swiss (jelly) roll tin (pan) with baking parchment.

2 Break the chocolate into squares and melt in a bowl over a pan of barely simmering water. Remove from the heat and leave to cool for about 5 minutes.

3 In a large bowl, whisk the sugar and egg yolks until light and fluffy. Stir in the melted chocolate.

4 Whisk the egg whites until stiff, but not dry, and then gently fold into the chocolate mixture.

5 Pour the chocolate mixture into the prepared tin, spreading it level with a palette knife (metal spatula). Bake for about 25 minutes, or until firm. Leave the cake in the tin and cover with a cooling rack, making sure that it does not touch the cake.

6 Cover the rack with a damp dishtowel, then wrap in clear film (plastic wrap). Leave in a cool place for 8 hours, preferably overnight.

7 Dust a sheet of greaseproof (waxed) paper with caster or icing sugar and turn out the roulade on to it. Peel off the lining paper.

8 To make the filling, whip the double cream until soft peaks form. Spread the cream over the roulade. Starting from one of the short ends, carefully roll it up, using the paper to help.

9 Place the roulade, seam side down, on to a serving plate and dust generously with more caster or icing sugar before serving.

200g/7oz plain (semisweet) chocolate

200g/7oz/1 cup caster (superfine) sugar, plus extra caster or icing (confectioners') sugar to dust

7 eggs, separated

300ml/^{1}/$_2$ pint/1^1/$_4$ cups double (heavy) cream

COOK'S TIP
For a special dessert, decorate the roulade with swirls of whipped cream and chocolate coffee beans or with clusters of raspberries and mint leaves.

Cherry Chocolate Brownies

This is a modern version of the classic Black Forest gâteau. Choose really good-quality bottled fruits because this will make all the difference to the end result. Look out for bottled fruits at Christmas-time, in particular, when supermarket shelves are packed with different varieties. Other types of fruit will work equally well – try slices of orange bottled in liqueur or pears bottled in brandy.

SERVES FOUR

1 Using a sharp knife, carefully cut the brownies in half crossways to make two thin slices. Place one brownie square on each of four serving plates.

2 Pour the cream into a large bowl and whip until soft but not stiff, then divide half the whipped cream between the four brownie squares.

3 Divide half the cherries among the cream-topped brownies, then place the remaining brownie halves on top of the cherries. Press down lightly.

4 Spoon the remaining cream on top of the brownies, then top each one with more cherries and serve immediately.

4 chocolate brownies

300ml/¹/₂ pint/1¹/₄ cups double (heavy) cream

20–24 bottled cherries in Kirsch

Coffee Mascarpone Creams

For the best results, use good quality coffee beans and make the coffee as strong as possible. These little desserts are very rich so you need a really robust shot of coffee to give the desired result. They are particularly good served with a glass of liqueur or a cup of espresso.

SERVES FOUR

1 Put the mascarpone in a bowl and add the coffee. Mix well until smooth and creamy. Sift in the icing sugar and stir until thoroughly combined.

2 Spoon the mixture into little china pots or ramekin dishes and chill for 30 minutes before serving.

115g/4oz/¹/₂ cup mascarpone cheese

45ml/3 tbsp strong espresso coffee

45ml/3 tbsp icing (confectioners') sugar

VARIATION *You can flavour mascarpone with almost anything you like to make a quick but elegant dessert. Try replacing the coffee with the same quantity of orange juice, Marsala or honey.*

Ice Creams and Frozen Desserts

ICE CREAMS AND ICED DESSERTS CAN MAKE A PERFECT,
REFRESHING END TO A MEAL. HOME-MADE ICES, WHETHER
A LIGHTLY PERFUMED SORBET, A CREAMY KULFI OR A RICH
AND CREAMY ICE CREAM GÂTEAU, ARE SURPRISINGLY
EASY TO MAKE AND A WONDERFUL TREAT TO SERVE
TO GUESTS AND FAMILY ALIKE.

Lemon Sorbet

This is probably the most classic sorbet of all. Refreshingly tangy and yet deliciously smooth, it quite literally melts in the mouth. Try to buy unwaxed lemons for recipes such as this one where the lemon rind is used. The wax coating can adversely affect the flavour of the rind.

SERVES SIX

200g/7oz/1 cup caster (superfine) sugar, plus extra for coating rind to decorate

4 lemons, well scrubbed

1 egg white

1 Put the sugar in a pan and pour in 300ml/½ pint/1¼ cups water. Bring to the boil, stirring occasionally until the sugar has just dissolved.

2 Using a swivel vegetable peeler, pare the rind thinly from two of the lemons so that it falls straight into the pan.

3 Simmer for 2 minutes without stirring, then take the pan off the heat. Leave to cool, then chill.

4 Squeeze the juice from all the lemons and add it to the syrup. Strain the syrup into a shallow freezerproof container, reserving the rind. Freeze the mixture for 4 hours, until it is mushy.

5 Process the sorbet (sherbet) in a food processor until it is smooth. Lightly whisk the egg white with a fork until it is just frothy. Replace the sorbet in the container, beat in the egg white and return the mixture to the freezer for 4 hours, or until it is firm.

6 Cut the reserved lemon rind into fine shreds and cook them in boiling water for 5 minutes, or until tender. Drain, then place on a plate and sprinkle generously with caster sugar. Scoop the sorbet into bowls or glasses and decorate with the sugared lemon rind.

Strawberry and Lavender Sorbet

A hint of lavender transforms a familiar strawberry sorbet into a perfumed dinner-party dessert. When buying strawberries look for plump, shiny fruit without any signs of staining or leakage at the bottom of the punnet – this suggests that the fruit at the bottom has been squashed. To hull strawberries, prise out the leafy top with a sharp knife or a specially designed strawberry huller.

SERVES SIX

1 Place the sugar in a pan and pour in 300ml/½ pint/1¼ cups water. Bring to the boil, stirring until the sugar has dissolved.

2 Take the pan off the heat, add the lavender flowers and leave to infuse (steep) for 1 hour. If time permits, chill the syrup in the refrigerator before using.

3 Process the strawberries in a food processor or in batches in a blender, then press the purée through a large sieve into a bowl.

4 Pour the purée into a freezerproof container, strain in the syrup and freeze for 4 hours, or until mushy. Transfer to a food processor and process until smooth. Whisk the egg white until frothy, and stir into the sorbet (sherbet). Spoon the sorbet back into the container and freeze until firm.

5 Serve in scoops, piled into tall glasses, and decorate with sprigs of lavender flowers.

150g/5oz/³/₄ cup
caster (superfine) sugar

**6 fresh lavender
flowers, plus extra
to decorate**

500g/1¹/₄lb/5 cups
strawberries, hulled

1 egg white

COOK'S TIP *The size of the lavender flowers can vary; if they are very small, you may need to use eight. To double check, taste a little of the cooled lavender syrup. If you think the flavour is too mild, add two or three more flowers, reheat and cool again before using.*

Blackcurrant Sorbet

Wonderfully sharp and bursting with flavour, blackcurrants make a really fabulous sorbet. Blackcurrants are more acidic than white or redcurrants and are very rarely eaten raw. Taste the mixture after adding the syrup, and if you find it a little too tart, add a little more sugar before freezing.

SERVES SIX

500g/1¹/₄lb/5 cups blackcurrants, trimmed, plus extra to decorate

150g/5oz/³/₄ cup caster (superfine) sugar

1 egg white

1 Put the blackcurrants in a pan and add 150ml/¼ pint/²/₃ cup water. Cover the pan and simmer for 5 minutes, or until the fruit is soft. Cool, then process to a purée in a food processor or blender.

2 Set a large sieve over a bowl, pour the purée into the sieve, then press it through the mesh with the back of a spoon to form a smooth liquid.

3 Pour 200ml/7fl oz/scant 1 cup water into a clean pan. Add the sugar and bring to the boil, stirring until the sugar has dissolved. Pour the syrup into a bowl. Cool, then chill.

4 Mix the blackcurrant purée and sugar syrup together. Spoon into a freezerproof container and freeze until mushy. Lightly whisk the egg white until just frothy. Process the sorbet (sherbet) in a food processor until smooth, then return it to the container and stir in the egg white. Freeze for 4 hours, or until firm.

5 Transfer the sorbet to the refrigerator about 15 minutes before serving. Serve in scoops, decorated with the blackcurrant sprigs.

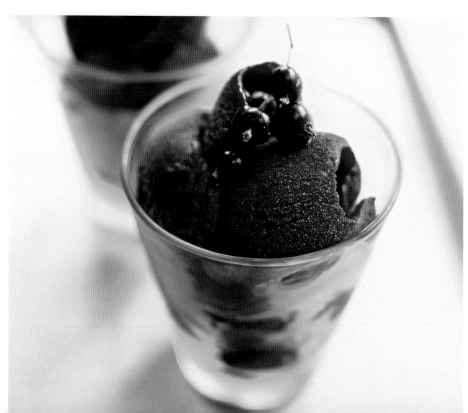

Damson Water Ice

Perfectly ripe damsons are sharp and full of flavour – if you can't find damsons, use another deep-red variety of plum or extra-juicy Victoria plums. To add an extra, nutty flavour to this mouthwatering ice, serve sprinkled with finely chopped toasted almonds.

SERVES SIX

500g/1¼lb ripe damsons, washed

150g/5oz/¾ cup caster (superfine) sugar

1 Put the damsons into a pan and add 150ml/¼ pint/⅔ cup water. Cover and simmer gently for 10 minutes, or until the damsons are tender.

2 Pour 300ml/½ pint/1¼ cups water into a second pan. Add the sugar and bring to the boil, stirring until the sugar has dissolved. Pour the syrup into a bowl, leave to cool, then chill.

3 Break up the cooked damsons in the pan with a wooden spoon and scoop out any free stones (pits). Pour the fruit and juices into a large sieve set over a bowl. Press the fruit through the sieve and discard the skins and any remaining stones from the sieve.

4 Pour the damson purée into a shallow plastic container. Stir in the syrup and freeze for 6 hours, beating once or twice to break up the ice crystals.

5 Spoon into tall serving glasses or dishes and serve the water ice with wafers.

VARIATION

Apricot water ice can be made in exactly the same way. Flavour the water ice with a little lemon or orange rind or add a broken cinnamon stick to the pan when poaching the fruit. Serve garnished with sprigs of mint or nasturtium flowers.

Peach and Cardamom Yogurt Ice

Make the most of spices that are familiar in savoury cooking by discovering their potential for sweet dishes. Cardamom, often used in Indian cooking, has a warm pungent aroma and a subtle lemon flavour. Although it is made with yogurt rather than cream, this ice cream has a luxurious velvety texture and it is a healthy choice, too.

SERVES FOUR

8 cardamom pods

6 peaches, total weight about 500g/1¹/₄lb, halved and stoned (pitted)

75g/3oz/6 tbsp caster (superfine) sugar

200ml/7fl oz/scant 1 cup natural (plain) yogurt

1 Put the cardamom pods on a board and crush them with the base of a ramekin, or place in a mortar and crush with a pestle.

2 Chop the peaches coarsely and put them in a pan. Add the crushed cardamom pods, with their black seeds, the sugar and 30ml/2 tbsp water. Cover and simmer for 10 minutes, or until the fruit is tender. Leave to cool.

3 Process the peach mixture in a food processor or blender until smooth, then press through a sieve placed over a bowl.

4 Mix the yogurt into the sieved purée and pour into a freezerproof container. Freeze for 5–6 hours, until firm, beating once or twice with a fork, electric whisk, or in a processor to break up the ice crystals.

5 Scoop the ice cream on to a large platter and serve.

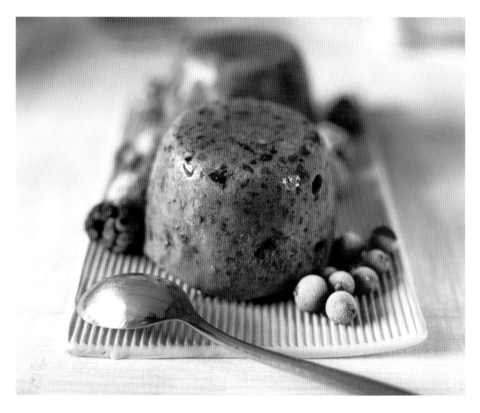

Summer Berry Frozen Yogurt

Any combination of summer fruits will work for this dish, as long as they are frozen, because this helps to create a chunky texture. Whole fresh or frozen berries make an attractive decoration.

SERVES SIX

350g/12oz/3 cups frozen summer fruits

200g/7oz/scant 1 cup Greek (US strained plain) yogurt

25g/1oz icing (confectioners') sugar

VARIATION *To make a rich and creamy ice cream, use double (heavy) cream in place of the yogurt. It's a lot less healthy but the taste is irresistible.*

1 Put all the ingredients into a food processor and process until combined but still quite chunky. Spoon the mixture into six 150ml/¼ pint/⅔ cup ramekin dishes.

2 Cover each dish with clear film (plastic wrap) and place in the freezer for about 2 hours, or until firm.

3 To turn out the frozen yogurts, dip the dishes briefly in hot water and invert them on to small serving plates. Tap the base of the dishes and the yogurts should come out. Serve immediately.

Raspberry Sherbet

Traditional sherbets are made in a similar way to sorbets but with added milk. This low-fat version is made from raspberry purée blended with sugar syrup and virtually fat-free fromage frais or yogurt.

SERVES SIX

175g/6oz/scant 1 cup caster (superfine) sugar

500g/1¹/₄lb/3¹/₂ cups raspberries, plus extra, to serve

500ml/17fl oz/2¹/₄ cups virtually fat-free fromage frais or yogurt

1 Put the sugar in a small pan with 150ml/¹/₄ pint/²/₃ cup water and bring to the boil, stirring until the sugar has dissolved completely. Pour into a jug (pitcher) and cool.

2 Put 350g/12oz/2¹/₂ cups of the raspberries in a food processor and blend to a purée. Press through a sieve into a large bowl and discard the seeds. Stir the sugar syrup into the raspberry purée and chill until very cold.

3 Add the fromage frais or yogurt to the chilled purée and whisk until smooth. Using an ice-cream maker, churn the mixture until it is thick but too soft to scoop. Scrape into a freezerproof container, then crush the remaining raspberries between your fingers and add to the ice cream. Mix lightly then freeze for 2–3 hours until firm. Scoop the ice cream into dishes and serve with extra raspberries.

Watermelon Ice

This simple, refreshing dessert is perfect after a hot, spicy meal. The aromatic flavour of kaffir lime leaves goes perfectly with watermelon.

SERVES FOUR TO SIX

90ml/6 tbsp caster (superfine) sugar

4 kaffir lime leaves, torn into small pieces

500g/1¼lb watermelon

1 Put the sugar and lime leaves in a pan with 105ml/7 tbsp water. Heat gently until the sugar has dissolved, then pour into a large bowl and set aside to cool.

2 Cut the watermelon into wedges with a large knife. Cut the flesh from the rind, remove the seeds and chop the flesh. Place the flesh in a food processor and process to a slush, then mix in the sugar syrup. Chill for 3–4 hours.

3 Strain the chilled mixture into a freezer container and freeze for 2 hours, then beat with a fork to break up the ice crystals. Return to the freezer and freeze for 3 hours more, beating at half-hourly intervals, then freeze until firm. Transfer the ice to the refrigerator about 30 minutes before serving.

Blackberry Ice Cream

There could scarcely be fewer ingredients in this delicious, vibrant ice cream, which is simple to make and ideal as a prepare-ahead dessert. Serve the ice cream with biscuits (cookies), such as shortbread or almond biscuits, to provide a delicious contrast in taste and texture.

SERVES FOUR TO SIX

500g/1¼lb/5 cups blackberries, hulled, plus extra to decorate

75g/3oz/6 tbsp caster (superfine) sugar

300ml/½ pint/1¼ cups whipping cream

crisp dessert biscuits (cookies), to serve

> **COOK'S TIP**
> *Frozen blackberries can be used instead of fresh. You will need to increase the cooking time to 10 minutes and stir occasionally.*

1 Put the blackberries into a pan, add 30ml/2 tbsp water and the sugar. Cover and simmer for 5 minutes, until just soft.

2 Tip the fruit into a sieve placed over a bowl and press it through the mesh, using a wooden spoon. Leave to cool, then chill.

3 Whip the cream until it is just thick but still soft enough to fall from a spoon, then mix it with the chilled fruit purée. Pour the mixture into a freezerproof container and freeze for 2 hours, or until it is part frozen.

4 Mash the mixture with a fork or process it in a food processor to break up the ice crystals. Return it to the freezer for 4 hours more, mashing or processing the mixture again after 2 hours.

5 Scoop the ice cream into dishes and decorate with extra blackberries. Serve with crisp dessert biscuits.

Coffee Ice Cream

This classic ice cream is always a favourite and, despite its simplicity, has an air of sophistication and elegance about it. If you have an ice cream maker, simply pour the mixture into it and churn until firm.

SERVES EIGHT

600ml/1 pint/2¹/₂ cups fresh ready-made custard

150ml/¹/₄ pint/²/₃ cup strong black coffee

300ml/¹/₂ pint/1¹/₄ cups double (heavy) cream

1 Put the custard in a large bowl and stir in the coffee. In a separate bowl, whip the cream until soft but not stiff and fold evenly into the coffee and custard mixture.

2 Pour the mixture into a freezerproof container and cover with a tight-fitting lid or clear film (plastic wrap) and freeze for about 2 hours.

3 Remove the ice cream from the freezer and beat with a fork to break up the ice crystals.

4 Return the ice cream to the freezer, freeze for a further 2 hours, then beat again. Return it to the freezer until completely frozen, then serve.

Kulfi

This favourite Indian ice cream is traditionally made by carefully boiling milk until it has reduced to about one-third of its original quantity. Although you can save time by using condensed milk, nothing beats the luscious result achieved by using the authentic method. When they are available, rose petals are a stylish decoration in addition to the pistachio nuts.

SERVES FOUR

1.5 litres/2¹/₂ pints/6¹/₄ cups full-fat (whole) milk

3 cardamom pods

25g/1oz/2 tbsp caster (superfine) sugar

50g/2oz/¹/₂ cup pistachio nuts, skinned

1 Pour the milk into a large, heavy pan. Bring to the boil, reduce the heat and simmer gently for 1 hour, stirring occasionally.

2 Put the cardamom pods in a mortar and crush them with a pestle. Add the pods and the seeds to the milk and continue to simmer, stirring frequently, for 1–1½ hours, or until the milk has reduced to about 475ml/16fl oz/2 cups. Strain the milk into a jug (pitcher), stir in the sugar and leave to cool.

3 Grind half the pistachios in a blender or nut grinder. Cut the remaining pistachios into thin slivers and set them aside for decoration. Stir the ground nuts into the milk mixture.

4 Pour the milk and pistachio mixture into four kulfi or lolly (popsicle) moulds. Freeze the mixture overnight or until firm.

5 To unmould the kulfi, half fill a plastic container or bowl with very hot water, stand the moulds in the water and count to ten. Immediately lift out the moulds and invert them on a baking sheet. Transfer the ice creams to individual plates and sprinkle sliced pistachios over the top.

Coconut Ice

The creamy taste and texture of this ice cream comes from the natural fat content of coconut as the mixture contains neither cream nor egg and is very refreshing. The lime adds a delicious tangy flavour as well as pretty green specks to the finished ice. Decorate with toasted coconut shavings or toasted desiccated (dry unsweetened shredded) coconut (this browns very quickly, so watch it constantly).

SERVES FOUR TO SIX

115g/4oz/generous ¹/₄ cup caster (superfine) sugar

2 limes

400ml/14fl oz can coconut milk

toasted coconut shavings, to decorate (optional)

1 Pour 150ml/¼ pint/⅔ cup water in a small pan. Tip in the caster sugar and bring to the boil, stirring constantly until the sugar has completely dissolved. Remove the pan from the heat and leave the syrup to cool, then chill well.

2 Grate the rind from the limes finely, taking care to avoid the bitter pith. Squeeze out their juice and add to the pan of syrup with the rind. Add the coconut milk.

3 Pour the mixture into a freezerproof container and freeze for 5–6 hours, or until firm. Beat twice with a fork or electric whisk, or process in a food processor to break up the crystals. Scoop into dishes and decorate with toasted coconut shavings, if you like.

COOK'S TIP *To make toasted coconut shavings, rinse the flesh from a coconut under cold water. Shave slices using a vegetable peeler, then toast under a moderate grill (broiler) until they are curled and the edges have turned golden.*

Gingered Semi-freddo

This Italian ice cream is rather like the original soft scoop ice cream. Made with a boiled sugar syrup rather than a traditional egg custard, and generously speckled with chopped stem ginger, this delicious ice cream will stay soft when frozen. For a really impressive dinner party dessert, serve the semi-freddo in plain (semisweet) chocolate cases.

SERVES SIX

1 Mix the sugar and 120ml/4fl oz/½ cup cold water in a pan and heat gently, stirring occasionally, until the sugar has dissolved.

2 Increase the heat and boil for 4–5 minutes, without stirring, until the syrup registers 119°C/238°F on a sugar thermometer. Alternatively, test by dropping a little of the syrup into a cup of cold water. Pour the water away and you should be able to mould the syrup into a small ball.

3 Put the egg yolks in a large heatproof bowl and whisk until frothy. Place the bowl over a pan of simmering water and whisk in the sugar syrup. Continue whisking until the mixture is very thick. Remove from the heat and whisk until cool.

4 Whip the cream and lightly fold it into the egg yolk mixture with the chopped stem ginger. Pour into a freezerproof container and freeze for 1 hour.

5 Stir the semi-freddo to bring any ginger that has sunk to the base of the container to the top, then return it to the freezer for 5–6 hours, until firm. Scoop into dishes or chocolate cases (*see* Cook's Tip). Decorate with slices of ginger and serve.

115g/4oz/generous ¹/₂ cup caster (superfine) sugar

4 egg yolks

300ml/¹/₂ pint/1¹/₄ cups double (heavy) cream

115g/4oz/²/₃ cup drained stem (preserved) ginger, finely chopped, plus extra slices, to decorate

COOK'S TIP

To make the cases, pour melted chocolate over squares of baking parchment and drape them over upturned glasses. Peel off the baking parchment when set.

Miniature Choc-ices

These little chocolate-coated ice creams make a fun alternative to the more familiar after-dinner chocolates, especially on hot summer evenings – although they need to be eaten quickly. Serve the choc-ices in fluted paper sweet (candy) cases. If you can, buy gold cases as they will contrast very prettily with the dark chocolate coating.

MAKES ABOUT TWENTY-FIVE

**750ml/1¹/₄ pints/
3 cups vanilla,
chocolate or
coffee ice cream**

**200g/7oz plain
(semisweet) chocolate,
broken into pieces**

**25g/1oz milk
chocolate, broken
into pieces**

**25g/1oz/¹/₄ cup
chopped hazelnuts,
lightly toasted**

1 Put a large baking sheet in the freezer for 10 minutes. Using a melon baller, scoop balls of ice cream and place these on the baking sheet. Freeze for at least 1 hour or until firm.

2 Line a second baking sheet with baking parchment and place in the freezer for 15 minutes. Melt the plain chocolate in a heatproof bowl set over a pan of gently simmering water. Melt the milk chocolate in a separate bowl.

3 Using a metal spatula, transfer the ice cream scoops to the parchment-lined sheet. Spoon a little plain chocolate over one scoop so that most of it is coated.

4 Sprinkle immediately with chopped nuts, before the chocolate sets. Coat half the remaining scoops in the same way, sprinkling each one with nuts before the chocolate sets. Spoon the remaining plain chocolate over all the remaining scoops.

5 Using a teaspoon, drizzle the milk chocolate over the choc-ices that are not topped with nuts. Freeze again until ready to serve.

White Chocolate Castles

With a little ingenuity, good-quality bought ice cream can masquerade as a culinary masterpiece – it's down to perfect presentation. For a professional finish, dust the castles and plates with a hint of cocoa powder or icing (confectioners') sugar.

225g/8oz white chocolate, broken into pieces

250ml/8fl oz/1 cup white chocolate ice cream

250ml/8fl oz/1 cup dark chocolate ice cream

115g/4oz/1 cup berries

SERVES SIX

1 Put the white chocolate in a heatproof bowl, set it over a pan of gently simmering water and leave until melted. Line a baking sheet with greaseproof (waxed) paper. Cut out six 30 x 13cm/12 x 5in strips of greaseproof paper, then fold each in half lengthways.

2 Stand a 7.5cm/3in pastry (cookie) cutter on the baking sheet. Roll one strip of paper into a circle and fit inside the cutter with the folded edge on the base paper. Stick the edges together with tape.

3 Remove the cutter and shape more paper collars in the same way, leaving the pastry cutter in place around the final collar.

4 Spoon a little of the melted chocolate into the base of the collar supported by the cutter. Using a teaspoon, spread the chocolate over the base and up the sides of the collar, making the top edge uneven. Carefully lift away the cutter.

5 Make five more chocolate cases in the same way, using the cutter for extra support each time. Leave the cases in a cool place or in the refrigerator to set.

6 Carefully peel away the paper from the sides of the chocolate cases, then lift the cases off the base. Transfer to serving plates.

7 Using a large melon baller or teaspoon, scoop the white and dark chocolate ice creams into the cases and decorate with berries. Serve immediately.

Caramel and Pecan Terrine

Frozen or long-life cream is a useful ingredient for making impressive desserts without having a mega shopping trip. Caramel and nuts transform cream to parfait in this recipe. Take care that the syrup does not become too dark, or the ice cream will taste bitter.

SERVES SIX

115g/4oz/generous ¹/₂ cup sugar

450ml/³/₄ pint/scant 2 cups double (heavy) cream

30ml/2 tbsp icing (confectioners') sugar

75g/3oz/³/₄ cup pecan nuts, toasted

COOK'S TIP *Watch the caramel syrup closely after removing it from the heat. If it starts to turn too dark, dip the base of the pan in cold water. If the syrup remains very pale, return the pan to the heat and cook it for a little longer.*

1 Heat the sugar and 75ml/5 tbsp water in a small, heavy pan until the sugar dissolves. Boil rapidly until the sugar has turned pale golden. Remove the pan from the heat and leave to stand until the syrup turns a rich brown colour.

2 Pour 90ml/6 tbsp of the cream over the caramel. Heat to make a smooth sauce. Leave to cool.

3 Rinse a 450g/1lb loaf tin (pan), then line the base and sides with clear film (plastic wrap). Whip a further 150ml/¼ pint/²/₃ cup of the cream with the icing sugar until it forms soft peaks. Whip the remaining cream separately and stir in the caramel sauce and the toasted pecan nuts.

4 Spoon one-third of the caramel cream into the prepared tin and spread with half the plain whipped cream. Spread half of the remaining caramel cream over the top, then top with the last of the plain cream. Finally, add the remaining caramel cream and level the surface. Freeze for 6 hours.

5 To serve, dip the tin in very hot water for 2 seconds, invert it on to a serving plate and peel away the film. Serve sliced.

Cookies and Sweet Treats

HOME-BAKED COOKIES AND SWEET SNACKS ARE THE
ULTIMATE INDULGENCE BUT ARE VIEWED BY MANY AS
TAKING TOO MUCH TIME AND EFFORT. HOWEVER, WITH
JUST A FEW BASIC INGREDIENTS, YOU CAN WHIP UP
FABULOUS CAKES, COOKIES AND CANDIES IN MOMENTS.
TRY DELICIOUS TREATS SUCH AS CHOCOLATE BROWNIES,
CHEWY FLAPJACKS OR QUICK AND EASY TEABREAD.

All Butter Cookies

Crisp, buttery cookies are perfect with strawberries and cream or any creamy dessert or fruit compote. These biscuits or cookies are known as refrigerator biscuits as the mixture is chilled until it is firm enough to cut neatly into thin biscuits. The dough can be frozen and when thawed enough to slice, can be freshly baked, but do allow a little extra cooking time.

MAKES TWENTY-EIGHT TO THIRTY

1 Put the flour in a food processor. Add the butter and process until the mixture resembles coarse breadcrumbs. Add the icing sugar and vanilla, and process until the mixture comes together to form a dough. Knead lightly and shape into a thick sausage, 30cm/12in long and 5cm/2in in diameter. Wrap and chill for at least 1 hour, until firm.

2 Preheat the oven to 200°C/400°F/Gas 6. Grease two baking sheets. Using a sharp knife, cut 5mm/¼in thick slices from the dough and space them slightly apart on the baking sheet.

3 Bake for 8–10 minutes, alternating the position of the baking sheets in the oven halfway through cooking, if necessary, until the biscuits are cooked evenly and have just turned pale golden around the edges. Leave for 5 minutes, then transfer to a wire rack to cool. Serve dusted with icing sugar.

275g/10oz/2½ cups plain (all-purpose) flour

90g/3½oz/scant 1 cup icing (confectioners') sugar, plus extra for dusting

10ml/2 tsp vanilla essence (extract)

FROM THE STORECUPBOARD

200g/7oz/scant 1 cup unsalted (sweet) butter

Almond Cookies

These short, light cookies have a melt-in-the-mouth texture. Their simplicity means they are endlessly versatile – irresistible with tea or coffee and stylish with special desserts.

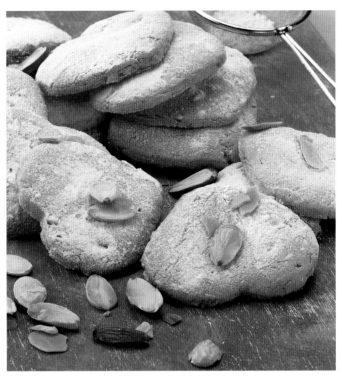

MAKES ABOUT TWENTY-FOUR

115g/4oz/1 cup plain (all-purpose) flour

175g/6oz/1¹/₂ cups icing (confectioners') sugar, plus extra for dusting

50g/2oz/¹/₂ cup chopped almonds, plus halved almonds to decorate

FROM THE STORECUPBOARD

115g/4oz/¹/₂ cup unsalted (sweet) butter, softened

1 Preheat the oven to 180°C/350°F/Gas 4. Combine the flour, sugar and chopped almonds in a bowl.

2 Put the softened unsalted butter in the centre of the flour and nut mixture and use a blunt knife or your fingertips to draw the dry ingredients into the butter until a dough is formed. Shape the dough into a ball.

3 Place the dough on a lightly floured surface and roll it out to a thickness of about 3mm/¹/₈in. Using a 7.5cm/3in cookie cutter, cut out about 24 rounds, re-rolling the dough as necessary. Place the cookie rounds on baking sheets, leaving a little space between them. Bake the cookies for about 25 minutes, until pale golden.

4 Leave the cookies on the baking sheet for 10 minutes, then transfer to wire racks to cool. Dust thickly with sifted icing sugar before serving, decorated with halved almonds.

Chewy Flapjacks

Flapjacks are popular with adults and children alike and they are so quick and easy to make. For alternative versions of the basic recipe, stir in 50g/2oz/¼cup finely chopped ready-to-eat dried apricots or sultanas (golden raisins). To make a really decadent treat, you can dip the cooled flapjack fingers into melted chocolate, to half cover.

MAKES TWELVE

1 Preheat the oven to 180°C/350°F/Gas 4. Line the base and sides of a 20cm/8in square cake tin (pan) with baking parchment.

2 Mix the butter, sugar and syrup in a pan and heat gently until the butter has melted. Add the oats and stir until all the ingredients are combined. Turn the mixture into the tin and level the surface.

3 Bake the flapjacks for 15–20 minutes, until just beginning to turn golden. Leave to cool slightly, then cut into fingers and remove from the tin. Store in an airtight container.

50g/2oz/¹/₄ cup caster (superfine) sugar

150g/5oz/generous ¹/₃ cup golden (light corn) syrup

250g/9oz/2¾ cups rolled oats

FROM THE STORECUPBOARD

175g/6oz/¾ cup unsalted (sweet) butter

Creamed Coconut Macaroons

Finely grated creamed coconut gives these soft-centred cookies a rich creaminess. Cooking the gooey mixture on baking parchment makes sure that the cookies are easily removed from the baking sheet. For a tangy flavour, add the grated rind of one lime to the mixture in step 2. The cooked macaroons can be stored in an airtight container for up to one week.

MAKES SIXTEEN TO EIGHTEEN

1 Preheat the oven to 180°C/350°F/Gas 4. Line a large baking sheet with baking parchment. Finely grate the creamed coconut.

2 Use an electric beater to whisk the egg whites in a large bowl until stiff. Whisk in the sugar, a little at a time, to make a stiff and glossy meringue. Fold in the grated creamed and desiccated coconut, using a large, metal spoon.

3 Place dessertspoonfuls of the mixture, spaced slightly apart, on the baking sheet. Bake for 15–20 minutes, until slightly risen and golden brown. Leave to cool on the parchment, then transfer to an airtight container.

50g/2oz creamed coconut, chilled

2 large (US extra large) egg whites

90g/3½oz/½ cup caster (superfine) sugar

75g/3oz/1 cup desiccated (dry unsweetened shredded) coconut

Orange and Pecan Scones

Serve these nutty orange scones with satiny orange or lemon curd or, for a simple, unsweetened snack, fresh and warm with unsalted (sweet) butter. Scones are best served on the day they are made, or they can be frozen. To freeze, place in an airtight container. To thaw, remove from the freezer and thaw at room temperature for an hour.

MAKES TEN

1 Preheat the oven to 220°C/425°F/Gas 7. Grease a baking sheet. Put the flour in a food processor with a pinch of salt and add the butter. Process the mixture until it resembles coarse breadcrumbs.

2 Add the orange rind. Reserve 30ml/2 tbsp of the orange juice and make the remainder up to 120ml/4fl oz/½ cup with water. Add the nuts and the juice mixture to the processor, process very briefly to a firm dough, adding a little water if the dough feels dry.

3 Turn the dough out on to a floured surface and roll out to 2cm/¾ in thick. Cut out scones using a round cutter and transfer them to the baking sheet. Re-roll the trimmings and cut more scones. Brush the scones with the reserved juice and bake for 15–20 minutes. Transfer to a wire rack to cool.

225g/8oz/2 cups self-raising (self-rising) flour

grated rind and juice of 1 orange

115g/4oz/1 cup pecan nuts, coarsely chopped

FROM THE STORECUPBOARD

50g/2oz/¼ cup unsalted (sweet) butter, chilled and diced

salt

Quick and Easy Teabread

This succulent, fruity teabread can be served just as it is, or spread with a little butter. The loaf can be stored, tightly wrapped in foil or in an airtight container, for up to five days. A great way to get children to eat some fruit, this teabread is ideal for packed lunches, picnics, or simply served with a cup of tea for afternoon tea.

SERVES EIGHT

1 Put the fruit in a bowl. Add 150ml/¼ pint/⅔ cup boiling water and leave to stand for 30 minutes.

2 Preheat the oven to 180°C/350°F/Gas 4. Grease and line the base and long sides of a 450g/1lb loaf tin (pan).

3 Beat the main quantity of sugar and the egg into the fruit. Sift the flour into the bowl and stir until combined. Turn into the prepared tin and level the surface. Sprinkle with the remaining sugar.

4 Bake the teabread for about 50 minutes, until risen and firm to the touch. When the bread is cooked, a skewer inserted into the centre will come out without any sticky mixture on it. Leave the loaf in the tin for 10 minutes before turning out on to a wire rack to cool.

350g/12oz/2 cups luxury mixed dried fruit

75g/3oz/scant ⅓ cup demerara (raw) sugar, plus 15ml/1 tbsp

1 large (US extra large) egg

175g/6oz/1½ cups self-raising (self-rising) flour

Cinnamon Pinwheels

These impressive sweet pastries go well with tea or coffee or as an accompaniment to ice cream and creamy desserts. If you find they turn soft during storage, re-crisp them briefly in the oven. Cinnamon is widely used in both sweet and savoury cooking: here ground cinnamon is used but it is also available as woody sticks. It has a delicious fragrant aroma and gives these simple-to-make pinwheels a warm spicy flavour.

MAKES TWENTY TO TWENTY-FOUR

50g/2oz/¹/₄ cup caster (superfine) sugar, plus a little extra for sprinkling

10ml/2 tsp ground cinnamon

250g/9oz puff pastry

beaten egg, to glaze

1 Preheat the oven to 220°C/425°F/Gas 7. Grease a large baking sheet. Mix the sugar with the cinnamon in a small bowl.

2 Roll out the pastry on a lightly floured surface to a 20cm/8in square and sprinkle with half the sugar mixture. Roll out the pastry to a 25cm/10in square so that the sugar is pressed into it.

3 Brush with the beaten egg and then sprinkle with the remaining sugar mixture. Loosely roll up the pastry into a log, brushing the end of the pastry with a little more egg to secure the edge in place.

4 Using a sharp knife, cut the log into thin slices and transfer them to the prepared baking sheet. Bake for 10 minutes, until golden and crisp. Sprinkle with more sugar and transfer to a wire rack to cool.

Almond Cigars

These simple, Moroccan-inspired pastries can be prepared in minutes. They are perfect served with strong black coffee or black tea, or as an after-dinner treat. They are also delicious served with traditional sweet Moroccan mint tea. To serve, the pastries look very pretty sprinkled with a little icing (confectioners') sugar as a simple finishing touch.

MAKES EIGHT TO TWELVE

250g/9oz marzipan

1 egg, lightly beaten

8–12 sheets filo pastry

FROM THE STORECUPBOARD

melted butter, for brushing

1 Knead the marzipan until soft and pliable, then put it in a mixing bowl and mix in the lightly beaten egg. Chill in the refrigerator for 1–2 hours.

2 Preheat the oven to 190°C/375°F/Gas 5. Lightly grease a baking sheet. Place a sheet of filo pastry on a piece of greaseproof (waxed) paper, keeping the remaining pastry covered with a damp cloth, and brush with the melted butter.

3 Shape 30–45ml/2–3 tbsp of the almond paste into a cylinder and place at one end of the pastry. Fold the pastry over to enclose the ends of the paste, then roll up to form a cigar shape. Place on the baking sheet and make 7–11 more cigars in the same way.

4 Bake the pastries in the preheated oven for about 15 minutes, or until golden brown in colour. Transfer to a wire rack to cool before serving.

Rich Chocolate Brownies

These brownies are packed with both milk and plain chocolate instead of adding sugar to the mixture. Serve them in small squares as they are very rich. When buying plain chocolate, bear in mind that the higher the percentage of cocoa solids, the higher the quality of the chocolate, and the less sugar it contains. The best quality has 70 per cent cocoa solids.

MAKES SIXTEEN

1 Preheat the oven to 180°C/350°F/Gas 4. Line the base and sides of a 20cm/8in square cake tin (pan) with baking parchment.

2 Break the plain chocolate and 90g/3½oz of the milk chocolate into pieces and put in a heatproof bowl with the butter. Melt over a pan of barely simmering water, stirring frequently.

3 Chop the remaining milk chocolate into chunky pieces. Stir the flour and eggs into the melted chocolate until combined. Stir in half the chopped milk chocolate and turn the mixture into the prepared tin, spreading it into the corners. Sprinkle with the remaining chopped chocolate.

4 Bake the brownies for 30–35 minutes, until risen and just firm to the touch. Leave to cool in the tin, then cut the mixture into squares. Store the brownies in an airtight container.

300g/11oz each plain (semisweet) and milk chocolate

75g/3oz/²⁄₃ cup self-raising (self-rising) flour

3 large (US extra large) eggs

FROM THE STORECUPBOARD

175g/6oz/³⁄₄ cup unsalted (sweet) butter

Rich Chocolate Biscuit Slice

This dark chocolate refrigerator cake is packed with crisp biscuit pieces and chunks of white chocolate for colour and flavour contrast. The slice is perfect served with strong coffee, either as a teatime treat or in place of dessert. Once set, cut the cake into slices and store the slices in an airtight container in the refrigerator until ready to serve.

SERVES EIGHT TO TEN

0275g/10oz fruit and nut plain (semisweet) chocolate

90g/3½oz digestive biscuits (graham crackers)

90g/3½oz white chocolate

FROM THE STORECUPBOARD

130g/4½oz/9 tbsp unsalted (sweet) butter

1 Grease and line the base and sides of a 450g/1lb loaf tin (pan) with baking parchment. Break the fruit and nut chocolate into pieces and place in a heatproof bowl with the butter. Place the bowl over a pan of barely simmering water and stir the chocolate gently until it is melted and smooth. Remove the bowl from the pan and leave to cool for 20 minutes.

2 Break the biscuits into small pieces. Finely chop the white chocolate. Stir the biscuits and white chocolate into the melted mixture until evenly combined. Turn the mixture into the prepared tin and pack down gently. Chill for about 2 hours, or until set. Cut the mixture into slices.

Stuffed Prunes

Prunes and plain chocolate are
delectable partners, especially when
the dried fruit is soaked in Armagnac.
Serve these sophisticated sweetmeats
dusted with cocoa powder as a dinner-
party treat with coffee.

MAKES ABOUT THIRTY

1 Put the prunes in a bowl and pour the Armagnac over. Stir, then cover with clear film (plastic wrap) and set aside for 2 hours, or until the prunes have absorbed the liquid.

2 Make a slit along each prune to remove the stone (pit), making a hollow for the filling, but leaving the fruit intact.

3 Heat the cream in a pan almost to boiling point. Put 115g/4oz of the chocolate in a bowl and pour over the hot cream.

4 Stir until the chocolate has melted and the mixture is smooth. Leave to cool, until it has the consistency of softened butter.

5 Fill a piping (pastry) bag with a small plain nozzle with the chocolate mixture. Pipe into the cavities of the prunes. Chill for about 20 minutes.

6 Melt the remaining chocolate in a heatproof bowl set over a pan of barely simmering water. Using a fork, dip the prunes, one at a time, into the chocolate to coat them generously. Place on baking parchment to set.

**225g/8oz/
1 cup unpitted prunes**

**50ml/2fl oz/
¹/₄ cup Armagnac**

**150ml/¹/₂ pint/²/₃ cup
double (heavy) cream**

**350g/12oz plain
(semisweet) chocolate,
broken into squares**

COOK'S TIP
Armagnac is a type of French brandy produced in the Gascogne region in the south-west of the country. It has a pale colour and a biscuity aroma. Other types of brandy can be used in this recipe.

Chocolate Truffles

Luxurious truffles are expensive to buy but very easy and fun to make. These rich melt-in-the-mouth treats are flavoured with coffee liqueur, but you could use whisky or brandy instead. The mixture can be rolled in cocoa powder or icing (confectioners') sugar instead of being dipped in melted chocolate. Remember to store the fresh-cream truffles in the refrigerator.

MAKES TWENTY-FOUR

1 Melt 225g/8oz of the plain chocolate in a heatproof bowl set over a pan of barely simmering water. Stir in the cream and liqueur, then chill the mixture for 4 hours, until firm.

2 Divide the mixture into 24 equal pieces and quickly roll each into a ball. Chill for about 1 hour, or until the truffles are firm again.

3 Melt the remaining plain, white or milk chocolate in separate small bowls. Using two forks, carefully dip eight of the truffles, one at a time, into the melted plain chocolate.

4 Repeat to cover the remaining 16 truffles with the melted white or milk chocolate. Place the truffles on a board or tray, covered with wax paper or foil. Leave to set before placing in individual mini paper cases or transferring to a serving dish.

350g/12oz plain (semisweet) chocolate

75ml/5 tbsp double (heavy) cream

30ml/2 tbsp coffee liqueur, such as Tia Maria, Kahlúa or Toussaint

225g/8oz good quality white or milk dessert chocolate

EXTRAS

Ring the changes by adding one of the following to the mixture:

GINGER
Stir in 40g/1½ oz/¼ cup finely chopped crystallized ginger.

CANDIED FRUIT
Stir in 50g/2oz/⅓ cup finely chopped candied fruit, such as pineapple and orange.

PISTACHIOS
Stir in 25g/1oz/¼ cup chopped skinned pistachio nuts.

HAZELNUTS
Roll each ball of chilled truffle mixture around a whole skinned hazelnut.

Chocolate Petit Four Cookies

Make these dainty cookies as stylish after-dinner snacks. If you do not have any amaretto liqueur, they will work well without it. Alternatively, you can substitute the same quantity of brandy or rum.

SERVES EIGHT

1 Preheat the oven according to the instructions on the cookie dough packet. Roll out the cookie dough on a floured surface to 1cm/^{1}/$_{2}$in thick. Using a 2.5cm/1in cutter, stamp out as many rounds from the dough as possible and transfer them to a lightly greased baking sheet. Bake for about 8 minutes, or until cooked through. Transfer to a wire rack to cool completely.

2 To make the filling, break the chocolate into small pieces and place in a heatproof bowl with the butter and Amaretto liqueur. Sit the bowl over a pan of gently simmering water and stir occasionally, until the chocolate has melted. Remove from the heat and set aside to cool.

3 Spread a small amount of the filling on the flat bottom of one of the cookies and sandwich together with another. Repeat until all the biscuits have been used.

350g/12oz carton chocolate chip cookie dough

115g/4oz plain (semisweet) chocolate

30ml/2 tbsp Amaretto di Sarone liqueur

FROM THE STORECUPBOARD

50g/2oz/^{1}/$_{4}$ cup butter

Praline Chocolate Bites

These delicate, mouthwatering little bites never fail to impress guests, but are quite simple to make. They are perfect for serving with coffee after dinner. Dust with icing sugar for a decorative finish.

SERVES FOUR

1 Put the sugar in a heavy pan with 90ml/6 tbsp water. Stir over a gentle heat until the sugar has dissolved. Bring the syrup to the boil and cook for about 5 minutes, without stirring, until the mixture is golden and caramelized.

2 Remove the pan from the heat and tip in the almonds, swirling the pan to immerse them in the caramel. Tip the mixture on to a lightly oiled baking sheet and set aside for 10–15 minutes, or until hardened. Meanwhile, melt the chocolate in a heatproof bowl set over a pan of simmering water.

3 Cover the hardened caramel mixture with clear film (plastic wrap) and break up with a rolling pin then place in a food processor. Process until finely chopped, then stir into the melted chocolate. Chill until set enough to roll into balls. Roll the mixture into 16 balls and place in mini paper cases to serve.

115g/4oz/1 cup caster (superfine) sugar

115g/4oz/^{2}/$_{3}$ cup whole blanched almonds

200g/7oz plain (semisweet) chocolate

COOK'S TIP *The mixture for these bites can be made ahead and stored in the freezer for up to 2 weeks. To use, thaw the mixture at room temperature until soft enough to roll into balls.*

Breads

THERE ARE FEW FOODS SO DELICIOUS AND COMFORTING
AS FRESHLY BAKED BREAD. THREE BASIC INGREDIENTS –
FLOUR, SALT AND YEAST – MIXED WITH WATER ARE ALL
THAT IS NEEDED TO MAKE A BASIC LOAF, WHILE THE
ADDITION OF A FOURTH INGREDIENT SUCH AS HERBS,
SUN-DRIED TOMATOES, OLIVE OIL OR MILK CAN
CREATE WONDERFUL, ENTICING VARIATIONS.

Scottish Morning Rolls

These soft, spongy bread rolls are irresistible while still warm and aromatic. Made with milk, rather than the more usual water, they have a rich flavour. In Scotland they are a firm favourite for breakfast with fried eggs and bacon. To speed up the rising time, place the rolls in the airing cupboard or on the top of the preheated oven.

MAKES TEN ROLLS

1 Grease two baking sheets. Sift the flour and salt together into a large bowl and make a well in the centre. Mix the yeast with the milk, then mix in 150ml/¼ pint/⅔ cup lukewarm water. Add to the centre of the flour and mix together to form a soft dough.

2 Knead the dough lightly in the bowl, then cover with lightly oiled clear film (plastic wrap) and leave to rise in a warm place for 1 hour, or until doubled in bulk. Turn the dough out on to a lightly floured surface and knock back (punch down).

3 Divide the dough into ten equal pieces. Knead lightly and, using a rolling pin, shape each piece of dough into a flat oval 10 x 7.5cm/ 4 x 3in, or a flat round 9cm/3½in.

4 Transfer to the prepared baking sheets, spaced well apart, and cover the rolls with oiled clear film. Leave to rise, in a warm place, for about 30 minutes.

5 Meanwhile, preheat the oven to 200°C/400°F/Gas 6. Press each roll in the centre with the three middle fingers to equalize the air bubbles and to help prevent blistering. Brush with milk and dust with flour. Bake for 15–20 minutes, or until lightly browned. Dust with more flour and cool slightly on a wire rack. Serve warm.

450g/1lb/4 cups unbleached strong white bread flour, plus extra for dusting

20g/³/₄oz fresh yeast

150ml/¹/₄ pint/²/₃ cup lukewarm milk, plus extra for glazing

FROM THE STORECUPBOARD

10ml/2 tsp salt

Panini all'Olio

Italian-style dough enriched and flavoured with extra virgin olive oil is versatile for making decorative rolls. Children will love helping to make and shape these rolls – they can try making twists, fingers or artichoke-shapes, or just about any shape they want. The rolls are sure to disappear as soon as they are cool enough to eat.

MAKES SIXTEEN ROLLS

450g/1lb/4 cups unbleached strong white bread flour

15g/¹/₂oz fresh yeast

60ml/4 tbsp extra virgin olive oil

FROM THE STORECUPBOARD

10ml/2 tsp salt

1 Lightly oil three baking sheets. Sift the flour and salt together in a large bowl and make a well in the centre. Measure 250ml/8fl oz/1 cup lukewarm water. Cream the yeast with half the water, then stir in the remainder. Add to the well with the oil and mix to a dough.

2 Turn the dough out on to a lightly floured surface and knead for 8–10 minutes, until smooth and elastic. Place in a lightly oiled bowl, cover with lightly oiled clear film (plastic wrap) and leave to rise in a warm place for about 1 hour, or until nearly doubled in bulk.

3 Turn the dough on to a lightly floured surface and knock back (punch down). Divide into 12 equal pieces and shape into rolls. To make twists, roll each piece of dough into a strip 30cm/12in long and 4cm/1½in wide. Twist each strip into a loose spiral and join the ends together to make a circle. Place on the baking sheets, spaced well apart. Brush lightly with olive oil, cover with lightly oiled clear film and leave to rise in a warm place for 20–30 minutes.

4 To make fingers, flatten each piece of dough into an oval and roll to about 23cm/9in long. Roll up from the wider end. Gently stretch the dough roll to 20–23cm/8–9in long. Cut in half. Place on the baking sheets, spaced well apart. Brush the dough with olive oil, cover with lightly oiled clear film and leave to rise in a warm place for 20–30 minutes.

5 To make artichoke-shapes, shape each piece of dough into a ball and space well apart on the baking sheets. Brush with oil, cover with lightly oiled clear film and leave to rise in a warm place for 20–30 minutes. Using scissors, snip 5mm/¼in deep cuts in a circle on the top of each ball, then make five larger horizontal cuts around the sides.

6 Preheat the oven to 200°C/400°F/Gas 6. Bake the rolls for 15 minutes.

French Baguette

Fine French flour is available from French delicatessens and superior supermarkets. If you cannot find any, try ordinary plain flour instead. Baguettes have a wide variety of uses: split horizontally and fill with meats, cheeses and salads; slice diagonally and toast the slices to serve with soup; or simply cut into chunks, spread with unsalted (sweet) butter and serve with French cheeses.

MAKES THREE LOAVES

500g/1¼lb/5 cups unbleached strong white bread flour

115g/4oz/1 cup fine French plain (all-purpose) flour

15g/½oz fresh yeast

FROM THE STORECUPBOARD

10ml/2 tsp salt

1 Sift the flours and salt into a bowl. Add the yeast to 550ml/18fl oz/2½ cups lukewarm water in another bowl and stir. Gradually beat in half the flour mixture to form a batter. Cover with clear film (plastic wrap) and leave for about 3 hours, or until nearly trebled in size.

2 Add the remaining flour a little at a time, beating with your hand. Turn out on to a lightly floured surface and knead for 8–10 minutes to form a moist dough. Place in a lightly oiled bowl, cover with lightly oiled clear film and leave to rise, in a warm place, for about 1 hour.

3 Knock back (punch down) the dough, turn out on to a floured surface and divide into three equal pieces. Shape each into a ball and then into a 15 x 7.5cm/6 x 3in rectangle. Fold the bottom third up lengthways and the top third down and press down. Seal the edges. Repeat two or three more times until each loaf is an oblong. Leave to rest in between folding for a few minutes.

4 Gently stretch each piece of dough into a 33–35cm/13–14in long loaf. Pleat a floured dishtowel on a baking sheet to make three moulds for the loaves. Place the loaves between the pleats, cover with lightly oiled clear film and leave to rise in a warm place for 45–60 minutes.

5 Preheat the oven to maximum, at least 230°C/450°F/Gas 8. Roll the loaves on to a baking sheet, spaced well apart. Slash the top of each loaf diagonally several times. Place at the top of the oven, spray the inside of the oven with water and bake for 20–25 minutes.

COOK'S TIP
Baguettes are difficult to reproduce at home as they require a very hot oven and steam. However, by using less yeast and a triple fermentation you can produce a bread with a superior taste and far better texture than mass-produced baguettes. It also helps if you spray the oven twice with water during the first 5 minutes of baking. These loaves are best eaten on the day of baking.

Rosemary Focaccia

If you do not need both loaves, freeze one for another time and warm it in the oven before serving. Sprinkle the loaves with finely chopped garlic, if you prefer.

MAKES TWO LOAVES

1 Put the flour and yeast in a large bowl with 5ml/1 tsp salt. Stir in 45ml/3 tbsp of the oil and 450ml/¾ pint/scant 2 cups lukewarm water. Mix with a round-bladed knife, then by hand to a soft dough, adding a little more lukewarm water if the dough feels dry.

2 Turn the dough out on to a lightly floured surface and knead for 10 minutes, until smooth and elastic. Put in a lightly oiled bowl and cover with oiled clear film (plastic wrap). Leave in a warm place for about 1 hour, until doubled in size.

3 Preheat the oven to 200°C/400°F/Gas 6. Turn out the dough on to a floured surface and cut in half. Roll out each half into a 25cm/10in round. Transfer to greased baking sheets, cover with lightly oiled clear film and leave for 20 minutes, until risen.

4 Press your fingers into the dough to make deep holes all over it about 3cm/1¼in apart. Leave for a further 5 minutes. Sprinkle with the rosemary and plenty of sea salt. Sprinkle with water to keep the crust moist and bake for 25 minutes, until pale golden. Remove from the oven and drizzle with the remaining olive oil. Transfer to a wire rack to cool.

675g/1½lb/4 cups strong white bread flour

15ml/1 tbsp easy-blend (rapid-rise) dried yeast

45ml/3 tbsp chopped fresh rosemary

FROM THE STORECUPBOARD

75ml/5 tbsp olive oil

Granary Cob

Mixing and shaping a simple round loaf is one of the most satisfying kitchen activities and the result is incomparably excellent. This bread is made with fresh yeast – it is a similar colour and texture to putty and should crumble easily when broken. For best results, buy fresh yeast in small quantities as required: it will keep for up to one month in the refrigerator.

MAKES ONE ROUND LOAF

450g/1lb/4 cups Granary
(multigrain) or malthouse flour

15g/¹/₂oz fresh yeast

wheat flakes or cracked wheat,
for sprinkling

FROM THE STORECUPBOARD

12.5ml/2¹/₂ tsp salt

1 Lightly flour a baking sheet. Mix the flour and 10ml/2 tsp of the salt together in a large bowl and make a well in the centre. Place in a very low oven for 5 minutes to warm.

2 Measure 300ml/½pint/1¼ cups lukewarm water. Mix the yeast with a little of the water, then blend in the rest. Pour the yeast mixture into the centre of the flour and mix to a dough.

3 Turn out on to a lightly floured surface and knead for about 10 minutes, until smooth and elastic. Place in a lightly oiled bowl, cover with lightly oiled clear film (plastic wrap) and leave to rise in a warm place for 1¼ hours, or until doubled in bulk.

4 Turn the dough out on to a lightly floured surface and knock back (punch down). Knead for 2–3 minutes, then roll into a ball. Place in the centre of the prepared baking sheet. Cover with an inverted bowl and leave to rise in a warm place for 30–45 minutes.

5 Preheat the oven to 230°C/450°F/Gas 8 towards the end of the rising time. Mix 30ml/2 tbsp water with the remaining salt and brush evenly over the bread. Sprinkle the loaf with wheat flakes or cracked wheat.

6 Bake the bread for 15 minutes, then reduce the oven temperature to 200°C/400°F/Gas 6 and bake for a further 20 minutes, or until the loaf is firm to the touch and sounds hollow when tapped on the base. Cool on a wire rack.

Grant Loaves

This quick and easy recipe was created by a baker called Doris Grant and was published in the 1940s. It is a dream for busy cooks as the dough requires no kneading and takes only a minute to mix. Nowadays we can make the recipe even quicker by using easy-blend yeast, which is added directly to the dry ingredients.

MAKES THREE LOAVES

1 Thoroughly grease three loaf tins (pans), each 21 x 11 x 6cm/ 8½ x 4½ x 2½in and set aside in a warm place. Sift the flour and salt together in a large bowl and warm slightly to take off the chill.

2 Sprinkle the dried yeast over 150ml/¼ pint/⅔ cup lukewarm water. After a couple of minutes, stir in the muscovado sugar. Leave the mixture for 10 minutes.

3 Make a well in the centre of the flour. Pour in the yeast mixture and add a further 900ml/1½ pints/3¾ cups lukewarm water. Stir to form a slippery dough. Mix for about 1 minute, working the dry ingredients from the sides into the middle.

4 Divide among the prepared tins, cover with oiled clear film (plastic wrap) and leave to rise in a warm place for 30 minutes, or until the dough has risen by about one-third to within 1cm/ ½in of the top of the tins.

5 Meanwhile, preheat the oven to 200°C/400°F/Gas 6. Bake for 40 minutes, or until the loaves are crisp and sound hollow when tapped on the base. Turn out on to a wire rack to cool.

1.3kg/3lb/12 cups wholemeal (whole-wheat) bread flour

15ml/1 tbsp easy-blend (rapid-rise) dried yeast

15ml/1 tbsp muscovado (molasses) sugar

FROM THE STORECUPBOARD

15ml/1 tbsp salt

Cottage Loaf

Create a culinary masterpiece from a few basic ingredients and experience the satisfaction of traditional baking. Serve this classic-shaped loaf to accompany home-made soup.

MAKES ONE LARGE ROUND LOAF

675g/1¹/₂lb/6 cups unbleached strong white bread flour

20g/³/₄oz fresh yeast

FROM THE STORECUPBOARD

10ml/2 tsp salt

1 Lightly grease two baking sheets. Sift the flour and salt together into a large bowl and make a well in the centre.

2 Mix the yeast in 150ml/¼ pint/²/₃ cup lukewarm water until dissolved. Pour into the centre of the flour and add a further 250ml/8fl oz/1 cup lukewarm water, then mix to a firm dough.

3 Knead the dough on a lightly floured surface for 10 minutes, until it is smooth and elastic. Place in a lightly oiled bowl, cover with lightly oiled clear film (plastic wrap) and leave to rise in a warm place for about 1 hour.

4 Turn out on to a lightly floured surface and knock back (punch down). Knead for 2–3 minutes, then divide the dough into two-thirds and one-third and shape each piece into a ball. Place the balls of dough on the prepared baking sheets. Cover with inverted bowls and leave to rise in a warm place for 30 minutes.

5 Gently flatten the top of the larger round of dough and cut a cross in the centre, about 4cm/1½in across. Brush with a little water and place the smaller round on top. Carefully press a hole through the middle of the top ball, down into the lower part, using your thumb and first two fingers. Cover with lightly oiled clear film and leave to rest in a warm place for about 10 minutes.

6 Preheat the oven to 220°C/425°F/Gas 7 and place the bread on the lower shelf of the oven. Bake for 35–40 minutes, or until a rich golden brown colour. Cool on a wire rack before serving.

Split Tin

The deep centre split down this loaf gives it its name. The split tin loaf slices well for making thick-cut sandwiches, or for serving hearty chunks of bread to accompany robust cheese.

MAKES ONE LOAF

500g/1¼lb/5 cups unbleached strong white bread flour, plus extra for dusting

15g/½oz fresh yeast

60ml/4 tbsp lukewarm milk

FROM THE STORECUPBOARD

10ml/2 tsp salt

1 Grease a 900g/2lb loaf tin (pan). Sift the flour and salt into a bowl and make a well in the centre. Mix the yeast with 150ml/¼ pint/⅔ cup lukewarm water. Stir in another 150ml/¼ pint/⅔ cup lukewarm water. Pour the yeast mixture into the centre of the flour and using your fingers, mix in a little flour to form a smooth batter.

2 Sprinkle a little more flour from around the edge over the batter and leave in a warm place for about 20 minutes to "sponge". Add the milk and remaining flour; mix to a firm dough.

3 Place on a lightly floured surface and knead for about 10 minutes, until smooth and elastic. Place in a lightly oiled bowl, cover with lightly oiled clear film (plastic wrap) and leave to rise in a warm place for 1–1¼ hours, or until nearly doubled in bulk.

4 Knock back (punch down) the dough and turn out on to a lightly floured surface. Shape it into a rectangle, the length of the prepared tin. Roll the dough up lengthways, tuck the ends under and place, seam side down, in the tin. Cover the loaf and leave to rise in a warm place for about 20–30 minutes.

5 Using a sharp knife, make one deep central slash. Dust the top of the loaf with a little sifted flour. Leave for 10–15 minutes. Meanwhile, preheat the oven to 230°C/450°F/Gas 8. Bake for 15 minutes, then reduce the oven temperature to 200°C/400°F/Gas 6. Bake for 20–25 minutes, until golden and it sounds hollow when tapped on the base. Cool on a wire rack.

Poppy-seeded Bloomer

This long, crusty loaf gets its fabulous flavour from poppy seeds. Cut into thick slices, the bread is perfect for mopping up the cooking juices of hearty stews, or for absorbing good dressing on summery salads. A variety of seeds can be used to add flavour, texture and colour to this loaf – try sunflower, pumpkin or sesame seeds as an alternative to the poppy seeds. Brushing the loaf with the salted water before baking helps to give it a crisp, crusty finish.

MAKES ONE LARGE LOAF

1 Lightly grease a baking sheet. Sift the flour and 10ml/2 tsp salt together into a large bowl and make a well in the centre.

2 Measure 450ml/¾ pint/scant 2 cups lukewarm water and stir about a third of it into the yeast in a bowl. Stir in the remaining water and pour into the centre of the flour. Mix, gradually incorporating the surrounding flour, to a firm dough.

3 Turn out on to a lightly floured surface and knead the dough very well, for at least 10 minutes, until smooth and elastic. Place the dough in a lightly oiled bowl, cover with lightly oiled clear film (plastic wrap) and leave to rise, at cool room temperature (about 15–18 C/60–65 F), for 5–6 hours, or until doubled in bulk.

4 Knock back (punch down) the dough, turn out on to a lightly floured surface and knead it thoroughly for about 5 minutes. Return the dough to the bowl and re-cover. Leave to rise, at cool room temperature, for a further 2 hours or slightly longer.

5 Knock back again and repeat the thorough kneading. Leave the dough to rest for 5 minutes, then roll out on a lightly floured surface into a rectangle 2.5cm/1in thick. Roll the dough up from one long side and shape it into a square-ended, thick baton shape about 33 x 13cm/13 x 5in.

6 Place the loaf, seam side up, on a lightly floured baking sheet. Cover with lightly oiled clear film and leave to rest for 15 minutes. Turn the loaf over and place on the greased baking sheet. Plump the loaf up by tucking the dough under the sides and ends. Using a sharp knife, cut six diagonal slashes on the top.

7 Leave to rest, covered, in a warm place, for 10 minutes. Meanwhile, preheat the oven to 230°C/450°F/Gas 8.

8 Mix the remaining salt with 30ml/2 tbsp water and brush this glaze over the bread. Sprinkle with poppy seeds.

9 Spray the oven with water, bake the bread immediately for 20 minutes, then reduce the oven temperature to 200°C/400°F/Gas 6. Bake for 25 minutes more, or until golden and it sounds hollow when tapped on the base. Transfer to a wire rack to cool.

675g/1½lb/6 cups unbleached strong white bread flour

15g/½oz fresh yeast

poppy seeds, for sprinkling

FROM THE STORECUPBOARD

12.5ml/2½ tsp salt

COOK'S TIP
The traditional cracked, crusty appearance of this loaf is difficult to achieve in a domestic oven. However, you can get a similar result by spraying the oven with water before baking. If the underneath of the loaf is not very crusty at the end of baking, turn it over on the baking sheet, switch off the heat and leave it in the oven for a further 5–10 minutes.

Traditional Irish Soda Bread

Irish soda bread contains no yeast and therefore does not need to be left to rise, so it is quick and easy to make. It is best eaten on the day that it is made, preferably while still warm. You can bake a loaf in the morning, ready to take on a picnic to serve with cheese and salads.

SERVES FOUR TO SIX

450g/1lb plain wholemeal (all-purpose whole-wheat) flour

10ml/2 tsp bicarbonate of soda (baking soda)

400ml/14fl oz/1²/₃ cups buttermilk

FROM THE STORECUPBOARD

5ml/1 tsp salt

1 Preheat the oven to 200°C/400°F/Gas 6. Place the flour in a large bowl and stir in the bicarbonate of soda and salt. Make a well in the centre.

2 Gradually pour the buttermilk into the well, beating in the flour from around the edges to form a soft, not sticky, dough.

3 Turn the dough out on to a lightly floured surface and knead for 5 minutes, until smooth. Shape into a 20cm/8in round and place on a lightly greased baking sheet.

4 Using a sharp knife, cut a deep cross on the top of the dough and bake for 30–35 minutes, or until slightly risen and cooked through. Cool slightly on a wire rack before serving.

Spring Onion Flatbreads

Use these flatbreads to wrap around barbecue-cooked meat and chunky vegetable salads, or serve with tasty dips such as hummus. They're at their best as soon as they're cooked.

MAKES SIXTEEN

1 Place the flour in a large mixing bowl and stir in the salt, yeast and spring onions. Make a well in the centre and pour in 300ml/½ pint/1¼ cups hand hot water. Mix to form a soft, but not sticky, dough.

2 Turn out the dough on to a floured work surface and knead for about 5 minutes, until smooth. Put the dough back in the bowl, cover with a damp dishtowel and leave in a warm place until doubled in size.

3 Knock back (punch down) the dough to get rid of any excess air and turn out on to a floured work surface. Divide the dough into 16 pieces and roll each piece into a smooth ball. Roll out each ball to a 13cm/5in round.

4 Heat a large frying pan until hot. Dust off any excess flour from one dough round and place in the frying pan. Cook for about 1 minute, then flip over and cook for a further 30 seconds. Repeat with the remaining dough rounds.

450g/1lb/4 cups strong white bread flour, plus extra for dusting

7g/¼ oz packet easy-blend (rapid-rise) dried yeast

4 spring onions (scallions), finely chopped

FROM THE STORECUPBOARD

5ml/1 tsp salt

VARIATION To make garlic flatbreads, use 2 finely chopped garlic cloves in place of the chopped spring onions. To add extra bite, mix in 1 finely chopped fresh red chilli as well.

Pitta Bread

Soft, slightly bubbly pitta bread is a pleasure to make. It can be eaten in a variety of ways, such as Mediterranean-style filled with salad or little chunks of meat cooked on the barbecue, or it can be torn into pieces and dipped in savoury dips such as hummus or tzatziki. Chop any leftover bread and incorporate into the Lebanese salad *fattoush* with parsley, mint, tomatoes and cucumber.

MAKES TWELVE

500g/1¹⁄₄lb/5 cups strong white bread flour, or half white and half wholemeal (whole-wheat)

12.5ml/2¹⁄₂ tsp easy-blend (rapid-rise) dried yeast

FROM THE STORECUPBOARD

15ml/1 tbsp olive oil

15ml/1 tbsp salt

1 Combine the flour, yeast and salt. Combine the oil and 250ml/8fl oz/1 cup water, then add half of the flour mixture, stirring in the same direction, until the dough is stiff. Knead in the remaining flour. Place the dough in a clean bowl, cover with a clean dishtowel and leave in a warm place for at least 30 minutes and up to 2 hours.

2 Knead the dough for 10 minutes, or until smooth. Lightly oil the bowl, place the dough in it, cover again and leave to rise in a warm place for about 1 hour, or until doubled in size.

3 Divide the dough into 12 equal pieces. With lightly floured hands, flatten each piece, then roll out into a round measuring about 20cm/8in and about 4mm–1cm/¼–½in thick. Keep the rolled breads covered while you make the remaining pittas.

4 Heat a heavy frying pan over a medium-high heat. When hot, lay one piece of flattened dough in the pan and cook for 15–20 seconds. Turn it over and cook the second side for about 1 minute.

5 When large bubbles start to form on the bread, turn it over again. It should puff up. Using a clean dishtowel, gently press on the bread where the bubbles have formed. Cook for a total of 3 minutes, then remove the pitta from the pan. Repeat with the remaining dough. Wrap the pitta breads in a clean dishtowel, stacking them as each one is cooked. Serve the pittas hot while they are soft and moist.

VARIATION To bake the breads, preheat the oven to 220°C/425°F/Gas 7. Fill an unglazed or partially glazed dish with hot water and place in the bottom of the hot oven. Alternatively, arrange a handful of unglazed tiles in the base of the oven. Use either a non-stick baking sheet or a lightly oiled baking sheet and heat in the oven for a few minutes. Place two or three pieces of flattened dough on to the hot baking sheet and place in the hottest part of the oven. Bake for 2–3 minutes until puffed up. Repeat with the remaining dough.

Yemeni Sponge Flat Breads

These flat breads, known as *lahuhs* and made from a batter, are bubbly and soft. They are eaten with soups but are also good with salads, dips or cheese.

SERVES FOUR

1 Measure 500ml/17fl oz/generous 2 cups lukewarm water. In a bowl, dissolve the dried yeast in about 75ml/5 tbsp of the water. Leave in a warm place for about 10 minutes, or until frothy.

2 Stir the remaining water, the flour, salt and melted butter or vegetable oil into the yeast mixture and mix until it forms a smooth batter. Cover with a clean dishtowel, then leave in a warm place for about 1 hour, until doubled in size.

3 Stir the thick, frothy batter and, if it seems too thick to ladle out, add a little extra water. Cover and leave the batter to stand in a warm place for about 1 hour.

4 Cook the flat breads in a non-stick frying pan. Ladle 45–60ml/ 3–4 tbsp of batter (or less for smaller breads) into the pan and cook over a low heat until the top is bubbling and the colour has changed. (Traditionally these breads are cooked on only one side, but they can be turned over and the second side cooked for just a moment, if you like.)

5 Remove the cooked flat bread from the frying pan with a spatula and keep warm in a clean dishtowel. Continue cooking until you have used up all the remaining batter.

15ml/1 tbsp dried active yeast

350g/12oz/ 3 cups plain (all-purpose) flour

FROM THE STORECUPBOARD

50g/2oz/¹/₄ cup butter, melted, or 60ml/4 tbsp vegetable oil

5ml/1 tsp salt

COOK'S TIP *Use two or three frying pans at the same time so that the flat breads are ready together and so can be eaten piping hot.*

West Indian Flat Breads

Eclectic Caribbean food is influenced by a wide range of international cultures. It is the Anglo-Indian connection that brought the Indian flat bread called roti to Trinidad in the West Indies. Serve these simple-to-make breads straight from the pan to accompany spicy seafood chowders, curries, or any other dish that has plenty of sauce for mopping up.

MAKES EIGHT

1 Mix the flour, baking powder and salt together in a large bowl and make a well in the centre. Gradually mix in 300ml/½ pint/ 1¼ cups water to make a firm dough.

2 Knead on a lightly floured surface until smooth. Place in a lightly oiled bowl, cover with lightly oiled clear film (plastic wrap). Leave to stand for 20 minutes.

3 Divide the dough into eight equal pieces and roll each one on a lightly floured surface into an 18cm/7in round. Brush the surface of each round with a little of the clarified butter or ghee, fold in half and half again. Cover the folded rounds with lightly oiled clear film (plastic wrap) and leave for 10 minutes.

4 Take one roti and roll out on a lightly floured surface into a round about 20–23cm/8–9in in diameter. Brush both sides with some clarified butter or ghee.

5 Heat a griddle or heavy frying pan, add the roti and cook for about 1 minute. Turn over and cook for 2 minutes, then turn over again and cook for 1 minute. Wrap in a clean dishtowel to keep warm while cooking the remaining rotis. Serve warm.

450g/1lb/4 cups atta or fine wholemeal (whole-wheat) flour

5ml/1 tsp baking powder

FROM THE STORECUPBOARD

115–150g/4–5oz/ 8–10 tbsp clarified butter or ghee, melted

5ml/1 tsp salt

Tandoori Rotis

Indian flat breads are fun to make at home: these may not be strictly authentic in terms of cooking method, but they taste fantastic. This bread would normally be baked in a tandoor, a clay oven that is heated with charcoal or wood. The oven becomes extremely hot, cooking the bread in minutes. The rotis are ready when light brown bubbles appear on the surface.

MAKES SIX

**350g/12oz/3 cups atta
or fine wholemeal
(whole-wheat) flour**

FROM THE
STORECUPBOARD

**30–45ml/2–3 tbsp
melted ghee or butter,
for brushing**

5ml/1 tsp salt

1 Sift the flour and salt into a large bowl. Add 250ml/8fl oz/1 cup water and mix to a soft dough. Knead on a lightly floured surface for 3–4 minutes, until smooth. Place the dough in a lightly oiled mixing bowl, cover with lightly oiled clear film (plastic wrap) and leave to rest for 1 hour.

2 Turn out on to a lightly floured surface. Divide the dough into six pieces and shape each piece into a ball. Press out into a larger round with the palm of your hand, cover with lightly oiled clear film (plastic wrap) and leave to rest for 10 minutes.

3 Meanwhile, preheat the oven to 230°C/450°F/Gas 8. Place three baking sheets in the oven to heat. Roll the rotis into 15cm/ 6in rounds, place two on each baking sheet and bake for 8–10 minutes. Brush with ghee or butter and serve warm.

Preserves, Pickles, Relishes and Sauces

SWEET AND SAVOURY PRESERVES, CONDIMENTS AND
SAUCES CAN ADD THE FINISHING TOUCH TO A SIMPLE DISH.
A SPOONFUL OF FRUIT JAM OR JELLY CAN TRANSFORM A
PLAIN SCONE INTO A TEATIME TREAT, WHILE PIQUANT
PICKLES AND RELISHES CAN ENLIVEN BREAD AND CHEESE,
AND A FLAVOURSOME SAUCE CAN TURN SIMPLY COOKED
FISH INTO A REALLY SPECIAL MEAL.

Bramble Jelly

The tart, fruity flavour of wild blackberries makes this jelly one of the best, especially for serving with hot buttered toast or English muffins. When picking the fruit, include a small proportion of red unripe berries for a good set. Redcurrant jelly is made in the same way, but with less sugar. Reduce the quantity to 350g/12oz/1½ cups of sugar for every 600ml/ 1 pint/2½ cups of fruit juice.

900g/2lb/ 8 cups blackberries

juice of 1 lemon

about 900g/2lb/ 4 cups caster (superfine) sugar

MAKES 900G/2LB

1 Put the blackberries and lemon juice into a large pan (use a preserving pan with two handles if possible). Add 300ml/½ pint/1¼ cups water. Cover the pan and cook for 15–30 minutes, or until the blackberries are very soft.

2 Ladle into a jelly bag or a large sieve lined with muslin (cheesecloth) and set over a large mixing bowl. Leave the fruit to drip overnight to obtain the maximum amount of juice. Do not disturb or squeeze the bag or the jelly will be cloudy.

3 Discard the fruit pulp. Measure the juice and allow 450g/1lb/2 cups sugar to every 600ml/ 1 pint/2½ cups juice. Place the juice and sugar in a large, heavy pan and bring to the boil, stirring constantly until the sugar has dissolved.

4 Boil the mixture rapidly until the jelly registers 105°C/220°F on a sugar thermometer, or test for setting by spooning a small amount on to a chilled saucer (keep a saucer in the freezer for this purpose). Chill for 3 minutes, then push the mixture with your finger: if wrinkles form on the surface of the jelly, it is ready.

5 Skim off any scum and immediately pour the jelly into warm sterilized jars. Cover and seal immediately, then label when the jars are cold.

Strawberry Jam

This is the classic fragrant preserve for English afternoon tea, served with freshly baked scones and clotted cream. It is also extremely good stirred into plain yogurt for breakfast. When choosing strawberries for making jam, pick undamaged, slightly under-ripe fruit if possible – the pectin content will be high and ensure a good set.

1kg/2¼lb/8 cups small strawberries

900g/2lb/4 cups granulated sugar

juice of 2 lemons

MAKES ABOUT 1.3KG/3LB

1 Layer the strawberries and sugar in a large bowl. Cover and leave overnight.

2 The next day, scrape the strawberries and their juice into a large, heavy pan. Add the lemon juice. Gradually bring to the boil over a low heat, stirring until the sugar has dissolved.

3 Boil steadily for 10–15 minutes, or until the jam registers 105°C/220°F on a sugar thermometer. Alternatively, test for setting by spooning a small amount on to a chilled saucer. Chill for 3 minutes, then push the jam with your finger: if wrinkles form on the surface, it is ready. Cool for 10 minutes.

4 Stir the jam before pouring it into warm sterilized jars, filling them right to the top. Cover with waxed paper discs immediately, but do not seal with lids until the jam is completely cold.

COOK'S TIP *For best results when making jam, don't wash the strawberries unless absolutely necessary. Instead, brush off any dirt, or wipe the strawberries with a damp cloth. If you have to wash any, pat them dry and then spread them out on a clean dishtowel to dry.*

Spiced Poached Kumquats

Warm cinnamon and star anise make a heady combination with the full citrus flavour of kumquats. Star anise is an attractive spice: it is an eight-pointed star that contains tiny aniseed-flavoured, amber coloured seeds. The kumquats go well with rich meats, such as roast pork or baked ham, or with punchy goat's milk cheese. They are also good with desserts and ice creams.

SERVES SIX

1 Cut the kumquats in half and discard the pips (seeds). Place the kumquats in a pan with the caster sugar, 150ml/¼ pint/⅔ cup water and the cinnamon stick and star anise. Cook over a gentle heat, stirring until the sugar has dissolved.

2 Increase the heat, cover the pan and boil the mixture for about 8–10 minutes, until the kumquats are tender. To bottle the kumquats, spoon them into warm, sterilized jars, seal and label.

3 If you want to serve the spiced kumquats soon after making them, let the mixture cool, then chill it.

450g/1lb/ 4 cups kumquats
115g/4oz/ ¹/₂ cup caster (superfine) sugar
1 small cinnamon stick
1 star anise

Three-fruit Marmalade

Bitter marmalade oranges have a powerful flavour and plenty of setting power to make an excellent preserve. Known as Seville oranges, they are usually only available for a short time in January – but sweet oranges can be used in this recipe if necessary.

MAKES 2.25KG/5LB

1 Wash the fruit, halve, and squeeze their juice. Pour into a large heavy pan or preserving pan. Tip the pips (seeds) and pulp into a square of muslin (cheesecloth), gather the sides into a bag and tie the neck. Tie the bag to the pan handle so that it dangles in the juice.

2 Remove and discard the membranes and pith from the citrus skins and cut the rinds into slivers. Add to the pan with 1.75 litres/3 pints/7½ cups water. Heat until simmering and then cook gently for 2 hours. Test the rinds for softness by pressing a cooled piece with a finger.

3 Lift out the muslin bag, squeezing out the juice into the pan. Discard the bag. Stir the sugar into the pan and heat very gently, stirring occasionally, until the sugar has dissolved.

4 Bring the mixture to the boil and boil for 10–15 minutes, or until the marmalade registers 105°C/220°F on a sugar thermometer. Alternatively, test the marmalade for setting by pouring a small amount on to a chilled saucer. Chill for 3 minutes, then push the marmalade with your finger: if wrinkles form on the surface, it is ready. Cool for 15 minutes.

5 Stir the marmalade and pour it into warm, sterilized jars. Cover with waxed paper discs. Seal and label when completely cold. Store in a cool dark cupboard.

2 Seville (Temple) oranges
2 lemons
1 grapefruit
1.5kg/3lb 6oz/ 6³/₄ cups granulated sugar

COOK'S TIP *Allow the marmalade to cool slightly before potting so that it is thick enough to stop the fruit from sinking in the jars.*

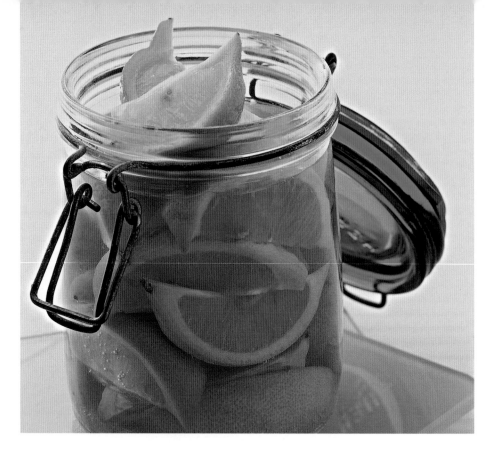

Preserved Lemons

These are widely used in Middle Eastern cooking, for which only the peel is used and not the pulp. In this recipe the lemons are cut into wedges instead of being preserved whole, in traditional style. The wedges are more practical for potting and they are also easy to prepare before use.

MAKES TWO JARS

1 Wash the lemons well and cut each into six to eight wedges. Press a generous amount of sea salt into the cut surfaces, pushing it into every crevice.

2 Pack the salted lemon wedges into two 1.2 litre/2 pint/5 cup sterilized jars. To each jar, add 30–45ml/2–3 tbsp salt and 90ml/6 tbsp lemon juice, then top up with boiling water to cover the lemons. (If using larger jars, use more lemon juice and less water.)

3 Cover the jars and leave to stand for 2–4 weeks before serving.

4 To serve, rinse the preserved lemons well to remove some of the salty flavour, then pull off and discard the flesh. Cut the lemon peel into strips or leave in chunks and use as you like.

10 unwaxed lemons

about 200ml/ 7fl oz/scant 1 cup fresh lemon juice or a combination of fresh and preserved

FROM THE STORECUPBOARD

sea salt

Middle Eastern Pickle

Beetroot brings attractive colour and its inimitable sweet, slightly earthy flavour to this Middle Eastern speciality. The pickle is delicious with falafel or cold roast beef. When buying beetroot, choose firm, unblemished, small- to medium-sized specimens. If you buy beetroot with green tops, reserve them and cook like spinach for a tasty vegetable accompaniment.

MAKES FOUR JARS

1kg/2¼lb
young turnips

3–4 raw
beetroot (beets)

juice of 1 lemon

FROM THE
STORECUPBOARD

about 45ml/3 tbsp
kosher salt or
coarse sea salt

1 Wash, but do not peel the turnips and beetroot. Then cut them into slices about 5mm/¼in thick. Put the salt in a bowl with about 1.5 litres/2½ pints/6¼ cups water, stir and leave on one side until the salt has completely dissolved.

2 Sprinkle the beetroot with lemon juice and divide among four 1.2 litre/2 pint/5 cup sterilized jars. Top with the sliced turnips, packing them in very tightly. Pour over the brine, making sure that the vegetables are completely covered.

3 Seal the jars and leave in a cool place for seven days for the flavours to develop before serving.

Horseradish and Beetroot Sauce

This is a traditional Jewish speciality. Known as *chrain*, it is often eaten at Pesah, the Passover meal, for which horseradish is one of the traditional bitter flavours. However, it complements a variety of foods and dishes of many different cooking styles, including roast meats and grilled fish.

SERVES ABOUT EIGHT

1 Put the horseradish and beetroot in a bowl and mix together, then season with sugar, vinegar and salt to taste.

2 Spoon the sauce into a sterilized jar, packing it down firmly, and seal. Store in the refrigerator, where it will keep for up to 2 weeks.

150g/5oz grated
fresh horseradish

2 cooked beetroot
(beets), grated

15ml/1 tbsp sugar

15–30ml/1–2 tbsp
red wine vinegar

FROM THE
STORECUPBOARD

salt

COOK'S TIP *Fresh horseradish is very potent and should be handled with care as it can make the skin burn as well as the eyes run. Wear fine rubber gloves to protect your hands.*

Yellow Pepper and Coriander Relish

Relishes are quick and easy to make and they are delicious with cold meats and cheese or as a sandwich filler. Here the ingredients are lightly cooked, then processed to a chunky consistency. Red or orange (bell) peppers will work just as well as yellow as they all have a sweet flavour. Don't use green peppers though, because they are not sweet.

SERVES FOUR TO SIX

1 Seed and coarsely chop the peppers. Heat the oil in a frying pan and gently cook the peppers, stirring frequently, for 8–10 minutes, until lightly coloured.

2 Meanwhile, seed the chilli and slice it as thinly as possible. Transfer the peppers and cooking juices to a food processor and process lightly until chopped. Transfer half the peppers to a bowl. Using a sharp knife, chop the fresh coriander, then add to the food processor and process briefly.

3 Tip the contents of the food processor into the bowl with the rest of the peppers and add the chilli and salt. Mix well, cover and chill until ready to serve.

3 large yellow (bell) peppers

1 large mild fresh red chilli

small handful of fresh coriander (cilantro)

FROM THE STORECUPBOARD

45ml/3 tbsp sesame oil

salt

COOK'S TIP *Other flavoured oils, such as lemon- or garlic-infused oil, can be used in place of the sesame oil.*

Hot Mango Salsa

For sweet, tangy results, select a really juicy, ripe mango for this salsa – it is not worth making the salsa with a firm, unripe mango as it will not taste as good as it should. Keep an unripe mango in the fruit bowl for a few days until it has ripened. This fruity salsa is a delicious accompaniment to chargrilled or barbecued chicken or fish.

SERVES FOUR TO SIX

1 To prepare the mango, cut the flesh off on either side of the flat stone (pit). Peel and finely dice the mango halves and cut off and chop the flesh that still clings to the stone.

2 Finely grate the lime rind and squeeze the juice. Seed and finely shred the fresh red chilli.

3 Finely chop the onion and mix it in a bowl with the mango, lime rind, 15ml/1 tbsp lime juice, the chilli and a little salt. Cover and chill until ready to serve.

1 **medium ripe mango**

1 **lime**

1 **large mild fresh red chilli**

^{1}/$_2$ **small red onion**

FROM THE STORECUPBOARD

salt

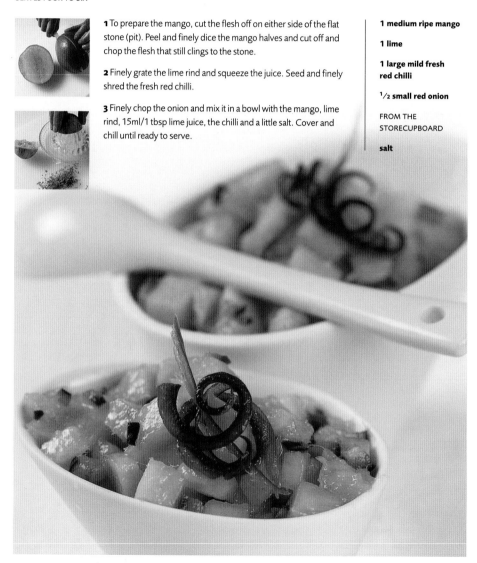

Harissa

This simplified version of harissa – the classic spicy North African sauce – is extremely quick to make. It can be served as a dip with wedges of Middle Eastern flat bread, as a condiment with couscous and other North African dishes, or as a flavouring to spice up meat and vegetable stews. This basic spice blend goes very well with other aromatic herbs and spices so you can vary the flavour by adding chopped fresh coriander (cilantro) or a pinch of caraway seeds along with the lemon juice, if you like.

SERVES FOUR TO SIX

1 Put the paprika, cayenne pepper, ground cumin and 250ml/8fl oz/ 1 cup water in a large, heavy pan.

2 Bring the spice mixture to the boil, then immediately remove the pan from the heat.

3 Stir in the lemon juice to taste and allow to cool completely before serving or using.

45ml/3 tbsp paprika

2.5–5ml/¹/₂–1 tsp cayenne pepper

1.5ml/¹/₄ tsp ground cumin

juice of ¹/₄–¹/₂ lemon

Aioli

This classic, creamy garlic mayonnaise from France is simple to make and absolutely delicious. Serve it with salads or as a dip with crudités, with potato wedges, or as a quick sauce for pan-fried salmon. Try to use extra virgin olive oil for this mayonnaise if you can – it has a rich and delicious flavour that really makes this sauce special.

SERVES FOUR TO SIX

1 Put the garlic cloves in a mortar, add a pinch of salt and pound to a smooth paste with a pestle.

2 Transfer the garlic paste to a bowl. Add the egg yolks and whisk for about 30 seconds, until creamy. Whisk in the olive oil, drop by drop, until the mixture begins to thicken, then add the oil in a slow drizzle until the mixture is thick and creamy.

3 Beat in the lemon juice and seasoning to taste. Serve immediately or cover with clear film (plastic wrap) and chill in the refrigerator until ready to use. Allow the aioli to return to room temperature before serving.

4 large garlic cloves, peeled

2 egg yolks

250ml/8fl oz/1 cup extra virgin olive oil

15–30ml/1–2 tbsp lemon juice

FROM THE STORECUPBOARD

salt

Roasted Garlic Sauce

A roasted garlic sauce has plenty of robust flavour without the harshness of some uncooked garlic sauces and dressings. This one keeps well in the refrigerator for several days. Serve it as an accompaniment to barbecued burgers or sausages, grilled steaks, lamb chops or pork steaks – the possibilities are endless.

SERVES SIX TO EIGHT

6 large heads of garlic

2 slices white bread, about 90g/3¹/₂oz

30–45ml/2–3 tbsp lemon juice

FROM THE STORECUPBOARD

120ml/4fl oz/¹/₂ cup olive oil

salt

1 Preheat the oven to 200°C/400°F/Gas 6. Slice the tops off the garlic and place the bulbs on a sheet of foil. Spoon over 30ml/2 tbsp of the oil and sprinkle with salt. Wrap the foil over the garlic and bake for 1 hour, until soft. Open out the foil and leave the garlic to cool.

2 Discard the crusts from the bread. Soak the bread in water for 1 minute, then squeeze dry and place in a food processor. Squeeze the garlic flesh into the processor. Process to a smooth paste.

3 Add 30ml/2 tbsp lemon juice with a little salt and pepper. With the machine running, gradually add the remaining oil in a thin stream to make a smooth paste. Check the seasoning, adding more lemon juice if needed. Turn into a bowl, cover and chill until required.

Watercress Sauce

This pretty green sauce is refreshingly tart and peppery. It is delicious served as an accompaniment to poached fish, or as a dip for simply grilled prawns (shrimp). Do not prepare the sauce more than a few hours ahead of serving, as the watercress will discolour the sauce. This peppery green sauce can also be made with rocket (arugula) leaves instead of the watercress.

SERVES SIX TO EIGHT

200g/7oz watercress leaves

300g/11oz/1¹/₄ cups mayonnaise

15–30ml/1–2 tbsp freshly squeezed lemon juice

FROM THE STORECUPBOARD

200g/7oz/scant 1 cup unsalted (sweet) butter

salt and ground black pepper

1 Remove the tough stems from the watercress leaves and finely chop the leaves by hand or in a food processor. Add the mayonnaise and the freshly squeezed lemon juice and process to mix.

2 Melt the unsalted butter, then add to the watercress mixture, a little at a time, processing or whisking in a bowl until the butter has been fully incorporated and the sauce is thick and smooth. Season to taste with salt and pepper, then cover and chill in the refrigerator for at least an hour before serving.

EXTRAS

Garlic makes a delicious addition to this sauce. Peel and finely chop 1–2 garlic cloves and combine with the chopped watercress leaves, mayonnaise and lemon juice, before adding the melted butter in step 2.

Shallots in Balsamic Vinegar

These whole shallots cooked in balsamic vinegar and herbs are a modern variation on pickled onions, but they have a much more gentle, smooth flavour. They are delicious served with cold pies, meats and cheese. A combination of bay leaves and thyme are used here but rosemary, oregano or marjoram sprigs would work just as well.

SERVES SIX

1 Put the unpeeled shallots in a bowl, cover with boiling water and leave for 2 minutes for the skins to loosen. Drain and peel the shallots, leaving them whole.

2 Put the sugar, bay leaves or thyme and vinegar in a heavy pan and bring to the boil. Add the shallots, cover and simmer gently for about 40 minutes, until the shallots are just tender.

3 Transfer the mixture to a sterilized jar, seal and label, then store in a cool, dark place. Alternatively, drain and transfer to a serving dish. Leave to cool, then chill until ready to serve.

500g/1^1/$_4$lb shallots

30ml/2 tbsp muscovado (molasses) sugar

several bay leaves or fresh thyme sprigs

300ml/^{1}/$_2$ pint/ 1^1/$_4$ cups balsamic vinegar

Barbecue Sauce

A wide selection of ready-made barbecue sauces are available in the supermarkets, but they really don't compare with the home-made variety. This 10-minute version can be used to transform baked or grilled chicken, sausages or fish into an interesting meal that needs no more than a mixed salad and baked potatoes as accompaniments.

1 Tip the cans of chopped tomatoes with herbs or garlic into a medium, heavy pan and add the finely chopped onion, black treacle and Worcestershire sauce.

2 Bring to the boil and cook, uncovered, until the mixture is thickened and pulpy, stirring frequently with a wooden spoon to stop the sauce catching on the base of the pan. Season lightly with salt and plenty of freshly ground black pepper and transfer to a serving dish or jug (pitcher). Serve the sauce warm or cold.

2 x 400g/14 oz cans chopped tomatoes with herbs or garlic

1 onion, finely chopped

15ml/1 tbsp black treacle (molasses)

45ml/3 tbsp Worcestershire sauce

FROM THE STORECUPBOARD

salt and ground black pepper

Mixed Herb and Peppercorn Sauce

This lovely, refreshing sauce relies on absolutely fresh herbs (any combination will do) and good-quality olive oil for its fabulous flavour. Make it a day in advance, to allow the flavours to mingle. Serve the sauce with simply cooked fish such as salmon or with grilled beef or lamb steaks.

SERVES FOUR TO SIX

1 Crush the cumin seeds using a mortar and pestle. Alternatively, put the seeds in a small bowl and pound them with the end of a rolling pin. Add the pink or green peppercorns and pound a little to break them up slightly.

2 Remove any tough stalks from the herbs. Put the herbs in a food processor with the cumin seeds, peppercorns, oil and salt and process until the herbs are finely chopped, scraping the sauce down from the sides of the bowl if necessary.

3 Turn the sauce into a small serving dish, cover with clear film (plastic wrap) and chill until ready to serve.

10ml/2 tsp cumin seeds

15ml/1 tbsp pink or green peppercorns in brine, drained and rinsed

25g/1oz/1 cup fresh mixed herbs, such as parsley, mint, chives and coriander (cilantro)

FROM THE STORECUPBOARD

45ml/3 tbsp lemon-infused olive oil

salt

Juices, Smoothies and Drinks

THERE IS SOMETHING REALLY ENTICING ABOUT FRESHLY

MADE BLENDED DRINKS AND HEALTHY JUICES. THEY CAN BE

CLEANSING, FRESH OR ZESTY, SMOOTH AND CREAMY OR

RICH AND DECADENT — EVERY GLASSFUL IS A TREAT. THIS

CHAPTER ALSO INCLUDES COOL COCKTAILS AND ENTICING

HOT DRINKS; WARM YOURSELF WITH A CUP OF

CARDAMOM HOT CHOCOLATE AND A RUM AND STAR

ANISE HOT TODDY OR CHILL OUT WITH A SEA BREEZE

OR MARGARITA COCKTAIL.

Leafy Apple Lift-off

This delicious blend of fruit and fresh green leaves is refreshing and healthy. The leaves are robustly flavoured and have a peppery, pungent taste. To prepare the leaves, discard any damaged and discoloured ones and rinse thoroughly in cold water to remove any grit. To prevent the juice from being watery, dry the leaves in a salad spinner or on kitchen paper before juicing.

SERVES ONE

1 Quarter the apple. Using a juice extractor, juice the fruit and watercress, rocket or spinach.

2 Add the lime juice to the apple, grape and leaf mixture and stir thoroughly to blend all the ingredients together. Pour the juice into a tall glass and serve immediately.

1 eating apple

150g/5oz white grapes

25g/1oz watercress, rocket (arugula) or spinach

15ml/1 tbsp lime juice

Fennel Fusion

The hearty combination of raw vegetables and apples makes a surprisingly delicious juice that is packed with natural goodness and is a truly wonderful pick-me-up. Use the remaining cabbage and fennel to make a really crunchy salad – slice and dress with French dressing or simply with olive oil, herb vinegar and plenty of freshly ground black pepper and sea salt to taste.

SERVES ONE

1 Coarsely slice the red cabbage and the fennel bulb and quarter the eating apples. Using a juice extractor, juice the vegetables and fruit.

2 Add the lemon juice to the red cabbage, fennel and apple mixture and stir thoroughly to blend all the ingredients together. Pour into a glass and serve immediately.

¹/₂ small red cabbage

¹/₂ fennel bulb

2 eating apples

15ml/1 tbsp lemon juice

Tropical Calm

This deliciously scented juice is packed with goodness to cleanse and calm the system. Orange fruits such as cantaloupe melons and papayas are rich in the phytochemical betacarotene, which is a valuable anti-oxidant and is thought to have many health-promoting properties.

SERVES ONE

1 papaya

¹/₂ cantaloupe melon

90g/3¹/₂oz seedless white grapes

1 Halve the papaya, remove the seeds and skin, then cut the flesh into coarse slices. Halve the melon, remove the seeds, cut into quarters, slice the flesh away from the skin and cut into chunks.

2 Using a juicer, juice the prepared fruit. Alternatively, blend the fruit in a food processor or blender for a thicker juice. Serve immediately.

Strawberry Soother

Relax with this comforting blend of just two fruits – it is rich in vitamin C and fabulous flavour. It's a perfect drink for summer when sweet strawberries, peaches and necatarines are in season.

SERVES ONE

225g/8oz/2 cups strawberries

1 peach or nectarine

1 Hull the strawberries. Using a sharp knife, quarter the peach or nectarine and pull out the stone (pit). Cut the flesh into coarse slices or chunks.

2 Using a juice extractor, juice the fruit. Alternatively, place the fruit in a food processor or blender and process until smooth. Serve immediately.

Carrot Revitalizer

This vibrant combination of vegetables and fruit makes a lively, health-giving drink. Carrots yield generous quantities of sweet juice, which goes perfectly with the sharp flavour of pear and the zesty taste of orange. This powerful drink will nourish and stimulate the system.

SERVES ONE

1 Scrub and trim the carrots and quarter the apples. Peel the orange and cut into rough segments.

2 Using a juice extractor, juice the carrots and fruit, pour into a glass and serve immediately.

3 carrots

2 apples

1 orange

Purple Pep

Jewel-coloured beetroot juice is well known for its detoxifying properties so this juice makes the perfect choice when you've been over-doing it. It offers an excellent supply of valuable nutrients that are essential for good health.

SERVES ONE

3 carrots

115g/4oz beetroot (beet)

25g/1oz baby spinach, washed and dried

2 celery sticks

1 Scrub and trim the carrots and beetroot. Using a sharp knife, cut the beetroot into large chunks.

2 Using a juice extractor, juice the carrots, beetroot, spinach and celery, then pour into a glass and serve immediately.

Tomato and Cucumber Juice with Basil

Some herbs don't juice well, losing their aromatic flavour and turning muddy and dull. Basil, on the other hand, is an excellent juicer, keeping its distinctive fresh fragrance. It makes the perfect partner for mild, refreshing cucumber and the ripest, juiciest tomatoes you can find. Try using cherry tomatoes for an extra sweet flavour.

SERVES TWO

½ cucumber, peeled

a handful of fresh basil

350g/12oz tomatoes

1 Quarter the cucumber lengthways. There's no need to remove the seeds. Push it through a juicer with the basil, then do the same with the tomatoes.

2 Pour the tomato, basil and cucumber juice over ice cubes in one tall or two short glasses and echo the herb flavour by adding a few basil sprigs for decoration.

Beetroot, Ginger and Orange Juice

Despite its firmness, beetroot can be juiced raw and its intense flavour goes perfectly with tangy citrus fruits and fresh root ginger. It has the highest sugar content of any vegetable and makes a delicious juice with a vibrant colour and rich but refreshing taste.

SERVES ONE

1 Scrub the beetroot, then trim them and cut into quarters. Push half the beetroot through a vegetable juicer, followed by the ginger and the remaining beetroot and pour the juice into a jug (pitcher).

2 Squeeze the juice from the orange, using a citrus juicer or by hand, and pour into the beetroot juice. Stir to combine.

3 Pour the juice over ice cubes in a glass or clear glass cup and serve immediately to enjoy the full benefit of all the nutrients. (Do not let the ice cubes melt into the juice or they will dilute its flavour.)

200g/7oz raw beetroot (beets)

1cm/^{1}/$_2$in piece fresh root ginger, peeled

1 large orange

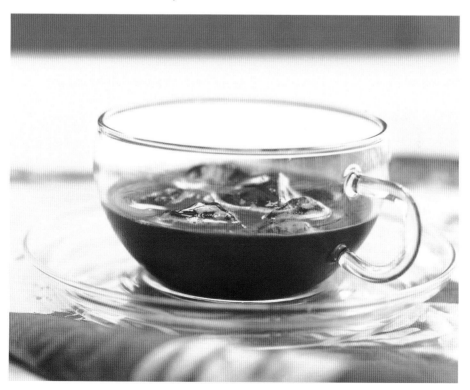

Melon Pick-me-up

Spicy fresh root ginger is delicious with melon and pear in this reviving and invigorating concoction. Charentais or Galia melon can be used instead of the cantaloupe melon in this recipe. To enjoy fresh root ginger at its best, buy it in small quantities and keep in a cool, dry place for up to a week. As it ages, the root will dry out and become hard.

SERVES ONE

1 Quarter the cantaloupe melon, remove the seeds using a teaspoon or a sharp knife, and carefully slice the flesh away from the skin, reserving any juice. Quarter the pears and reserve any juice.

2 Using a juice extractor, juice the melon flesh and juice, quartered pears and juice and the fresh root ginger. Pour the juice into a tall glass and serve immediately.

^{1}/$_2$ cantaloupe melon

2 pears

2.5cm/1in piece of fresh root ginger

Apple Shiner

This refreshing fusion of sweet apple, honeydew melon, red grapes and lemon provides a reviving burst of energy and a feel-good sensation. Serve as a drink or use to pour over muesli (granola) for a quick and healthy breakfast.

SERVES ONE

1 eating apple

^{1}/$_2$ honeydew melon

90g/3^1/$_2$oz red grapes

15ml/1 tbsp lemon juice

1 Quarter the apple and remove the core. Cut the melon into quarters, remove the seeds and slice the flesh away from the skin.

2 Using a juice extractor, juice the apple, melon and grapes. Alternatively, process the fruit in a food processor or blender for 2–3 minutes, until smooth. Pour the juice into a long, tall glass, stir in the lemon juice and serve immediately.

Citrus Sparkle

Zesty citrus fruits are packed with vitamin C, which is necessary for a healthy immune system. Pink grapefruit have a sweeter flavour than the yellow varieties – in fact, the pinker they are, the sweeter they are likely to be. For a lighter drink to serve two, divide the juice between two glasses and top up with sparkling mineral water or soda water (club soda) and ice cubes.

SERVES ONE

1 Cut the pink grapefruit and orange in half and squeeze out the juice using a citrus fruit squeezer.

2 Pour the juice into a glass, stir in 15ml/1 tbsp lemon juice, add the remaining lemon juice if required and serve immediately.

1 pink grapefruit

1 orange

30ml/2 tbsp freshly squeezed lemon juice

Hum-zinger

Aromatic tropical fruits make a drink that is bursting with flavour and energy. Enjoy a glass first thing in the morning to kick-start your day.

SERVES ONE

$^1/_2$ pineapple, peeled

1 small mango, peeled and stoned (pitted)

$^1/_2$ small papaya, seeded and peeled

1 Remove any "eyes" left in the pineapple, then cut all the fruit into fairly coarse chunks.

2 Using a juice extractor, juice the fruit. Alternatively, use a food processor or blender and process for about 2–3 minutes until smooth. Pour into a glass and serve immediately.

Grapefruit and Pear Juice

This deliciously refreshing rose-tinged blend will keep you bright-eyed and bushy-tailed. Its sharp yet sweet flavour is perfect for breakfast or as a pick-me-up when energy levels are flagging. If the grapefruit are particularly tart, serve the juice with a little bowl of brown sugar, or even brown sugar stirrers.

SERVES TWO

1 Take a thin slice from one grapefruit half and halve it. Cut a few thin slices of pear. Squeeze the juice from the grapefruit halves, then the pears using a juicer.

2 Combine the fruit juices and pour into two glasses. Add a few ice cubes to each glass and decorate with the grapefruit and pear slices. Serve immediately.

2 pink grapefruit, halved

2 ripe pears

Strawberry Apple Slush

Sweet, juicy strawberries make a delicately fragrant juice, with a consistency that's not too thick and not too thin. The addition of apple juice and just a hint of vanilla creates a tantalizing treat that's perfect for sipping on a lazy summer's afternoon.

SERVES TWO

300g/11oz/2³/₄ cups ripe strawberries

2 small, crisp eating apples

10ml/2 tsp vanilla syrup

1 Reserve a couple of strawberries and hull the remaining ones. Roughly chop the apples and push all the fruits through a juicer. Stir in the vanilla syrup.

2 Half-fill two tall glasses with crushed ice. Pour over the juice, decorate with the reserved strawberries (slicing them if you like) and serve immediately.

Honey and Watermelon Tonic

This refreshing juice will help to cool the body, calm the digestion and cleanse the system, and may even have aphrodisiac qualities. On hot days add ice cubes to keep the juice cool. The distinctive pinkish-red flesh of the watermelon gives this tonic a beautiful hue – decorate with a few fresh mint leaves to provide a stunning colour contrast.

SERVES FOUR

1 Cut the watermelon flesh into chunks, cutting away the skin and discarding the black seeds. Place in a large bowl, pour the chilled water over and leave to stand for 10 minutes.

2 Tip the mixture into a large sieve set over a bowl. Using a wooden spoon, press gently on the fruit to extract all the liquid.

3 Stir in the lime juice and sweeten to taste with honey. Pour into a jug (pitcher) or glasses and serve.

1 watermelon

1 litre/1³/₄ pints/ 4 cups chilled still mineral water

juice of 2 limes

clear honey, to taste

Cranberry, Ginger
and Cinnamon Spritzer

Partially freezing fruit juice gives it a refreshingly slushy texture.
The combination of cranberry and apple juice is tart and clean. Add
a few fresh or frozen cranberries to decorate each glass, if you like.

SERVES FOUR

**600ml/1 pint/2¹/₂ cups
chilled cranberry juice**

**150ml/¹/₄ pint/²/₃ cup clear
apple juice**

4 cinnamon sticks

**about 400ml/14fl oz/
1²/₃ cups chilled ginger ale**

1 Pour the cranberry juice into a shallow freezerproof container and freeze for about 2 hours, or until a thick layer of ice crystals has formed around the edges.

2 Mash the semi-frozen juice with a fork to break up the ice, then return the mixture to the freezer for a further 2–3 hours or until it is almost solid.

3 Pour the apple juice into a small pan, add two cinnamon sticks and bring to just below boiling point. Pour into a jug (pitcher) and leave to cool, then remove the cinnamon sticks and set them aside. Cool, then chill the juice.

4 Spoon the cranberry ice into a food processor or blender. Add the cinnamon-flavoured apple juice and process briefly until slushy. Pile the mixture into cocktail glasses, top up with chilled ginger ale, decorate with cinnamon sticks and serve immediately.

Lavender Orange Lush

This fragrant, lavender-scented juice is guaranteed to perk up a jaded palate in no time at all. It has a heavenly aroma and distinct yet subtle taste. Make plenty and keep it in the refrigerator. Use extra lavender sprigs as fun stirrers or a pretty garnish.

SERVES FOUR TO SIX

10–12 lavender flowers

45ml/3 tbsp caster (superfine) sugar

8 large oranges

1 Pull the lavender flowers from their stalks and put them into a bowl with the sugar and 120ml/4fl oz/¹/₂ cup boiling water. Stir briskly until the sugar has dissolved, then leave the lavender to steep for 10 minutes.

2 Squeeze the oranges using a citrus juicer and pour the juice into a jug (pitcher).

Ice Cool Currant

Intensely flavoured blackcurrants, whizzed in a blender with crushed ice, make a drink so thick and slushy that you might want to serve it with long spoons. If you have a glut of blackcurrants, make a double quantity of the juice and store it in the refrigerator for up to a week, ready to blend with ice.

SERVES TWO

125g/4¹/₄oz/generous 1 cup blackcurrants

60ml/4 tbsp light muscovado (brown) sugar

good pinch of mixed (apple pie) spice (optional)

VARIATION *Redcurrants or a mixture of redcurrants and blackcurrants could also be used instead of blackcurrants if you like. The juice will have a lighter taste.*

1 Put the blackcurrants and sugar in a pan. (There is no need to string the blackcurrants first.) Add the mixed spice, if using, and pour in 100ml/3¹/₂fl oz/scant ¹/₂ cup water. Bring the mixture to the boil and cook for 2–3 minutes, or until the blackcurrants are completely soft.

2 Press the mixture through a sieve into a bowl, pressing the pulp with the back of a dessertspoon to extract as much juice as possible. Set aside to cool completely.

3 Put 225g/8oz crushed ice in a food processor or blender with the cooled juice and process for about 1 minute until slushy and thoroughly mixed. Scrape the drink into tall glasses and serve immediately.

Lemon Float

Traditional lemonade made with freshly squeezed lemons and served with scoops of ice cream and soda water makes the ultimate refresher. The lemonade can be stored in the refrigerator for up to two weeks, so make a double batch when the weather is hot.

SERVES FOUR

6 lemons

200g/7oz/1 cup caster (superfine) sugar

8 scoops vanilla ice cream

1 Finely grate the rind from the lemons, then squeeze out the juice using a citrus juicer. Put the rind in a bowl with the sugar and pour over 600ml/1 pint/2$^1\!/_2$ cups boiling water. Stir until the sugar dissolves, then leave to cool.

2 Stir the lemon juice into the cooled syrup. Strain and chill for several hours. To serve, put a scoop of ice cream in each glass, then half-fill with the lemonade and add plenty of lemon slices. Top up with soda water (club soda) and add another scoop of ice cream to each glass and serve immediately.

Blue Lagoon

Blueberries are not only an excellent source of betacarotene and vitamin C, but they are also rich in flavonoids, which help to cleanse the system. Mixed with other dark red fruits, such as blackberries and grapes, they make a highly nutritious and extremely delicious blend that can be stored in the refrigerator and enjoyed throughout the day.

SERVES ONE

90g/3¹/₂oz/scant 1 cup blackcurrants or blackberries

150g/5oz red grapes

130g/4¹/₂oz/generous 1 cup blueberries

1 If using blackcurrants, gently pull the stalks through the tines of a fork to remove the fruit, then remove the stalks from the grapes.

2 Push all the fruits through a juicer, saving a few for decoration. Place some ice in a medium glass and pour over the juice. Decorate with the reserved fruit and serve.

Strawberry and Banana Smoothie

The blend of perfectly ripe bananas and strawberries creates a drink that is both fruity and creamy, with a luscious texture. Papaya, mango or pineapple can be used instead of strawberries for a tropical drink. Popular with adults and children alike, this is a great way to get children to enjoy fruit – much healthier than commercial milkshakes, too.

SERVES FOUR

200g/7oz/1³/₄ cups
strawberries, plus
extra, sliced,
to decorate

2 ripe bananas

300ml/¹/₂ pint/1¹/₄
cups skimmed milk

10 ice cubes

1 Hull the strawberries. Peel the bananas and chop them into fairly large chunks.

2 Put the fruit in a food processor or blender. Process to a thick, coarse purée, scraping down the sides of the goblet as necessary.

3 Add the skimmed milk and ice cubes, crushing the ice first unless you have a heavy-duty processor. Process until smooth and thick. Pour into tall glasses and top each with strawberry slices to decorate. Serve immediately.

EXTRAS For a rich and velvety drink, add 120ml/ 4fl oz/¹/₂cup coconut milk and process as above. Reduce the volume of milk to 175ml/6fl oz/³/₄ cup.

Raspberry and Orange Smoothie

Sharp-sweet raspberries and zesty oranges taste fabulous combined with the light creaminess of yogurt. This smoothie takes just minutes to prepare, making it perfect for breakfast – or any other time of the day. If you like a really tangy drink add freshly squeezed lemon or lime juice to taste.

SERVES TWO TO THREE

1 Place the raspberries and yogurt in a food processor or blender and process for about 1 minute, until smooth and creamy.

2 Add the orange juice to the raspberry and yogurt mixture and process for about 30 seconds, or until thoroughly combined. Pour into tall glasses and serve immediately.

250g/9oz/1¹/₂ cups
fresh raspberries,
chilled

200ml/7fl oz/scant
1 cup natural (plain)
yogurt, chilled

300ml/¹/₂pint/1¹/₄
cups freshly squeezed
orange juice, chilled

COOK'S TIP For a super-chilled version, use frozen raspberries or a combination of frozen summer berries such as strawberries, redcurrants and blueberries instead of fresh. You may need to blend the raspberries and yogurt slightly longer for a really smooth result.

New York Egg Cream

No one knows precisely why this legendary drink is called egg cream, but some say it was a witty way of describing richness at a time when no one could afford to put both expensive eggs and cream together in a drink. Use full-fat (whole) milk for a really creamy taste. Dust a little cocoa powder over the top of the egg cream before serving, if you like.

SERVES ONE

45–60ml/3–4 tbsp good quality
chocolate syrup

120ml/4fl oz/¹/₂ cup chilled milk

175ml/6fl oz/³/₄ cup chilled
sparkling mineral water

1 Carefully pour the chocolate syrup into the bottom of a tall glass avoiding dripping any on the inside of the glass.

2 Pour the chilled milk into the glass on to the chocolate syrup.

3 Gradually pour the chilled sparkling mineral water into the glass, sip up any foam that rises to the top of the glass and carefully continue to add the remaining chilled sparkling mineral water. Stir well before drinking.

COOK'S TIP *An authentic egg cream is made with an old-fashioned seltzer dispenser that you press and spritz. In any case, you can use soda water (club soda) rather than mineral water, if you like.*

Banana and Maple Flip

This satisfying drink is packed with so much goodness that it makes a complete breakfast in a glass – great for when you're in a hurry. Be sure to use a really fresh free-range egg. The glass can be decorated with a slice of orange or lime to serve.

SERVES ONE

1 small banana, peeled and halved

50ml/2fl oz/¼ cup thick Greek (US strained plain) yogurt

1 egg

30ml/2 tbsp maple syrup

1 Put the peeled and halved banana, thick Greek yogurt, egg and maple syrup in a food processor or blender. Add 30ml/ 2 tbsp chilled water.

2 Process the ingredients constantly for about 2 minutes, or until the mixture turns a really pale, creamy colour and has a nice frothy texture.

3 Pour the banana and maple flip into a tall, chilled glass and serve immediately. Decorate the glasses with an orange or lime slice, if you like.

COOK'S TIPS

To chill the drinking glass quickly, place it in the freezer while you are preparing the drink.

For a hint of sharpness, add 5ml/1 tsp lemon or lime juice or use a slightly tangy yogurt.

Chocolate Brownie Milkshake

This truly indulgent drink is so simple, yet utterly rich and luxurious, so take a quiet moment to yourself and just sit back, relax and enjoy. For an even more indulgent treat, spoon over whipped cream and sprinkle with grated chocolate to serve.

SERVES ONE

40g/1¹/₂oz chocolate brownies

200ml/7fl oz/scant 1 cup full cream (whole) milk

2 scoops vanilla ice cream

1 Crumble the chocolate brownies into a food processor or blender and add the milk. Blend until the mixture is smooth.

2 Add the ice cream to the chocolate milk mixture and blend until the shake is really smooth and frothy. Pour into a tall glass and serve immediately.

Peppermint Candy Crush

The next time you see peppermint candy canes that are on sale at Christmas time, buy a few sticks and make this fun kid's drink. All you need to do is whizz up the candy with some milk and freeze until slushy, so it's ready and waiting for thirsty youngsters.

SERVES FOUR

90g/3¹/₂oz pink peppermint candy canes, plus four extra to serve

750ml/1¹/₄ pints/3 cups milk

a few drops of pink food colouring (optional)

1 While the candy canes are still in their wrappers, break into small bits using a rolling pin. (If it is unwrapped, put the candy in a polythene bag before you crush it.) Tip the pieces into a food processor or blender.

2 Pour the milk over the candy and add a few drops of pink food colouring, if using. Process until the cane is broken up into tiny pieces, then pour the mixture into a shallow freezer container and freeze for 2 hours, or until frozen around the edges.

3 Beat the mixture with a fork, breaking up the semi-frozen areas and stirring them into the centre. Re-freeze and repeat the process once or twice more until the mixture is slushy. Spoon into tall glasses and serve with candy cane stirrers.

Rum and Star Anise Hot Toddy

Hot toddies are normally made with whisky but rum works really well too and produces a deliciously warming drink that's perfect for a cold winter evening – or even a winter afternoon after a hearty walk out in the freezing cold countryside. You can also flavour this toddy with different spices such as a vanilla pod (bean) or cinnamon stick.

SERVES FOUR

300ml/¹/₂ pint/1¹/₄ cups dark rum

45ml/3 tbsp caster (superfine) sugar

1 star anise

1 Pour the rum into a heatproof jug (pitcher) and add the sugar and star anise. Pour in 450ml/³/₄ pint/scant 2 cups boiling water and stir thoroughly until the sugar has dissolved.

2 Carefully pour the hot toddy into heatproof glasses or mugs and serve immediately.

Cardamom Hot Chocolate

Hot chocolate is a wonderful treat at any time of day – for breakfast with a warm croissant, as a teatime treat on a cold winter afternoon or before bed to help you sleep. Adding spicy cardamom gives this hot chocolate an extra rich, fragrant aroma.

SERVES FOUR

900ml/1¹/₂ pints/3³/₄ cups milk

2 cardamom pods, bruised

200g/7oz plain (semisweet) chocolate, broken into pieces

1 Put the milk in a pan with the cardamom pods and bring to the boil. Add the chocolate and whisk until melted.

2 Using a slotted spoon, remove the cardamom pods and discard. Pour the hot chocolate into heatproof glasses, mugs or cups and serve with whipped cream.

Atole

This drink, rather like a thick milkshake in consistency, is made from Mexican cornflour (masa harina) and flavoured with piloncillo (Mexican unrefined brown sugar). Ground cinnamon and/or fresh fruit purées are often added before serving, and some recipes introduce ground almonds.

SERVES SIX

1 Combine the milk with 600ml/ 1 pint/2¹/₂ cups cold water. Put the masa harina in a heavy pan and gradually beat in the milk and water mixture to make a smooth paste.

2 Place the pan over a moderate heat, add the vanilla pod and bring the mixture to the boil, stirring constantly until it thickens. Beat in the sugar and stir until the sugar has dissolved. Remove from the heat, discard the vanilla and serve.

200g/7oz/1³/₄ cups white masa harina

600ml/1 pint/ 2¹/₂ cups milk

1 vanilla pod (bean)

50g/2oz/¹/₄ cup piloncillo or soft dark brown sugar

EXTRAS

Process 115g/4oz/ 1 cup strawberries, chopped pineapple or orange segments in a food processor or blender until smooth, then press the purée through a sieve. Stir the purée into the corn mixture and return the pan to the heat until warmed through. Remove the vanilla pod and serve.

Café de Olla

This spiced black coffee is one of the most popular drinks in Mexico. The name means out of the pot, which refers to the heavy earthenware cooking pot, or *olla*, in which the coffee is made. Piloncillo is the local unrefined brown sugar, but any soft dark brown sugar can be used. French or Viennese roast coffees work particularly well in this hot drink.

SERVES FOUR

115g/4oz/¹/₂ cup piloncillo or soft dark brown sugar

4 cinnamon sticks, each about 15cm/ 6in long

50g/2oz/²/₃ cup freshly ground coffee, from dark-roast coffee beans

1 Pour 1 litre/1¾ pints/4 cups water into a pan. Add the sugar and cinnamon sticks. Heat gently, stirring occasionally to make sure that the sugar dissolves, then bring to the boil. Boil rapidly for about 20 minutes, until the syrup has reduced by one-quarter.

2 Add the ground coffee to the syrup and stir well, then bring the liquid back to the boil. Remove from the heat, cover the pan and leave to stand for about 5 minutes.

3 Strain the coffee through a fine sieve (strainer), and pour into cups.

Vanilla Caffè Latte

This luxurious vanilla and chocolate version of the classic coffee drink can be served at any time of the day topped with whipped cream, with cinnamon sticks to stir and flavour the drink. Caffè latte is a popular breakfast drink in Italy and France, and is now widely available elsewhere.

SERVES TWO

1 Pour the milk into a small pan and bring to the boil, then remove from the heat. Mix the espresso or very strong coffee with 500ml/16fl oz/ 2 cups of the boiled milk in a large heatproof jug (pitcher). Sweeten with vanilla sugar to taste.

2 Return the remaining boiled milk in the pan to the heat and add the 45ml/3 tbsp vanilla sugar. Stir constantly until dissolved. Bring to the boil, then reduce the heat. Add the dark chocolate and continue to heat, stirring constantly until all the chocolate has melted and the mixture is smooth and glossy.

3 Pour the chocolate milk into the jug of coffee and whisk thoroughly. Serve in tall mugs or glasses topped with whipped cream and with cinnamon sticks to stir.

700ml/24fl oz/scant 3 cups milk

250ml/8fl oz/1 cup espresso or very strong coffee

45ml/3 tbsp vanilla sugar, plus extra to taste

115g/4oz dark (bittersweet) chocolate, grated

Frothy Hot Chocolate

Real hot chocolate doesn't come as a powder in a packet – it is made with the best chocolate you can afford, whisked in hot milk until really frothy. This recipe uses dark (bittersweet) chocolate, but for a special treat you could use Mexican chocolate, which is flavoured with almonds, cinnamon and vanilla, and sweetened with sugar. All the ingredients are crushed together in a special mortar, and heated over coals. The powdered mixture is then shaped into discs, which can be bought in specialist stores.

SERVES FOUR

1 Pour the milk into a pan. Split the vanilla pod lengthways using a sharp knife to reveal the seeds, and add it to the milk; the vanilla seeds and the pod will flavour the milk.

2 Add the chocolate. The amount to use depends on personal taste – start with a smaller amount if you are unsure of the flavour and taste at the beginning of step 3, adding more if necessary.

3 Heat the chocolate milk gently, stirring until all the chocolate has melted and the mixture is smooth, then whisk with a wire whisk until the mixture boils. Remove the vanilla pod from the pan and divide the drink among four mugs or heatproof glasses. Serve the hot chocolate immediately.

1 litre/1³/₄pints/ 4 cups milk

50–115g/2–4oz dark (bittersweet) chocolate, grated

1 vanilla pod (bean)

Cuba Libre

Rum and coke takes on a much livelier, citrus flavour in this vibrant Caribbean cocktail that's sure to put you in the mood to party. The refreshing flavour and aroma of freshly squeezed limes is the dominant taste in this blend, and the dark rum really packs a punch when combined with the sweet, syrupy cola drink.

SERVES EIGHT

9 limes

250ml/8fl oz/1 cup dark rum

800ml/1¹/₃ pints/3¹/₂ cups cola drink

1 Thinly slice one lime then, using a citrus juicer, squeeze the juice from the rest of the limes.

2 Put plenty of ice cubes into a large glass jug (pitcher), tucking the lime slices around them, then pour in the lime juice.

3 Pour the rum into the jug and stir well with a long-handled spoon. Top up with cola drink and serve immediately in tall glasses with stirrers.

Tropical Fruit Royale

Based on the Kir Royale, a blend of champagne and crème de cassis, this elegant cocktail is made with tropical fruits and sparkling wine. Remember to blend the fruits ahead of time to give the mango ice cubes time to freeze.

SERVES SIX

1 Peel the mangoes, cut the flesh off the stone (pit), then put the flesh in a food processor or blender. Process until smooth, scraping the mixture down from the sides of the bowl.

2 Fill an ice cube tray with a good half of the mango purée and freeze for 2 hours until solid.

3 Cut six wedges from one or two of the passion fruits and scoop the pulp from the rest into the remaining mango purée. Process until well blended.

4 Spoon the mixture into six stemmed glasses. Divide the mango ice cubes among the glasses, top up with sparkling wine and add the passion fruit wedges. Serve with stirrers.

2 large mangoes

6 passion fruit

sparkling wine

Lemon Vodka

Very similar to the deliciously moreish Italian liqueur, Limoncello, this lemon vodka should be drunk in small quantities due to its hefty alcoholic punch. Blend the sugar, lemons and vodka and keep in a bottle in the refrigerator, ready for pouring over crushed ice, or topping up with soda or sparkling water.

SERVES TWELVE TO FIFTEEN

10 large lemons

275g/10oz/generous 1¹/₄ cups caster (superfine) sugar

250ml/8fl oz/1 cup vodka

1 Squeeze the lemons using a citrus juicer. Pour the juice into a jug (pitcher), add the sugar and whisk well until all the sugar has dissolved.

2 Strain the sweetened lemon juice into a clean bottle or narrow-necked jar and add the vodka. Shake the mixture well to combine and chill for up to 2 weeks.

3 To serve, fill small glasses with ice and pour over the lemon vodka or pour into larger, ice-filled glasses and top up with chilled soda water (club soda).

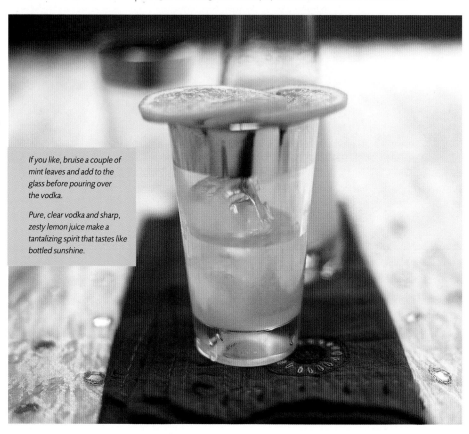

If you like, bruise a couple of mint leaves and add to the glass before pouring over the vodka.

Pure, clear vodka and sharp, zesty lemon juice make a tantalizing spirit that tastes like bottled sunshine.

Quick Bloody Mary

Using vodka flavoured with chilli gives this drink the perfect spicy kick. You can make your own chilli vodka, simply by slipping a fresh red chilli into a bottle of vodka and leaving the flavours to infuse.

SERVES FOUR

250ml/8fl oz/1 cup chilli vodka

1.2 litres/2 pints/5 cups tomato juice

5ml/1 tsp celery salt

FROM THE STORECUPBOARD

2.5ml/¹/₂ tsp ground black pepper

1 Quarter-fill four tall glasses with a handful of ice cubes and pour over the chilli vodka. (If there's a chilli in the bottle, be careful not to pour it out!)

2 Pour the tomato juice into a jug (pitcher) and add the celery salt and pepper. Stir well to combine.

3 Pour the flavoured tomato juice over the vodka, mix well using a long-handled spoon or stirrer, and serve with a stick of celery in each glass.

Gin Fizz

The combination of sourness and fizziness in this 19th-century recipe is what makes it so refreshing.

SERVES ONE

1 Shake the gin, lemon juice and sugar with ice until the sugar is properly dissolved. Pour out into a frosted, tall, narrow glass half-filled with ice, and top up with soda.

2 Add two straws. There should be a little less soda than the other combined ingredients.

2 measures/3 tbsp gin

juice of half a large lemon

5ml/1 tsp caster (superfine) sugar

soda water

Sea Breeze

One of today's most requested cocktails, Sea Breeze was one of the first popular cocktails to use cranberry juice. Ocean Spray is one of the most famous brands, but the supermarkets nearly all have a proprietary version.

SERVES ONE

COOK'S TIP

Cranberry juice is a sugar-and-water product. It is possible to buy apple juice with cranberry if you want neither sugar nor water.

2 measures/3 tbsp vodka

2 measures/3 tbsp grapefruit juice

3 measures/4¹/₂ tbsp cranberry juice

1 Shake all the ingredients well with plenty of ice, and pour everything into a chilled highball glass.

2 Add a wedge of lime and a few cranberries.

Perfect Manhattan

When making Manhattans it's a matter of preference whether you use sweet vermouth, dry vermouth or a mixture of the two. Both of the former require a dash of Angostura bitters. The last, given here, is such a harmoniously balanced mixture that it doesn't need it.

SERVES ONE

2 measures/3 tbsp rye whiskey

$^1/_4$ measure/1 tsp dry vermouth

$^1/_4$ measure/1 tsp sweet red vermouth

1 Pour the whiskey and vermouths into a bar glass half-full of ice. Stir well for 30 seconds to mix and chill.

2 Strain on the rocks or straight up into a chilled cocktail glass.

3 Pare away a small strip of lemon rind. Tie it into a knot to help release the oils from the rind, and drop it into the cocktail.

4 Add a maraschino cherry with its stalk left intact. As any Manhattan drinker wil tell you, the cherry is essential.

Margarita

With the Tequila Sunrise, Margarita, created in Tijuana in the late 1940s, is probably the best-known tequila cocktail of them all. Its saltiness and sourness make it a great aperitif. Some recipes use lemon juice instead of lime, but lime juice sharpens its bite.

SERVES ONE

1¹/₂ **measures/6 tsp silver tequila**

¹/₂ **measure/2 tsp Cointreau**

juice of a lime

FROM THE STORECUPBOARD

salt

1 Rub the rim of a cocktail glass with a wedge of fresh lime, and then dip it in fine salt.

2 Shake the tequila, Cointreau and lime juice with ice, and strain into the prepared glass. Garnish with a twist of cucumber rind or a half-slice of lime.

Nutritional Information

The nutritional analysis below is **per portion**, unless otherwise stated.

p10 Hummus
Energy 125Kcal/523kJ; Protein 6g; Carbohydrate 9g, of which sugars 0g; Fat 7g, of which saturates 1g; Cholesterol 0mg; Calcium 92mg; Fibre 3.1g; Sodium 100mg.

p11 Baba Ghanoush
Energy 395Kcal/1635kJ; Protein 13g; Carbohydrate 5g, of which sugars 4g; Fat 3g, of which saturates 5g; Cholesterol 0mg; Calcium 92mg; Fibre 8.1g; Sodium 100mg.

p12 Cannellini Bean Pâté
Energy 252Kcal/1635kJ; Protein 13g; Carbohydrate 21g, of which sugars 2g; Fat 13g, of which saturates 4g; Calcium 12mg; Calcium 120mg; Fibre 7.6g; Sodium 900mg.

p13 Chicken Liver and Brandy Pâté
Energy 263Kcal/1091kJ; Protein 16g; Carbohydrate 0g, of which sugars 0g; Fat 20g, of which saturates 12g; Cholesterol 170mg; Calcium 91mg; Fibre 0g; Sodium 400mg.

p14 Peperonata
Energy 140Kcal/583kJ; Protein 2g; Carbohydrate 8g, of which sugars 8g; Fat 11g, of which saturates 2g; Cholesterol 0mg; Calcium 19mg; Fibre 2.0g; Sodium 100mg.

p14 Artichoke and Cumin Dip Energy 37Kcal/155kJ; Protein 2g; Carbohydrate 2g, of which sugars 1g; Fat 3g, of which saturates 0g; Cholesterol 0mg; Calcium 29mg; Fibre 0.1g; Sodium 100mg.

p16 Sweet and Salty Vegetable Crisps
Energy 64Kcal/265kJ; Protein 1g; Carbohydrate 3g, of which sugars 3g; Fat 0g, of which saturates 1g; Cholesterol 0mg; Calcium 8mg; Fibre 0.7g; Sodium 100mg.

p17 Sizzling Prawns

Energy 109Kcal/450kJ; Protein 2g; Carbohydrate 1g, of which sugars 0g; Fat 11g, of which saturates 2g; Cholesterol 17mg; Calcium 8mg; Fibre 0.1g; Sodium 100mg.

p18 Potted shrimps
Energy 326Kcal/1389kJ; Protein 11g; Carbohydrate 0g, of which sugars 0g; Fat 31g, of which saturates 26g; Cholesterol 170mg; Calcium 91mg; Fibre 0g; Sodium 400mg.

p18 Marinated Feta with Lemon and Oregano
Energy 803Kcal/3308kJ; Protein 8g; Carbohydrate 1g, of which sugars 1g; Fat 85g, of which saturates 18g; Cholesterol 35mg; Calcium 199mg; Fibre 0g; Sodium 700mg.

p20 Mushroom Caviar
Energy 101Kcal/417kJ; Protein 3g; Carbohydrate 23g, of which sugars 92g; Fat 9g, of which saturates 1g; Cholesterol 0mg; Calcium 14mg; Fibre 1.7g; Sodium 100mg.

p21 Brandade of Salt Cod
Energy 627Kcal/2583kJ; Protein 10g; Carbohydrate 1g, of which sugars 1g; Fat 64g, of which saturates 20g; Cholesterol 57mg; Calcium 96mg; Fibre 0.1g; Sodium 100mg.

p22 Chopped Egg and Onions Energy 245Kcal/1017kJ; Protein 12g; Carbohydrate 3g, of which sugars 2g; Fat 20g, of which saturates 5g; Cholesterol 389mg; Calcium 70mg; Fibre 0.5g; Sodium 200mg.

p22 Israeli Cheese with Green Olives
Energy 252Kcal/1040kJ; Protein 4g; Carbohydrate 0g, of which sugars 0g; Fat 26g, of which saturates 16g; Cholesterol 53mg; Calcium 116mg; Fibre 0.5g; Sodium 800mg.

p24 Bacon-rolled Enokitake Mushrooms
Energy 116Kcal/483kJ; Protein 9g; Carbohydrate 1g, of which sugars 0g; Fat 9g, of which saturates 3g; Cholesterol 27mg; Calcium 10mg; Fibre 1.2g; Sodium 500mg.

p25 Walnut and Goat's Cheese Bruschetta
Energy 520Kcal/2159kJ; Protein 16g; Carbohydrate 26g, of which sugars 7g; Fat 42g, of which saturates 13g; Cholesterol 47mg; Calcium 113mg; Fibre 0.6g; Sodium 500mg.

p28 Spanish Salted Almonds
Energy 206Kcal/853kJ; Protein 8g; Carbohydrate 2g, of which sugars 1g; Fat 19g, of which saturates 1g; Cholesterol 0mg; Calcium 80mg; Fibre 2.5g; Sodium 300mg.

p29 Golden Gruyère and Basil Tortillas
Energy 430Kcal/1795kJ; Protein 20g; Carbohydrate 33g, of which sugars 1g; Fat 25g, of which saturates 13g; Cholesterol 58mg; Calcium 613mg; Fibre 1.3g; Sodium 700mg.

p30 Polenta Chips
Per chip: Energy 35Kcal/144kJ; Protein 1g; Carbohydrate 3g, of which sugars 0g; Fat 2g, of which saturates 1g; Cholesterol 4mg; Calcium 20mg; Fibre 0.1g; Sodium 100mg.

p31 Parmesan Tuiles
Energy 48Kcal/199kJ; Protein 4g; Carbohydrate 0g, of which sugars 0g; Fat 3g, of which saturates 2g; Cholesterol 11mg; Calcium 118mg; Fibre 0g; Sodium 100mg.

p32 Yogurt Cheese in Olive Oil Energy 1927kcal/7943kJ; Protein 32g; Carbohydrate 10g,of which sugars 10g; Fat 201g, of which saturates 47g; Cholesterol 0mg; Calcium 758mg; Fibre 0.0g; Sodium 400mg.

p33 Eggs Mimosa
Energy 77Kcal/318kJ; Protein 4g; Carbohydrate 0g, of which sugars 0g; Fat 7g, of which saturates 2g; Cholesterol 116mg; Calcium 18mg; Fibre 0.5g; Sodium 100mg.

p34 Marinated Smoked Salmon with Lime and Coriander Energy 65Kcal/271kJ; Protein 9g; Carbohydrate 0g, of which sugars 0g; Fat 3g, of which saturates 1g; Cholesterol 12mg; Calcium 9mg; Fibre 0g; Sodium 600mg.

p34 Blinis with Caviar and Crème Fraîche
Energy 96Kcal/398kJ; Protein 2g; Carbohydrate 5g, of which sugars 3g; Fat 8g, of which saturates 5g; Cholesterol 39mg; Calcium 19mg; Fibre 0.2g; Sodium 200mg.

p36 Marinated Anchovies
Energy 112Kcal/469kJ; Protein 14g; Carbohydrate 1g, of which sugars 1g; Fat 6g, of which saturates 1g; Cholesterol 35mg; Calcium 172mg; Fibre 0.1g; Sodium 500mg.

p37 Chilli Prawn Skewers
Energy 51Kcal/215kJ; Protein 7g; Carbohydrate 5g, of which

sugars 4g; Fat 0g, of which saturates 0g; Cholesterol 78mg; Calcium 37mg; Fibre 0.3g; Sodium 700mg.

p38 Salt Cod and Potato Fritters
Energy 718Kcal/2980kJ; Protein 21.1g; Carbohydrate 33.1g, of which sugars 1.9g; Fat 56.5g, of which saturates 8.3g; Cholesterol 165mg; Calcium 67mg; Fibre 1.6g; Sodium 196mg.

p39 Asian-style Crab Cakes
Energy 70Kcal/209kJ; Protein 6g; Carbohydrate 2g, of which sugars 0g; Fat 4g, of which saturates 1g; Cholesterol 20mg; Calcium 4mg; Fibre 0.1g; Sodium 100mg.

p40 Crab and Water-chestnut Wontons Energy 41Kcal/175kJ; Protein 6g; Carbohydrate 4g, of which sugars 1g; Fat 0g, of which saturates 0g; Cholesterol 21mg; Calcium 36mg; Fibre 0.1g; Sodium 300mg.

p40 Chilli-spiced Chicken Wings Energy 428Kcal/1781kJ; Protein 30g; Carbohydrate 12g, of which sugars 4g; Fat 29g, of which saturates 6g; Cholesterol 129mg; Calcium 60mg; Fibre 0.3g; Sodium 200mg.

p42 Vietnamese Spring Rolls with Pork
Energy 218Kcal/910kJ; Protein 20g; Carbohydrate 3g, of which sugars 0g; Fat 14g, of which saturates 1g; Cholesterol 0mg; Calcium 2mg; Fibre 0g; Sodium 400mg.

p43 Curried Lamb Samosas
Energy 57Kcal/238kJ; Protein 4g; Carbohydrate 1g, of which sugars 0g; Fat 4g, of which saturates 2g; Cholesterol 18mg; Calcium 8mg; Fibre 0g; Sodium 100mg.

p46 Avocado Soup Energy 301Kcal/1240kJ; Protein 4g; Carbohydrate 3g, of which sugars 3g; Fat 30g, of which saturates 12g; Cholesterol 45mg; Calcium 86mg; Fibre 2.5g; Sodium 600mg.

p47 Vichyssoise
Energy 186kcal/781kJ; Protein

5g; Carbohydrate 16g, of which sugars 4g; Fat 4g, of which saturates 2g; Cholesterol 17mg; Calcium 8mg; Fibre 0.1g; Sodium 100mg.

p48 Avgolemono
Energy 117Kcal/495kJ; Protein 7g; Carbohydrate 15g, of which sugars 1g; Fat 4g, of which saturates 1g; Cholesterol 116mg; Calcium 26mg; Fibre 0.6g; Sodium 400mg.

p49 Simple Cream of Onion Soup Energy 499kcal/2073kJ; Protein 4g; Carbohydrate 21g, of which sugars 15g; Fat 45g, of which saturates 28g; Cholesterol 118mg; Calcium 89mg; Fibre 3.5g; Sodium 900mg.

p50 Capelletti in Broth
Energy 130Kcal/551kJ; Protein 6g; Carbohydrate 22g, of which sugars 1g; Fat 3g, of which saturates 1g; Cholesterol 5mg; Calcium 68mg; Fibre 1g; Sodium 600mg.

p50 Tiny Pasta in Broth
Energy 86Kcal/366kJ; Protein 4g; Carbohydrate 15g, of which sugars 1g; Fat 2g, of which saturates 1g; Cholesterol 2mg; Calcium 33mg; Fibre 0.8g; Sodium 500mg.

p52 Potato and Roasted Garlic Broth
Energy 122Kcal/515 kJ; Protein 5g; Carbohydrate 25g, of which sugars 1g; Fat 1g, of which saturates 0g; Cholesterol 0mg; Calcium 12mg; Fibre 2.2g; Sodium 900mg.

p53 Winter Squash Soup with Tomato Salsa
Energy 255Kcal/1059kJ; Protein 3g; Carbohydrate 18g, of which sugars 12g; Fat 19g; of which saturates 3g; Cholesterol 0mg; Calcium 86mg; Fibre 3.1g; Sodium 100mg.

p54 Butter Bean, Sun-dried Tomato and Pesto Soup
Energy 305Kcal/1276kJ; Protein 14g; Carbohydrate 23g, of which sugars 3g; Fat 18g, of which saturates 4g; Cholesterol 8mg; Calcium 136mg; Fibre 7.5g;

Sodium 1.5g.

p55 Stilton and Watercress Soup Energy 162Kcal/671kJ; Protein 8g; Carbohydrate 1g, of which sugars 1g; Fat 14g, of which saturates 9g; Cholesterol 38mg; Calcium 169mg; Fibre 0.6g; Sodium 400mg.

p58 Baked Eggs with Creamy Leeks Energy 219Kcal/905kJ; Protein 9g; Carbohydrate 2g, of which sugars 2g; Fat 19g, of which saturates 10g; Cholesterol 261mg; Calcium 61g; Fibre 1.2g; Sodium 100mg.

p59 Red Onion and Olive Pissaladière
Energy 436Kcal/1815kJ; Protein 6g; Carbohydrate 37g, of which sugars 6g; Fat 31g, of which saturates 2g; Cholesterol 0mg; Calcium 77mg; Fibre 1.5g; Sodium 500mg.

p60 Figs with Prosciutto and Roquefort
Energy 192Kcal/808kJ; Protein 10g; Carbohydrate 19g, of which sugars 19g; Fat 9g, of which saturates 5g; Cholesterol 17mg; Calcium 142mg; Fibre 1.7g; Sodium 700mg.

p61 Pea and Mint Omelette
Energy 216Kcal/898kJ; Protein 17g; Carbohydrate 2g, of which sugars 1g; Fat 15g, of which saturates 5g; Cholesterol 469mg; Calcium 87mg; Fibre 1.3g; Sodium 400mg.

p62Warm Penne with Fresh Tomatoes and Basil Energy 556Kcal/2356kJ; Protein 16g; Carbohydrate 99g, of which sugars 7g; Fat 14g, of which saturates 2g; Cholesterol 0mg; Calcium 46mg; Fibre 5.1g; Sodium 100mg.

p63 Broccoli and Chilli Spaghetti
Energy 675Kcal/ 2835kJ; Protein 16g; Carbohydrate 67g, of which sugars 5g; Fat 40g, of which saturates 6g; Cholesterol 0mg; Calcium 86mg; Fibre 5.5g; Sodium 100mg.

p64 Grilled Aubergine, Mint and Couscous Salad Energy 264Kcal/1101kJ; Protein 5g; Carbohydrate 35g, of which sugars 5g; Fat 12g, of which saturates 2g; Cholesterol 0mg; Calcium 39mg; Fibre 4.5g; Sodium 200mg.

p65 Marinated Courgette and Flageolet Bean Salad
Energy 155Kcal/647kJ; Protein 8g; Carbohydrate 11g, of which sugars 2g; Fat 9g, of which saturates 1g; Cholesterol 0mg; Calcium 57mg; Fibre 4.7g; Sodium 300mg.

p66 Roasted Pepper and Hummus Wrap
Energy 370Kcal/1533kJ; Protein 11g; Carbohydrate 53g, of which sugars 14g; Fat 14g, of which saturates 1g; Cholesterol 0mg; Calcium 101mg; Fibre 6g; Sodium 800mg.

p66 Focaccia with Sardines and Roast Tomatoes Energy 507Kcal/2134kJ; Protein 29g; Carbohydrate 54g, of which sugars 5g; Fat 21g, of which saturates 4g; Cholesterol 20mg; Calcium 205mg; Fibre 3.1g; Sodium 800mg.

p68 Jansson's Temptation
Energy 688kcal/2859kJ; Protein 15g; Carbohydrate 51g, of which sugars 1g; Fat 49g, of which saturates 29g; Cholesterol 134mg; Calcium 182mg; Fibre 4.6g; Sodium 1g.

p69 Crisp Fried Whitebait
Energy 591Kcal/2446kJ; Protein 22g; Carbohydrate 6g, of which sugars 0g; Fat 53g, of which saturates 0g; Cholesterol 0mg; Calcium 968mg; Fibre 0.2g; Sodium 300mg.

p70 Seared Tuna Niçoise
Energy 325Kcal/1358kJ; Protein 39g; Carbohydrate 0g, of which sugars 0g; Fat 18g, of which saturates 4g; Cholesterol 158mg; Calcium 42mg; Fibre 0g; Sodium 200mg.

p70 Creamy Parmesan-Baked Eggs
Energy 194Kcal/803kJ; Protein 11g; Carbohydrate 0g, of which sugars 0g; Fat 17g, of which saturates 8g; Cholesterol 280mg; Calcium 98mg; Fibre 0g; Sodium 200mg.

p72 Toasted Sourdough with Goat's Cheese Energy 414Kcal/1722kJ; Protein 13g; Carbohydrate 20g, of which sugars 2g; Fat 32g, of which saturates 11g; Cholesterol 44mg; Calcium 127mg; Fibre 0.7g; Sodium 600mg.

p73 Steak and Blue Cheese Sandwiches Energy 816Kcal/ 3418kJ; Protein 64g; Carbohydrate 52g, of which sugars 3g; Fat 41g, of which saturates 19g; Cholesterol 174mg; Calcium 434mg; Fibre 2.3g; Sodium 1.8g.

p74 Spicy Chorizo Sausage and Spring Onion Hash
Energy 442Kcal/1843kJ; Protein 23g; Carbohydrate 23g, of which sugars 6g; Fat 29g, of which saturates 11g; Cholesterol 41mg; Fibre 1.8g; Sodium 800mg.

p75 Baked Sweet Potatoes

with Leeks and Gorgonzola
Energy 352Kcal/1474kJ; Protein 10g; Carbohydrate 45g, of which sugars 24g; Fat 16g, of which saturates 7g; Cholesterol 26mg; Calcium 223mg; Fibre 7.2g; Sodium 700mg.

p78 Mussels in White Wine
Energy 300Kcal/1252kJ; Protein 17g; Carbohydrate 5g, of which sugars 1g; Fat 13g, of which saturates 7g; Cholesterol 87mg; Calcium 83mg; Fibre 0.4g; Sodium 600mg.

p79 Crab and Cucumber Wraps Energy 310Kcal/1312kJ; Protein 15g; Carbohydrate 59g, of which sugars 2g; Fat 3g, of which saturates 0g; Cholesterol 25mg; Calcium 117mg; Fibre 2.4g; Sodium 2.8g.

p80 Scallops with Fennel and Bacon
Energy 452Kcal/1870kJ; Protein 20g; Carbohydrate 4g, of which sugars 3g; Fat 40g, of which saturates 22g; Cholesterol 108mg; Calcium 114mg; Fibre 3.6g; Sodium 800mg.

p81 Prawn and New Potato Stew Energy 271Kcal/1147kJ; Protein 22g; Carbohydrate 35g, of which sugars 6g; Fat 6g, of which saturates 2g; Cholesterol 219mg; Calcium 113mg; Fibre 2.9g; Sodium 1.5g.

p82 Haddock with Fennel Butter Energy 220Kcal/921kJ; Protein 29g; Carbohydrate 1g, of which sugars 1g; Fat 11g, of which saturates 7g; Cholesterol 81mg; Calcium 123mg; Fibre 0.3g; Sodium 200mg.

p83 Baked Salmon with Caraway Seeds
Energy 665Kcal/2758kJ; Protein 51g; Carbohydrate 0g, of which sugars 0g; Fat 34g, of which saturates 20g; Cholesterol 186mg; Calcium 61mg; Fibre 0g; Sodium 300mg.

p84 Sea Bass in a Salt Crust
Energy 200Kcal/842kJ; Protein 39g; Carbohydrate 0g, of which sugars 0g; Fat 5g, of which saturates 1g; Cholesterol 160mg; Calcium 261mg; Fibre 0g; Sodium 2.2g.

p85 Roast Cod wrapped in Prosciutto Energy 342Kcal/1427kJ; Protein 38g; Carbohydrate 3g, of which sugars 3g; Fat 20g, of which saturates 4g; Cholesterol 98mg; Calcium 25mg; Fibre 1g; Sodium 400mg.

p86 Grilled Hake with Lemon and Chilli Energy 206Kcal/862kJ; Protein 27g; Carbohydrate 0g, of which sugars 0g; Fat 11g, of which saturates 2g; Cholesterol 35mg; Calcium 26mg; Fibre 0g; Sodium 300mg.

p87 Trout with grilled Serrano Ham Energy 236Kcal/980kJ; Protein 19g; Carbohydrate 0g, of which sugars 0g; Fat 18g, of which saturates 9g; Cholesterol 43mg; Calcium 7mg; Fibre 0g; Sodium 1.2g.

p88 Poached Fish in Spicy Tomato Sauce Energy 217Kcal/915kJ; Protein 36g; Carbohydrate 7g, of which sugars 3g; Fat 5g, of which saturates 2g; Cholesterol 94mg; Calcium 33mg; Fibre 1.1g; Sodium 400mg.

p89 Fish with Tomato and Pine Nuts Energy 308Kcal/1294kJ; Protein 42g; Carbohydrate 6g, of which sugars 3g; Fat 13g, of which saturates 2g; Cholesterol 80mg; Calcium 94mg; Fibre 1.0g; Sodium 400mg.

p90 Teriyaki Salmon Energy 618Kcal/2558kJ; Protein 31g; Carbohydrate 2g, of which sugars 2g; Fat 54g, of which saturates 7g; Cholesterol 75mg; Calcium 36mg; Fibre 0g; Sodium 1.4g.

p91 Roast Mackerel in Spicy Chermoula Paste Energy 591Kcal/2449kJ; Protein 39g; Carbohydrate 6g, of which sugars 4g; Fat 46g, of which saturates 9g; Cholesterol 108mg; Calcium 66mg; Fibre 1.1g; Sodium 200mg.

p92 Pan-fried Skate Wings Energy 160Kcal/671kJ; Protein 23g; Carbohydrate 0g, of which sugars 0g; Fat 7g, of which saturates 4g; Cholesterol 18mg; Calcium 64mg; Fibre 0.1g; Sodium 300mg.

p93 Sea Bass with Parsley and Lime Butter Energy 213Kcal/890kJ; Protein 29g; Carbohydrate 0g, of which sugars 0g; Fat 11g, of which saturates 5g; Cholesterol 138mg; Calcium 199mg; Fibre 0.1g; Sodium 200mg.

p96 Beef Patties with Onions and Peppers Energy 339Kcal/1416 kJ; Protein 30g; Carbohydrate 15g, of which sugars 11g; Fat 18g, of which saturates 6g; Cholesterol 70mg; Calcium 60mg; Fibre 4.0g; Sodium 100mg.

p97 Steak with Warm Tomato Salsa Energy 175Kcal/736kJ; Protein 25g; Carbohydrate 3g, of which sugars 7g; Fat 3g, of which saturates 69g; Cholesterol 69mg; Calcium 18mg; Fibre 0.9g; Sodium 100mg.

p98 Meatballs in Tomato Sauce Energy 309Kcal/1290kJ; Protein 22g; Carbohydrate 12g, of which sugars 7g; Fat 20g, of which saturates 8g; Cholesterol 70mg; Calcium 89mg; Fibre 2.0g; Sodium 800mg.

p99 Beef Cooked in Red Wine Energy 244Kcal/1021kJ; Protein 24g; Carbohydrate 1g, of which sugars 0g; Fat 7g, of which saturates 3g; Cholesterol 69mg; Calcium 14mg; Fibre 0.1g; Sodium 100mg.

p100 Pan-fried Gaelic steaks Energy 738Kcal/3062kJ; Protein 54.1g; Carbohydrate 1.3g, of which sugars 1.3g; Fat 54.2g, of which saturates 31.6g; Cholesterol 226mg; Calcium 49mg; Fibre 0g; Sodium 200mg.

p101 Thai-style Rare Beef and Mango Salad Energy 316Kcal/1330kJ; Protein 28g; Carbohydrate 22g, of which sugars 22g; Fat 14g, of which saturates 4g; Cholesterol 57mg; Calcium 26mg; Fibre 3.9g; Sodium 900mg.

p102 North African Lamb Energy 412Kcal/1716 kJ; Protein 34g; Carbohydrate 16g, of which sugars 14g; Fat 24g, of which saturates 11g; Cholesterol 127mg; Calcium 36mg; Fibre 2.7g; Sodium 200mg.

p103 Lamb Steaks with Redcurrant Glaze Energy 301Kcal/1258kJ; Protein 24g; Carbohydrate 12g, of which sugars 12g; Fat 17g, of which saturates 8g; Cholesterol 94mg; Calcium 10mg; Fibre 0.0g; Sodium 100mg.

p104 Lamb Chops with a Mint Jelly Crust Energy 201Kcal/845kJ; Protein 22g; Carbohydrate 11g, of which sugars 2g; Fat 8g, of which saturates 3g; Cholesterol 67mg; Calcium 41mg; Fibre 0.3g; Sodium 300mg.

p105 Marinated Lamb with Oregano and Basil Energy 251Kcal/1042kJ; Protein 21g; Carbohydrate 0g,

of which sugars 0g; Fat 19g, of which saturates 5g; Cholesterol 67mg; Calcium 29mg; Fibre 0g; Sodium 1.2g.

p106 Roast Shoulder of Lamb with Whole Garlic Cloves Energy 296Kcal/1244kJ; Protein 28g; Carbohydrate 19g, of which sugars 2g; Fat 13g, of which saturates 6g; Cholesterol 90mg; Calcium 16mg; Fibre 1.4g; Sodium 100mg.

p107 Roast Leg of Lamb with Rosemary and Garlic Energy 223Kcal/931kJ; Protein 28g; Carbohydrate 0g, of which sugars 0g; Fat 12g, of which saturates 4g; Cholesterol 99mg; Calcium 9mg; Fibre 0g; Sodium 100mg.

p108 Sweet-and-sour Lamb Energy 237Kcal/988kJ; Protein 20g; Carbohydrate 8g, of which sugars 8g; Fat 13g, of which saturates 4g; Cholesterol 74mg; Calcium 13mg; Fibre 0g; Sodium 200mg.

p109 Roast Lamb with Figs Energy 446Kcal/1859kJ; Protein 33g; Carbohydrate 11g, of which sugars 11g; Fat 27g, of which saturates 11g; Cholesterol 125mg; Calcium 39mg; Fibre 1.2g; Sodium 200mg.

p110 Paprika Pork Energy 249Kcal/1049kJ; Protein 31g; Carbohydrate 15g, of which sugars 8g; Fat 8g, of which saturates 2g; Cholesterol 88mg; Calcium 44mg; Fibre 3.0g; Sodium 200mg.

p111 Pork Kebabs Energy 218Kcal/916kJ; Protein 28g; Carbohydrate 8g, of which sugars 8g; Fat 8g, of which saturates 3g; Cholesterol 79mg; Calcium 22mg; Fibre 0.5g; Sodium 400mg.

p112 Fragrant Lemon Grass and Ginger Pork Patties Energy 187Kcal/782kJ; Protein 24g; Carbohydrate 0g, of which sugars 0g; Fat 10g, of which saturates 2g; Cholesterol 71mg; Calcium 8mg; Fibre 0g; Sodium 200mg.

p113 Pan-fried Gammon with Cider Energy 448Kcal/1860kJ; Protein 40g; Carbohydrate 1g, of which sugars 1g; Fat 30g, of which saturates 11g; Cholesterol 72mg; Calcium 26mg; Fibre 0g; Sodium 2.1g.

p114 Caramelized Onion and Sausage Tarte Tatin Energy 569Kcal/2368kJ; Protein 16g; Carbohydrate 37g, of which sugars 6g; Fat 41g, of which saturates 7g; Cholesterol 42mg; Calcium 143mg; Fibre 1.6g; Sodium 1.2g.

p115 Roast Pork with Juniper Berries and Bay Energy 238Kcal/1003kJ; Protein 42g; Carbohydrate 0g,

of which sugars 0g; Fat 8g, of which saturates 2g; Cholesterol 126mg; Calcium 11mg; Fibre 0g; Sodium 200mg.

p116 Sticky Glazed Pork Ribs Energy 622Kcal/2605kJ; Protein 64g; Carbohydrate 16g, of which sugars 14g; Fat 34g, of which saturates 12g; Cholesterol 218mg; Calcium 78mg; Fibre 0g; Sodium 200mg.

p116 Chinese Spiced Pork Chops Energy 231Kcal/961kJ; Protein 27g; Carbohydrate 1g, of which sugars 0g; Fat 13g, of which saturates 4g; Cholesterol 76mg; Calcium 31mg; Fibre 0g; Sodium 500mg.

p120 Pot-roasted Chicken with Preserved Lemons Energy 280Kcal/1180kJ; Protein 36g; Carbohydrate 19g, of which sugars 1g; Fat 7g, of which saturates 1g; Cholesterol 135mg; Calcium 15mg; Fibre 1.5g; Sodium 200mg.

p121 Honey Mustard Chicken Energy 244Kcal/1028kJ; Protein 27g; Carbohydrate 12g, of which sugars 12g; Fat 10g, of which saturates 2g; Cholesterol 130mg; Calcium 33mg; Fibre 0.7g; Sodium 400mg.

p122 Drunken Chicken Energy 343Kcal/1437kJ; Protein 39g; Carbohydrate 1g, of which sugars 1g; Fat 11g, of which saturates 3g; Cholesterol 158mg; Calcium 38mg; Fibre 0.1g; Sodium 100mg.

p123 Soy-marinated Chicken Energy 67Kcal/703kJ; Protein 34g; Carbohydrate 4g, of which sugars 3g; Fat 2g, of which saturates 0g; Cholesterol 88mg; Calcium 36mg; Fibre 1.7g; Sodium 500mg.

p124 Stir-fried Chicken with Thai Basil Energy 209Kcal/878kJ; Protein 31g; Carbohydrate 5g, of which sugars 5g; Fat 7g, of which saturates 1g; Cholesterol 88mg; Calcium 22mg; Fibre 1.3g; Sodium 200mg.

p124 Crème Fraîche and Coriander Chicken Energy 164Kcal/682kJ; Protein 16g; Carbohydrate 0g, of which sugars 0g; Fat 11g, of which saturates 5g; Cholesterol 96mg; Calcium 18mg; Fibre 0g;

Sodium 200mg.

p126 Chicken Escalopes with Lemon and Serrano Ham Energy 253Kcal/1058kJ; Protein 36g; Carbohydrate 0g, of which sugars 0g; Fat 12g, of which saturates 6g; Cholesterol 109mg; Calcium 9mg; Fibre 0g; Sodium 500mg.

p127 Roast Chicken with Herb Cheese, Chilli and Lime Stuffing Energy 220Kcal/921kJ; Protein 29g; Carbohydrate 0g, of which sugars 0g; Fat 12g, of which saturates 6g; Cholesterol 131mg; Calcium 27mg; Fibre 0g; Sodium 200mg.

p128 Tandoori Chicken Energy 592Kcal/2479kJ; Protein 44g; Carbohydrate 77.5g, of which sugars 4.5g; Fat 11.4g, of which saturates 1.1g; Cholesterol 105mg; Calcium 54g; Fibre 0.4g; Sodium 826mg.

p129 Roast Chicken with Black Pudding and Sage Energy 297Kcal/1246kJ; Protein 36g; Carbohydrate 5g, of which sugars 0g; Fat 15g, of which saturates 7g; Cholesterol 161mg; Calcium 87mg; Fibre 0g; Sodium 500mg.

p130 Spatchcock Poussins with Herb Butter Energy 810Kcal/3364kJ; Protein 51g; Carbohydrate 1g, of which sugars 0g; Fat 67g, of which saturates 29g; Cholesterol 341mg; Calcium 38mg; Fibre 0.3g; Sodium 400mg.

p131 Chilli-spiced Poussin Energy 337Kcal/1403kJ; Protein 25g; Carbohydrate 0g, of which sugars 0g; Fat 27g, of which saturates 6g; Cholesterol 131mg; Calcium 28mg; Fibre 0g; Sodium 200mg.

p132 Turkey Patties Energy 155Kcal/651kJ; Protein 26g; Carbohydrate 1g, of which sugars 1g; Fat 5g, of which saturates 1g; Cholesterol 79mg; Calcium 11mg; Fibre 0.1g; Sodium 100mg.

p133 Guinea Fowl with Whisky Sauce Energy 449Kcal/1866kJ; Protein 34g; Carbohydrate 1g, of which sugars 1g; Fat 29g, of which saturates 13g; Cholesterol 51mg; Calcium 56mg; Fibre 0g; Sodium 200mg.

p134 Pheasant Cooked in Port with Mushrooms Energy 457Kcal/1902kJ; Protein 31g; Carbohydrate 9g, of which sugars 9g; Fat 24g, of which saturates 11g; Cholesterol 263mg; Calcium 46mg; Fibre 0.8g; Sodium 200mg.

p135 Roast Pheasant with Sherry and Mustard Sauce Energy 393Kcal/1632kJ; Protein 30g; Carbohydrate 3g, of which sugars 3g; Fat 23g, of which saturates 11g; Cholesterol 263mg; Calcium 39mg; Fibre 0g; Sodium 400mg.

p136 Marmalade and Soy Roast Duck Energy 273Kcal/1144kJ; Protein 32g; Carbohydrate 8g, of which sugars 7g; Fat 13g, of which saturates 4g; Cholesterol 144mg; Calcium 20mg; Fibre 0g; Sodium 700mg.

p137 Duck with Plum Sauce Energy 334Kcal/1405kJ; Protein 33g; Carbohydrate 22g, of which sugars 21g; Fat 13g, of which saturates 4g; Cholesterol 144mg; Calcium 48mg; Fibre 2.8g; Sodium 100mg.

p140 Minty Courgette Linguine Energy 580Kcal/2442kJ; Protein 15g; Carbohydrate 87g, of which sugars 4g; Fat 21g, of which saturates 3g; Cholesterol 0mg; Calcium 61mg; Fibre 4.4g; Sodium 100mg.

p141 Pasta with Roast Tomatoes and Goat's Cheese Energy 749Kcal/3156kJ; Protein 28g; Carbohydrate 95g, of which sugars 12g; Fat 31g, of which saturates 13g; Cholesterol 49mg; Calcium 419mg; Fibre 6.5g; Sodium 500mg.

p142 Linguine with Anchovies and Capers Energy 527Kcal/2228kJ; Protein 15g; Carbohydrate 85g, of which sugars 3g; Fat 16g, of which saturates 2g; Cholesterol 4mg; Calcium 48mg; Fibre 3.5g; Sodium 300mg.

p142 Home-made Potato Gnocchi Energy 683Kcal/2892kJ; Protein 24g; Carbohydrate 136g, of which sugars 4g; Fat 8g, of which saturates 2g; Cholesterol 232mg; Calcium 164mg; Fibre 8.2g; Sodium 2.1g.

p144 Spaghettini with Roasted Garlic Energy 637Kcal/2670kJ; Protein 14g; Carbohydrate 77g, of which sugars 4g; Fat 33g, of which saturates 5g; Cholesterol 2mg; Calcium 53mg; Fibre 3.1g; Sodium 100mg.

p145 Spaghetti with Lemon Energy 450Kcal/1895kJ; Protein 11g; Carbohydrate 65g,

of which sugars 3g; Fat 18g, of which saturates 3g; Cholesterol 0mg; Calcium 23mg; Fibre 2.6g; Sodium 100mg.

p146 Fettuccine all'Alfredo Energy 697Kcal/2917kJ; Protein 16g; Carbohydrate 67g, of which sugars 3g; Fat 42g, of which saturates 26g; Cholesterol 107mg; Calcium 172mg; Fibre 2.7g; Sodium 200mg.

p147 Pansotti with Walnut Sauce Energy 550Kcal/2282kJ; Protein 11g; Carbohydrate 24g, of which sugars 2g; Fat 47g, of which saturates 13g; Cholesterol 41mg; Calcium 136mg; Fibre 1.9g; Sodium 200mg.

p148 Fettuccine with Butter and Parmesan Energy 560Kcal/2362kJ; Protein 22g; Carbohydrate 76g, of which sugars 3g; Fat 21g, of which saturates 12g; Cholesterol 53mg; Calcium 322mg; Fibre 3.1g; Sodium 300mg.

p149 Penne with Cream and Smoked Salmon Energy 475Kcal/2005kJ; Protein 18g; Carbohydrate 67g, of which sugars 3g; Fat 17g, of which saturates 9g; Cholesterol 48mg; Calcium 64mg; Fibre 2.7g; Sodium 200mg.

p150 Oven-baked Porcini Risotto Energy 288Kcal/1218kJ; Protein 6g; Carbohydrate 52g, of which sugars 2g; Fat 8g, of which saturates 1g; Cholesterol 0mg; Calcium 43mg; Fibre 1.6g; Sodium 100mg.

p151 Persian Baked Rice Energy 573Kcal/2389kJ; Protein 11g; Carbohydrate 91g, of which sugars 1g; Fat 18g, of which saturates 7g; Cholesterol 27mg; Calcium 54mg; Fibre 0.9g; Sodium 200mg.

p152 Rosemary Risotto with Borlotti Beans Energy 362Kcal/1517 kJ; Protein 11g; Carbohydrate 38g, of which sugars 4g; Fat 20g, of which saturates 8g; Cholesterol 19mg; Calcium 80mg; Fibre 65g; Sodium 900mg.

p153 Pancetta and Broad Bean Risotto Energy 526Kcal/2211kJ; Protein 18g; Carbohydrate 72g, of which sugars 4g; Fat 21g, of which saturates 6g; Cholesterol 29mg; Calcium 81mg; Fibre 3.4g; Sodium 2.4g.

p154 Mussel Risotto Energy 348Kcal/459kJ; Protein 15g; Carbohydrate 31g, of which sugars 4g; Fat 19g, of which saturates 7g; Cholesterol 351mg; Calcium 83mg; Fibre 6.5g; Sodium 700mg.

p155 Crab Risotto

Energy 345Kcal/1458kJ; Protein 20g; Carbohydrate 54g, of which sugars 0g; Fat 7g, of which saturates 1g; Cholesterol 54mg; Calcium 35mg; Fibre 0.3g; Sodium 900mg.

p138 Coconut Rice Energy 472Kcal/2009kJ; Protein 8g; Carbohydrate 114g, of which sugars 16g; Fat 1g, of which saturates 0g; Cholesterol 0mg; Calcium 40mg; Fibre 0.6g; Sodium 400mg.

p157 Savoury Ground Rice Energy 333Kcal/1392kJ; Protein 7g; Carbohydrate 59g, of which sugars 4g; Fat 7g, of which saturates 4g; Cholesterol 18mg; Calcium 111mg; Fibre 1.5g; Sodium 100mg.

p160 Aubergines with Cheese Sauce Energy 509Kcal/2111kJ; Protein 22g; Carbohydrate 13g, of which sugars 7g; Fat 41g, of which saturates 19g; Cholesterol 80mg; Calcium 640mg; Fibre 2.2g; Sodium 900mg.

p161 Mushroom Stroganoff Energy 318Kcal/1316kJ; Protein 10g; Carbohydrate 13g, of which sugars 7g; Fat 26g, of which saturates 13g; Cholesterol 56mg; Calcium 194mg; Fibre 2.7g; Sodium 400mg.

p162 Red Onion and Goat's Cheese Pastries Energy 554Kcal/2308kJ; Protein 13g; Carbohydrate 48g, of which sugars 8g; Fat 36g, of which saturates 6g; Cholesterol 27mg; Calcium 128mg; Fibre 1.6g; Sodium 500mg.

p163 Baked Leek and Potato Gratin Energy 574Kcal/2394kJ; Protein 20g; Carbohydrate 43g, of which sugars 5g; Fat 37g, of which saturates 23g; Cholesterol 108mg; Calcium 257mg; Fibre 4.6g; Sodium 300mg.

p164 Mushroom Polenta Energy 518Kcal/2155kJ; Protein 19g; Carbohydrate 46g, of which sugars 0g; Fat 26g, of which saturates 16g; Cholesterol 69mg; Calcium 333mg; Fibre 2.5g; Sodium 400mg.

p165 Tomato and Tapenade Tarts Energy 603Kcal/2512kJ; Protein 9g; Carbohydrate 50g, of which sugars 5g; Fat 43g, of which saturates 7g; Cholesterol

21mg; Calcium 117mg; Fibre 1.7g; Sodium 800mg.

p166 Stuffed Baby Squash Energy 469Kcal/1951kJ; Protein 14g; Carbohydrate 48g, of which saturates 10g; Cholesterol 36mg; Calcium 316mg; Fibre 2g; Sodium 300mg.

p167 Roasted Peppers with Halloumi and Pine Nuts Energy 361Kcal/1504kJ; Protein 18g; Carbohydrate 16g, of which sugars 16g; Fat 26g, of which saturates 12g; Cholesterol 58mg; Calcium 105mg; Fibre 4.3g; Sodium 400mg.

p168 Spicy Chickpea Samosas Energy 580Kcal/2437kJ; Protein 20g; Carbohydrate 72g, of which sugars 12g; Fat 24g, of which saturates 6g; Cholesterol 17mg; Calcium 91mg; Fibre 8.3g; Sodium 500mg.

p169 Tofu and Pepper Kebabs Energy 177Kcal/738kJ; Protein 10g; Carbohydrate 13g, of which sugars 12g; Fat 10g, of which saturates 2g; Cholesterol 0mg; Calcium 342mg; Fibre 3.6g; Sodium 800mg.

p170 Mixed Bean and Tomato Chilli Energy 216Kcal/911kJ; Protein 12g; Carbohydrate 30g, of which sugars 6g; Fat 6g, of which saturates 2g; Cholesterol 10mg; Calcium 47mg; Fibre 8.9g; Sodium 1g.

p171 Cheese and Tomato Soufflès Energy 317Kcal/ 1319kJ; Protein 19g; Carbohydrate 6g, of which sugars 3g; Fat 25g, of which saturates 10g; Cholesterol 203mg; Calcium 395mg; Fibre 0.1g; Sodium 600mg.

p172 Classic Margherita Pizza Energy 552Kcal/2317kJ; Protein 22g; Carbohydrate 59g, of which sugars 4g; Fat 27g, of which saturates 12g; Cholesterol 46mg; Calcium 362mg; Fibre 2.4g; Sodium 800mg.

p173 Cheesy Leek and Couscous Cake Energy 474Kcal/1973kJ; Protein 19g; Carbohydrate 41g, of which sugars 2g; Fat 27g, of which

saturates 12g; Cholesterol 49mg; Calcium 408mg; Fibre 2.2g; Sodium 500mg.

p174 Potato and Onion Tortilla Energy 512Kcal/2132kJ; Protein 15g; Carbohydrate 40g, of which sugars 5g; Fat 34g, of which saturates 6g; Cholesterol 285mg; Calcium 73mg; Fibre 3.7g; Sodium 100mg.

p175 Spiced Lentils Energy 326Kcal/1372kJ; Protein 24g; Carbohydrate 34g, of which sugars 4g; Fat 11g, of which saturates 7g; Cholesterol 35mg; Calcium 235mg; Fibre 6.2g, Sodium 800mg.

p176 Roast Acorn Squash with Spinach and Gorgonzola Energy 317Kcal/ 1312kJ; Protein 12g; Carbohydrate 10g, of which sugars 2g; Fat 25g, of which saturates 12g; Cholesterol 45mg; Calcium 404mg; Fibre 3.6g; Sodium 1g.

p177 Creamy Red Lentil Dhal Energy 156Kcal/658kJ; Protein 9g; Carbohydrate 21g, of which sugars 1g; Fat 4g, of which saturates 0g; Cholesterol 0mg; Calcium 27mg; Fibre 1.8g; Sodium 200mg.

p178 Wild Mushroom and Fontina Tart Energy 508Kcal/2110kJ; Protein 14g; Carbohydrate 25g, of which sugars 1g; Fat 40g, of which saturates 15g; Cholesterol 63mg; Calcium 309mg; Fibre 2.0g; Sodium 500mg.

p179 Parmigiana di Melanzane Energy 218Kcal/ 904kJ; Protein 7g; Carbohydrate 5g, of which sugars 4g; Fat 19g, of which saturates 5g; Cholesterol 13mg; Calcium 168mg; Fibre 2.8g; Sodium 200mg.

p182 Japanese-style Spinach with Toasted Sesame Seeds Energy 51Kcal/210kJ; Protein 4g; Carbohydrate 2g, of which sugars 2g; Fat 3g, of which saturates 0g; Cholesterol 0mg; Calcium 213mg; Fibre 2.6g; Sodium 600mg.

p183 Braised Lettuce and Peas with Spring Onions Energy 206Kcal/851kJ; Protein 8g; Carbohydrate 17g, of which sugars 8g; Fat 12g, of which saturates 7g; Cholesterol 27mg; Calcium 109mg; Fibre 6.5g; Sodium 100mg.

p184 Asparagus with Lemon Sauce Energy 84Kcal/349kJ; Protein 6g; Carbohydrate 7g, of which sugars 4g; Fat 3g, of which saturates 1g; Cholesterol 90mg; Calcium 58mg; Fibre 2.9g; Sodium 100mg.

p185 Caramelized Shallots Energy 109Kcal/450kJ; Protein

1g; Carbohydrate 10g, of which sugars 8g; Fat 7g, of which saturates 4g; Cholesterol 18mg; Calcium 23mg; Fibre 1.2g; Sodium 100mg.

p186 Green Beans with Almond Butter and Lemon Energy 192Kcal/790kJ; Protein 4g; Carbohydrate 4g, of which sugars 3g; Fat 18g, of which saturates 7g; Cholesterol 27mg; Calcium 65mg; Fibre 2.9g; Sodium 200mg.

p186 Garlicky Green Salad with Raspberry Dressing Energy 83Kcal/344kJ; Protein 1g; Carbohydrate 1g, of which sugars 1g; Fat 9g, of which saturates 1g; Cholesterol 0mg; Calcium 14mg; Fibre 0.5g; Sodium 100mg.

p188 Cauliflower with Garlic Crumbs Energy 289Kcal/1201kJ; Protein 8g; Carbohydrate 18g, of which sugars 4g; Fat 21g, of which saturates 3g; Cholesterol 0mg; Calcium 61mg; Fibre 4.0g; Sodium 200mg.

p189 Summer Squash and Baby New Potatoes in Warm Dill Sour Cream Energy 261Kcal/1093kJ; Protein 5g; Carbohydrate 27g, of which sugars 9g; Fat 15g, of which saturates 9g; Cholesterol 45mg; Calcium 129mg; Fibre 2.7g; Sodium 100mg.

p190 Roast Asparagus with Crispy Prosciutto Energy 141Kcal/582kJ; Protein 7g; Carbohydrate 2g, of which sugars 2g; Fat 11g, of which saturates 3g; Cholesterol 18mg; Calcium 38mg; Fibre 1.5g; Sodium 400mg.

p191 Garlicky Roasties Energy 324Kcal/1356kJ; Protein 6g; Carbohydrate 45g, of which sugars 2g; Fat 14g, of which saturates 2g; Cholesterol 0mg; Calcium 15mg; Fibre 3.9g; Sodium 100mg.

p192 Leek Fritters Energy 331Kcal/1380kJ; Protein 11g; Carbohydrate 34g, of which sugars 6g; Fat 17g, of which saturates 3g; Cholesterol 116mg; Calcium 84mg; Fibre 5.5g; Sodium 100mg.

p193 Deep-fried Artichokes Energy 111Kcal/459kJ; Protein 2g; Carbohydrate 2g, of which sugars 1g; Fat 11g, of which saturates 2g; Cholesterol 0mg; Calcium 24mg; Fibre 0g; Sodium 100mg.

p194 Stir-fried Broccoli with Soy Sauce and Sesame Seeds Energy 130Kcal/538kJ; Protein 6g; Carbohydrate 4g, of which sugars 2g; Fat 10g, of which saturates 2g; Cholesterol 0mg; Calcium 267mg; Fibre 4.4g; Sodium 600mg.

p195 Stir-fried Brussels

Sprouts with Bacon and Caraway Seeds Energy 130Kcal/542kJ; Protein 7g; Carbohydrate 5g, of which sugars 3g; Fat 10g, of which saturates 2g; Cholesterol 9mg; Calcium 40mg; Fibre 4.6g; Sodium 300mg.

p196 Bocconcini with Fennel and Basil Energy 243Kcal/1008kJ; Protein 14g; Carbohydrate 0g, of which sugars 0g; Fat 21g, of which saturates 11g; Cholesterol 44mg; Calcium 282mg; Fibre 0g; Sodium 400mg.

p197 Noodles with Sesame-roasted Spring Onions Energy 268Kcal/1121kJ; Protein 3g; Carbohydrate 50g, of which sugars 3g; Fat 3g, of which saturates 1g; Cholesterol 0mg; Calcium 51mg; Fibre 0.5g; Sodium 400mg.

p198 Spicy Potato Wedges Energy 205Kcal/860kJ; Protein 4g; Carbohydrate 30g, of which sugars 1g; Fat 9g, of which saturates 1g; Cholesterol 0mg; Calcium 16mg; Fibre 2.2g; Sodium 100mg.

p198 Crisp and Golden Roast Potatoes with Goose Fat and Garlic Energy 202Kcal/848kJ; Protein 4g; Carbohydrate 30g, of which sugars 1g; Fat 1g, of which saturates 0.8g; Cholesterol 7mg; Calcium 10mg; Fibre 2.6g; Sodium 100mg.

p200 Tomato and Aubergine Gratin Energy 229Kcal/952kJ; Protein 6g; Carbohydrate 6g, of which sugars 6g; Fat 20g, of which saturates 5g; Cholesterol 9mg; Calcium 125mg; Fibre 40g; Sodium 100mg.

p201 Bubble and Squeak Energy 205Kcal/854kJ; Protein 3g; Carbohydrate 23g, of which sugars 4g; Fat 12g, of which saturates 1g; Cholesterol 0mg; Calcium 30mg; Fibre 2.8g; Sodium 100mg.

p202 Cheesy Creamy Leeks Energy 333Kcal/1376kJ; Protein 9g; Carbohydrate 6g, of which sugars 5g; Fat 30g, of which saturates 17g; Cholesterol 70mg; Calcium 205mg; Fibre 4.4g; Sodium 200mg.

p203 Creamy Polenta with

Dolcelatte Energy 271Kcal/1130kJ; Protein 11g; Carbohydrate 21g, of which sugars 7g; Fat 16g, of which saturates 6g; Cholesterol 23mg; Calcium 274mg; Fibre 0.4g; Sodium 400mg.

p204 Fennel, Potato and Garlic Mash
Energy 374Kcal/1560kJ; Protein 7g; Carbohydrate 38g, of which sugars 7g; Fat 23g, of which saturates 6g; Cholesterol 17mg; Calcium 73mg; Fibre 6.2g; Sodium 100mg.

p205 Champ
Energy 445Kcal/1858kJ; Protein 8g; Carbohydrate 49g, of which sugars 7g; Fat 25g, of which saturates 16g; Cholesterol 66mg; Calcium 143mg; Fibre 3.7g; Sodium 200mg.

p208 Sour Cucumber with Fresh Dill
Energy 18Kcal/75kJ; Protein 1g; Carbohydrate 2g, of which sugars 2g; Fat 0g, of which saturates 0g; Cholesterol 0mg; Calcium 50mg; Fibre 0.9g; Sodium 100mg.

p209 Beetroot with Fresh Mint Energy 75Kcal/314kJ; Protein 2g; Carbohydrate 10g, of which sugars 9g; Fat 3g, of which saturates 0g; Cholesterol 0mg; Calcium 41mg; Fibre 2.4g; Sodium 100mg.

p210 Globe Artichokes with Green Beans and Garlic Dressing Energy 371kcal/1528kJ; Protein 4g; Carbohydrate 5g, of which sugars 3g; Fat 38g, of which saturates 6g; Cholesterol 0mg; Calcium 60mg; Fibre 1.2g; Sodium 100mg.

p211 Halloumi and Grape Salad Energy 274Kcal/1139kJ; Protein 10g; Carbohydrate 9g, of which sugars 9g; Fat 22g, of which saturates 10g; Cholesterol 14mg; Calcium 241mg; Fibre 0.6g; Sodium 1g.

p212 Watermelon and Feta Salad Energy 211Kcal/884kJ; Protein 8g; Carbohydrate 16g, of which sugars 15g; Fat 13g, of which saturates 5g; Cholesterol 23mg; Calcium 145mg; Fibre 1.1g; Sodium 700mg.

p213 Tomato, Bean and Fried Basil Salad
Energy 201Kcal/837kJ; Protein 6g; Carbohydrate 13g, of which sugars 3g; Fat 14g, of which saturates 2g; Cholesterol 0mg; Calcium 30mg; Fibre 4.5g; Sodium 400mg.

p214 Moroccan Date, Orange and Carrot Salad
Energy 147Kcal/619kJ; Protein 4g; Carbohydrate 26g, of which sugars 25g; Fat 4g, of which saturates 0g; Cholesterol 0mg; Calcium 98mg; Fibre 4.9g; Sodium 100mg.

p215 Pink Grapefruit and Avocado Salad
Energy 216Kcal/892kJ; Protein 2g; Carbohydrate 8g, of which sugars 7g; Fat 20g, of which saturates 3g; Cholesterol 6mg; Calcium 34mg; Fibre 3.8g; Sodium 100mg.

p217 Turnip Salad
Energy 107Kcal/443kJ; Protein 2g; Carbohydrate 8g, of which sugars 7g; Fat 8g, of which saturates 5g; Cholesterol 23mg; Calcium 82mg; Fibre 2.4g; Sodium 100mg.

p218 Moroccan Carrot Salad
Energy 85Kcal/350kJ; Protein 0g; Carbohydrate 4g, of which sugars 4g; Fat 8g, of which saturates 1g; Cholesterol 0mg; Calcium 18mg; Fibre 1.3g; Sodium 100mg.

p218 Warm Chorizo and Spinach Salad
Energy 273Kcal/1127kJ; Protein 8g; Carbohydrate 2g, of which sugars 2g; Fat 26g, of which saturates 8g; Cholesterol 0mg; Calcium 96mg; Fibre 1.2g; Sodium 300mg.

p219 Potato and Olive Salad
Energy 296Kcal/1246kJ; Protein 5g; Carbohydrate 48g, of which sugars 4g; Fat 11g, of which saturates 2g; Cholesterol 0mg; Calcium 40mg; Fibre 3.3g; Sodium 300mg.

p220 Asparagus, Bacon and Leaf Salad
Energy 239Kcal/989kJ; Protein 13g; Carbohydrate 5g, of which sugars 5g; Fat 19g, of which saturates 4g; Cholesterol 19mg; Calcium 54mg; Fibre 2.7g; Sodium 800mg.

p221 Anchovy and Roasted Pepper Salad
Energy 86Kcal/366kJ; Protein 6g; Carbohydrate 12g, of which sugars 11g; Fat 2g, of which saturates 0g; Cholesterol 8mg; Calcium 57mg; Fibre 4.0g; Sodium 500mg.

p224 Plum and Almond Tart
Energy 491Kcal/2061kJ; Protein 7g; Carbohydrate 61g, of which sugars 28g; Fat 27g, of which saturates 0g; Cholesterol 0mg; Calcium 84mg; Fibre 1.9g; Sodium 300mg.

p225 Baked Apples with Marsala Energy 215Kcal/901kJ; Protein 1g; Carbohydrate 22g, of which sugars 22g; Fat 11g, of which saturates 7g; Cholesterol 27mg; Calcium 40mg; Fibre 3.3g; Sodium 100mg.

p226 Grilled Peaches with Meringues Energy 123Kcal/526kJ; Protein 2g; Carbohydrate 31g, of which sugars 31g; Fat 0g, of which saturates 0g; Cholesterol 0mg; Calcium 24mg; Fibre 2.3g; Sodium 100mg.

p227 Summer Berries in Sabayon Glaze
Energy 217Kcal/914kJ; Protein 4g; Carbohydrate 29g, of which sugars 29g; Fat 6g, of which saturates 2g; Cholesterol 202mg; Calcium 72mg; Fibre 3.4g; Sodium 100mg.

p228 Baked Ricotta Cakes with Red Sauce
Energy 176Kcal/741kJ; Protein 8g; Carbohydrate 21g, of which sugars 21g; Fat 7g, of which saturates 4g; Cholesterol 31mg; Calcium 173mg; Fibre 1.4g; Sodium 100mg.

p229 Apricot and Ginger Gratin Energy 414Kcal/1731kJ; Protein 4g; Carbohydrate 44g, of which sugars 35g; Fat 26g, of which saturates 16g; Cholesterol 48mg; Calcium 94mg; Fibre 2.4g; Sodium 200mg.

p230 Deep-fried Cherries
Energy 146Kcal/612kJ; Protein 4g; Carbohydrate 18g, of which sugars 10g; Fat 7g, of which saturates 2g; Cholesterol 61mg; Calcium 65mg; Fibre 1.0g; Sodium 100mg.

p231 Hot Blackberry and Apple Soufflé
Energy 128Kcal/543kJ; Protein 2g; Carbohydrate 31g, of which sugars 31g; Fat 0g, of which saturates 0g; Cholesterol 0mg; Calcium 28mg; Fibre 2.2g; Sodium 100mg.

p232 Caramelized Upside-down Pear Pie
Energy 322Kcal/1347kJ; Protein 1g; Carbohydrate 37g, of which sugars 25g; Fat 20g, of which saturates 7g; Cholesterol 31mg; Calcium 18mg; Fibre 0.8g; Sodium 100mg.

p234 Blueberry and Almond Tart Energy 316Kcal/1324kJ; Protein 6g; Carbohydrate 41g, of which sugars 23g; Fat 16g, of which saturates 0g; Cholesterol 0mg; Calcium 41mg; Fibre 1.5g; Sodium 100mg.

p235 Baked Bananas with Ice Cream and Toffee Sauce Energy 368Kcal/1545kJ; Protein 4g; Carbohydrate 55g, of which sugars 52g; Fat 16g, of which saturates 10g; Cholesterol 40mg; Calcium 81mg; Fibre 1.1g; Sodium 400mg.

p236 Roast Peaches with Amaretto Energy 111Kcal/472kJ; Protein 2g; Carbohydrate 24g, of which sugars 24g; Fat 0g, of which saturates 0g; Cholesterol 0mg; Calcium 11mg; Fibre 2.3g; Sodium 100mg.

p237 Passion Fruit Soufflés
Energy 57Kcal/243kJ; Protein 4g; Carbohydrate 9g, of which sugars 6g; Fat 1g, of which saturates 1g; Cholesterol 4mg; Calcium 72mg; Fibre 0.4g; Sodium 100mg.

p238 Zabaglione Energy 131Kcal/548kJ; Protein 3g; Carbohydrate 14g, of which sugars 14g; Fat 5g, of which saturates 2g; Cholesterol 202mg; Calcium 26mg; Fibre 0.0g; Sodium 100mg.

p239 Grilled Pineapple and Rum Cream Energy 454Kcal/1869kJ; Protein 1g; Carbohydrate 4g, of which sugars 4g; Fat 45g, of which saturates 28g; Cholesterol 116mg; Calcium 43mg; Fibre 0.3g; Sodium 100mg.

p242 Oranges in Syrup
Energy 236Kcal/1001kJ; Protein 3g; Carbohydrate 48g, of which sugars 48g; Fat 5g, of which saturates 1g; Cholesterol 0mg; Calcium 82mg; Fibre 3.0g; Sodium 100mg.

p242 Fresh Fig Compote
Energy 156Kcal/667kJ; Protein 2g; Carbohydrate 38g, of which sugars 38g; Fat 0g, of which saturates 0g; Cholesterol 0mg; Calcium 67mg; Fibre 2.5g; Sodium 100mg.

p244 Pistachio and Rose Water Oranges
Energy 94Kcal/400kJ; Protein 3g; Carbohydrate 18g, of which sugars 18g; Fat 2g, of which saturates 0g; Cholesterol 0mg; Calcium 102mg; Fibre 3.7g; Sodium 100mg.

p245 Lychee and Elderflower Sorbet
Energy 249Kcal/1063kJ; Protein 1g; Carbohydrate 65g, of which sugars 65g; Fat 0g, of which saturates 0g; Cholesterol 0mg; Calcium 12mg; Fibre 0.9g; Sodium 100mg.

p246 Papayas in Jasmine Flower Syrup
Energy 251Kcal/1057kJ; Protein 1g; Carbohydrate 38g, of which sugars 38g; Fat 0g, of which saturates 0g; Cholesterol 0mg; Calcium 39mg; Fibre 5.5g; Sodium 100mg.

p247 Mango and Lime Fool
Energy 289Kcal/1204kJ; Protein 2g; Carbohydrate 21g, of which sugars 21g; Fat 22g, of which saturates 14g; Cholesterol 51mg; Calcium 62mg; Fibre 0.7g; Sodium 0mg.

p248 Tangy Raspberry and Lemon Tartlets
Energy 206Kcal/868kJ; Protein

4g; Carbohydrate 37g, of which sugars 20g; Fat 6g, of which saturates 2g; Cholesterol 5mg; Calcium 59mg; Fibre 1.5g; Sodium 200mg.

p249 Crispy Mango Stacks with Raspberry Coulis Energy 189Kcal/791kJ; Protein 3g; Carbohydrate 21g, of which sugars 13g; Fat 11g, of which saturates 7g; Cholesterol 27mg; Calcium 18mg; Fibre 3.0g; Sodium 100mg.

p250 Rhubarb and Ginger Trifles Energy 690Kcal/2852kJ; Protein 4g; Carbohydrate 26g, of which sugars 13g; Fat 34g, of which saturates 39g; Cholesterol 154mg; Calcium 99mg; Fibre 0.6g; Sodium 100mg.

p251 Strawberry Cream Shortbreads Energy 890Kcal/3673kJ; Protein 4g; Carbohydrate 22g, of which sugars 10g; Fat 88g, of which saturates 55g; Cholesterol 225mg; Calcium 105mg; Fibre 1.0g; Sodium 100mg.

p252 Blackberries in Port Energy 220Kcal/923kJ; Protein 1g; Carbohydrate 34g, of which sugars 34g; Fat 0g, of which saturates 0g; Cholesterol 0mg; Calcium 51mg; Fibre 3.5g; Sodium 100mg.

p252 Baby Summer Puddings Energy 212Kcal/904kJ; Protein 5g; Carbohydrate 48g, of which sugars 23g; Fat 1g, of which saturates 0g; Cholesterol 0mg; Calcium 72mg; Fibre 1.9g; Sodium 300mg.

p254 Raspberry Brûlée Energy 152Kcal/649kJ; Protein 3g; Carbohydrate 34g, of which sugars 30g; Fat 2g, of which saturates 1g; Cholesterol 6mg; Calcium 114mg; Fibre 0.7g; Sodium 100mg.

p255 Portuguese Custard Tarts Energy 90Kcal/379kJ; Protein 2g; Carbohydrate 11g, of which sugars 4g; Fat 5g, of which saturates 0g; Cholesterol 1mg; Calcium 31mg; Fibre 0.0g; Sodium 100mg.

p256 Chocolate Banana Fools Energy 265Kcal/1180kJ; Protein 5g; Carbohydrate 42g, of which sugars 37g; Fat 10g, of which saturates 6g; Cholesterol 8mg; Calcium 117mg; Fibre

1.3g; Sodium 100mg.

p256 Lemon Posset Energy 917Kcal/3801kJ; Protein 2g; Carbohydrate 49g, of which sugars 49g; Fat 81g, of which saturates 50g; Cholesterol 206mg; Calcium 79mg; Fibre 0g; Sodium 100mg.

p258 Chilled Chocolate and Espresso Mousse Energy 710Kcal/2974kJ; Protein 13g; Carbohydrate 71g, of which sugars 70g; Fat 43g, of which saturates 24g; Cholesterol 253mg; Calcium 74mg; Fibre 2.8g; Sodium 100mg.

p259 Meringue Pyramid with Chocolate Mascarpone Energy 216Kcal/907kJ; Protein 3g; Carbohydrate 28g, of which sugars 28g; Fat 11g, of which saturates 7g; Cholesterol 12mg; Calcium 20mg; Fibre 0.5g; Sodium 100mg.

p261 Classic Chocolate Roulade Energy 434Kcal/1815kJ; Protein 9g; Carbohydrate 43g, of which sugars 43g; Fat 26g, of which saturates 15g; Cholesterol 208mg; Calcium 72mg; Fibre 0.7g; Sodium 100mg.

p262 Cherry Chocolate Brownies Energy 522Kcal/2159kJ; Protein 3g; Carbohydrate 23g, of which sugars 12g; Fat 47g, of which saturates 27g; Cholesterol 128mg; Calcium 62mg; Fibre 0.5g; Sodium 100mg.

p262 Coffee Mascarpone Creams Energy 146Kcal/604kJ; Protein 1g; Carbohydrate 5g, of which sugars 5g; Fat 14g, of which saturates 9g; Cholesterol 27mg; Calcium 29mg; Fibre 0g; Sodium 100mg.

p266 Lemon Sorbet Energy 135Kcal/577kJ; Protein 1g; Carbohydrate 35g, of which sugars 35g; Fat 0g, of which saturates 0g; Cholesterol 0mg; Calcium 6mg; Fibre 0g; Sodium 100mg.

p267 Strawberry and Lavender Sorbet Energy 123Kcal/522kJ; Protein 1g; Carbohydrate 31g, of which sugars 31g; Fat 0g, of which saturates 0g; Cholesterol 0mg; Calcium 16mg; Fibre 0.9g; Sodium 100mg.

p268 Blackcurrant Sorbet Energy 124Kcal/529kJ; Protein 1g; Carbohydrate 32g, of which sugars 32g; Fat 0g, of which saturates 0g; Cholesterol 0mg; Calcium 53mg; Fibre 3g; Sodium 100mg.

p269 Damson Water Ice Energy 130Kcal/555kJ; Protein 0g; Carbohydrate 34g, of which sugars 34g; Fat 0g, of which saturates 0g; Cholesterol 0mg;

Calcium 23mg; Fibre 1.5g; Sodium 100mg.

p270 Peach and Cardamom Yogurt Ice Energy 155Kcal/659kJ; Protein 4g; Carbohydrate 33g, of which sugars 33g; Fat 2g, of which saturates 0g; Cholesterol 1mg; Calcium 126mg; Fibre 1.9g; Sodium 100mg.

p271 Summer Berry Frozen Yogurt Energy 74Kcal/311kJ; Protein 3g; Carbohydrate 10g, of which sugars 10g; Fat 3g, of which saturates 2g; Cholesterol 0mg; Calcium 61mg; Fibre 0.7g; Sodium 100mg.

p272 Raspberry Sherbet Energy 179Kcal/763kJ; Protein 8g; Carbohydrate 39g, of which sugars 39g; Fat 0g, of which saturates 0g; Cholesterol 1mg; Calcium 132mg; Fibre 2.3g; Sodium 100mg.

p273 Watermelon Ice Energy 85Kcal/363kJ; Protein 0g; Carbohydrate 22g, of which sugars 22g; Fat 0g, of which saturates 0g; Cholesterol 0mg; Calcium 7mg; Fibre 0.1g; Sodium 100mg.

p274 Blackberry Ice Cream Energy 391Kcal/1621kJ; Protein 3g; Carbohydrate 28g, of which sugars 28g; Fat 30g, of which saturates 19g; Cholesterol 79mg; Calcium 97mg; Fibre 3.9g; Sodium 100mg.

p275 Coffee Ice Cream Energy 164Kcal/686kJ; Protein 3g; Carbohydrate 13g, of which sugars 9g; Fat 11g, of which saturates 7g; Cholesterol 32mg; Calcium 115mg; Fibre 0g; Sodium 100mg.

p276 Kulfi Energy 334Kcal/1389kJ; Protein 14g; Carbohydrate 24g, of which sugars 24g; Fat 20g, of which saturates 10g; Cholesterol 53mg; Calcium 455mg; Fibre 0.6g; Sodium 200mg.

p277 Coconut Ice Energy 137Kcal/583kJ; Protein 0g; Carbohydrate 35g, of which sugars 35g; Fat 0g, of which saturates 0g; Cholesterol 0mg; Calcium 33mg; Fibre 0g; Sodium 100mg.

p278 Gingered Semi-freddo Energy 397Kcal/1694kJ; Protein 3g; Carbohydrate 29g, of which sugars 28g; Fat 31g, of which saturates 18g; Cholesterol 203mg; Calcium 45mg; Fibre 0g; Sodium 100mg.

p279 Miniature Choc-ices Energy 106Kcal/442kJ; Protein 2g; Carbohydrate 12g, of which sugars 11g; Fat 6g, of which saturates 3g; Cholesterol 8mg; Calcium 36mg; Fibre 0.3g; Sodium 100mg.

p280 White Chocolate Castles Energy

352Kcal/1476kJ; Protein 6g; Carbohydrate 43g, of which sugars 42g; Fat 18g, of which saturates 11g; Cholesterol 22mg; Calcium 198mg; Fibre 0.5g; Sodium 100mg.

p281 Caramel and Pecan Terrine Energy 553Kcal/2292kJ; Protein 2g; Carbohydrate 27g, of which sugars 27g; Fat 49g, of which saturates 26g; Cholesterol 103mg; Calcium 46mg; Fibre 0.6g; Sodium 100mg.

p284 All Butter Cookies Energy 99Kcal/419kJ; Protein 1g; Carbohydrate 11g, of which sugars 3g; Fat 6g, of which saturates 4g; Cholesterol 16mg; Calcium 15mg; Fibre 0.3g; Sodium 100mg.

p285 Almond Cookies Energy 94Kcal/394kJ; Protein 1g; Carbohydrate 12g, of which sugars 8g; Fat 5g, of which saturates 3g; Cholesterol 11mg; Calcium 13mg; Fibre 0.3g; Sodium 100mg.

p286 Chewy Flapjacks Energy 276Kcal/1038kJ; Protein 3g; Carbohydrate 29g, of which sugars 14g; Fat 14g, of which saturates 8g; Cholesterol 34mg; Calcium 16mg; Fibre 1.4g; Sodium 100mg.

p287 Creamed Coconut Macaroons Energy 83Kcal/344kJ; Protein 1g; Carbohydrate 6g, of which sugars 6g; Fat 10g, of which saturates 5g; Cholesterol 29mg; Calcium 7mg; Fibre 0.6g; Sodium 100mg.

p288 Orange and Pecan Scones Energy 192Kcal/806kJ; Protein 3g; Carbohydrate 18g, of which sugars 1g; Fat 12g, of which saturates 3g; Cholesterol 12mg; Calcium 87mg; Fibre 1.2g; Sodium 100mg.

p289 Quick and Easy Teabread Energy 239Kcal/1017kJ; Protein 4g; Carbohydrate 56g, of which sugars 40g; Fat 1g, of which saturates 0g; Cholesterol 32mg; Calcium 116mg; Fibre 1.6g; Sodium 600mg.

p290 Cinnamon Pinwheels Energy 45Kcal/189kJ; Protein 1g; Carbohydrate 6g, of which sugars 2g; Fat 2g, of which saturates 0g; Cholesterol 5mg; Calcium 9mg; Fibre 0.0g; Sodium 100mg.

p291 Almond Cigars
Energy 171Kcal/721kJ; Protein 4g; Carbohydrate 28g, of which sugars 22g; Fat 5g, of which saturates 1g; Cholesterol 29mg; Calcium 25mg; Fibre 0.8g; Sodium 100mg.

p292 Rich Chocolate Brownies
Energy 213Kcal/892kJ; Protein 4g; Carbohydrate 14g, of which sugars 11g; Fat 16g, of which saturates 10g; Cholesterol 77mg; Calcium 67mg; Fibre 0.3g; Sodium 100mg.

p293 Rich Chocolate Biscuit Slice Energy 408Kcal/1711kJ; Protein 3g; Carbohydrate 36g, of which sugars 30g; Fat 29g, of which saturates 18g; Cholesterol 44mg; Calcium 55mg; Fibre 1.1g; Sodium 100mg.

p294 Stuffed Prunes
Energy 98Kcal/411kJ; Protein 1g; Carbohydrate 10g, of which sugars 10g; Fat 6g, of which saturates 4g; Cholesterol 8mg; Calcium 9mg; Fibre 0.7g; Sodium 100mg.

p295 Chocolate Truffles
Energy 143Kcal/596kJ; Protein 2g; Carbohydrate 15g, of which sugars 15g; Fat 9g, of which saturates 5g; Cholesterol 5mg; Calcium 32mg; Fibre 0.4g; Sodium 100mg.

p296 Chocolate Petit Four Cookies Energy 366Kcal/1533kJ; Protein 4g; Carbohydrate 43g, of which sugars 26g; Fat 21g, of which saturates 11g; Cholesterol 15mg; Calcium 47mg; Fibre 1.4g; Sodium 200mg.

p296 Praline Chocolate Bites Energy 544Kcal/2280kJ; Protein 9g; Carbohydrate 64g, of which sugars 63g; Fat 30g, of which saturates 10g; Cholesterol 3mg; Calcium 88mg; Fibre 3.4g; Sodium 100mg.

p300 Scottish Morning Rolls
Energy 165Kcal/701kJ; Protein 6g; Carbohydrate 35g, of which sugars 1g; Fat 1g, of which saturates 0g; Cholesterol 2mg; Calcium 2mg; Fibre 1.4g; Sodium 200mg.

p301 Panini all'Olio Energy 121Kcal/510kJ; Protein 3g; Carbohydrate 21g, of which sugars 0g; Fat 3g, of which saturates 0g; Cholesterol 0mg; Calcium 40mg; Fibre 0.9g; Sodium 200mg.

p302 French Baguette
Energy 702Kcal/3285kJ; Protein 23g; Carbohydrate 155g, of which sugars 3g; Fat 3g, of which saturates 0g; Cholesterol 0mg; Calcium 289mg; Fibre 6.4g; Sodium 1.3g.

p303 Rosemary Focaccia
Energy 1504Kcal/6349kJ; Protein 42g; Carbohydrate 255g, of which sugars 5g; Fat 42g, of which saturates 6g; Cholesterol 0mg; Calcium 490mg; Fibre 10.5g; Sodium 100mg.

p304 Granary Cob
Per loaf: Energy 1403Kcal/5965kJ; Protein 59g; Carbohydrate 288g, of which sugars 9g; Fat 10g, of which saturates 1g; Cholesterol 0mg; Calcium 176mg; Fibre 40.5g; Sodium 4.9g.

p305 Grant Loaves Per loaf: Energy 1371Kcal/5831kJ; Protein 57g; Carbohydrate 282g, of which sugars 14g; Fat 10g, of which saturates 1g; Cholesterol 0mg; Calcium 17.1mg; Fibre 39g; Sodium 2g.

p306 Cottage Loaf
Per loaf: Energy 2312Kcal/9839kJ; Protein 80g; Carbohydrate 508g, of which sugars 9g; Fat 10g, of which saturates 1g; Cholesterol 0mg; Calcium 951mg; Fibre 20.9g; Sodium 4g.

p307 Split Tin
Per loaf: Energy 1770kcal/7527kJ; Protein 65g; Carbohydrate 380g, of which sugars 10g; Fat 10g, of which saturates 3g; Cholesterol 8mg; Calcium 784mg; Fibre 15.5g; Sodium 4g.

p309 Poppy-seeded Bloomer Per loaf: Energy 2310Kcal/9828kJ; Protein 82g; Carbohydrate 508g, of which sugars 9g; Fat 15g, of which saturates 2g; Cholesterol 0mg; Calcium 1140mg; Fibre 20.9g; Sodium 4.9g.

p310 Traditional Irish Soda Bread Energy 257Kcal/1093kJ; Protein 12g; Carbohydrate 5g, of which sugars 2g; Fat 0g, of which saturates 0g; Cholesterol 11mg; Calcium 109mg; Fibre 6.8g; Sodium 800mg.

p310 Spring Onion Flatbreads Energy 97Kcal/414kJ; Protein 3g; Carbohydrate 21g, of which sugars 0g; Fat 0g, of which saturates 0g; Cholesterol 0mg; Calcium 41mg; Fibre 0.9g; Sodium 100mg.

p312 Pitta Bread
Energy 151Kcal/641kJ; Protein 5g; Carbohydrate 31g, of which sugars 1g; Fat 2g, of which saturates 0g; Cholesterol 0mg; Calcium 59mg; Fibre 1.3g; Sodium 500mg.

p313 Yemeni Sponge Flat Breads Energy 393Kcal/1660kJ; Protein 8g; Carbohydrate 68g, of which sugars 1g; Fat 11g, of which saturates 7g; Cholesterol 27mg; Calcium 126mg; Fibre 2.7g; Sodium 600mg.

p314 West Indian Flat Breads Energy 316Kcal/1322kJ; Protein 7g; Carbohydrate 36g, of which sugars 1g; Fat 17g, of which saturates 10g; Cholesterol 44mg; Calcium 27mg; Fibre 5.1g; Sodium 300mg.

p315 Tandoori Rotis
Energy 218Kcal/922kJ; Protein 7g; Carbohydrate 37g, of which sugars 1g; Fat 5g, of which saturates 3g; Cholesterol 11mg; Calcium 23mg; Fibre 5.3g; Sodium 400mg.

p318 Bramble Jelly
Per 15ml/1 tbsp: Energy 63Kcal/268kJ; Protein 0g; Carbohydrate 17g, of which sugars 17g; Fat 0g, of which saturates 0g; Cholesterol 0mg; Calcium 8mg; Fibre 0g; Sodium 0mg.

p319 Strawberry Jam
Per 15ml/1 tbsp: Energy 42Kcal/161kJ; Protein 0g; Carbohydrate 11g, of which sugars 11g; Fat 0g, of which saturates 0g; Cholesterol 0mg; Calcium 3mg; Fibre 0.1g; Sodium 0mg.

p320 Spiced Poached Kumquats
Energy 108Kcal/459kJ; Protein 1g; Carbohydrate 27g, of which sugars 0g; Fat 0g, of which saturates 0g; Cholesterol 0mg; Calcium 21mg; Fibre 2.9g; Sodium 100mg.

p320 Three-fruit Marmalade
Per jar: Energy 1225Kcal/5223kJ; Protein 1324g; Carbohydrate 324g, of which sugars 324g; Fat 0g, of which saturates 0g; Cholesterol 0mg; Calcium 71mg; Fibre 0.1g; Sodium 2.2g.

p322 Preserved Lemons
Per jar: Energy 41Kcal/174kJ; Protein 2g; Carbohydrate 7g, of which sugars 7g; Fat 1g, of which saturates 0g; Cholesterol 0mg; Calcium 71mg; Fibre 0.1g; Sodium 2.2g.

p323 Middle Eastern Pickles
Per jar: Energy 86Kcal/365kJ; Protein 4g; Carbohydrate 18g, of which sugars 17g; Fat 1g, of which saturates 0g; Cholesterol 0mg; Calcium 137mg; Fibre 7.4g; Sodium 4.5g.

p324 Horseradish and Beetroot Sauce Energy 28Kcal/121kJ; Protein 1g; Carbohydrate 6g, of which sugars 5g; Fat 0g, of which saturates 0g; Cholesterol 0mg; Calcium 28mg; Fibre 1.5g; Sodium 100mg.

p325 Yellow Pepper and Coriander Relish
Energy 77Kcal/324kJ; Protein 1g; Carbohydrate 6g, of which sugars 5g; Fat 6g, of which saturates 1g; Cholesterol 0mg; Calcium 12mg; Fibre 1.7g;

Sodium 100mg.

p326 Hot Mango Salsa
Energy 18Kcal/76kJ; Protein 0g; Carbohydrate 4g, of which sugars 4g; Fat 0g, of which saturates 0g; Cholesterol 0mg; Calcium 6mg; Fibre 0.7g; Sodium 100mg.

p327 Harissa
Energy 35Kcal/148kJ; Protein 2g; Carbohydrate 4g, of which sugars 0g; Fat 2g, of which saturates 0g; Cholesterol 0mg; Calcium 23mg; Fibre 0.0g; Sodium 100mg.

p328 Aioli
Energy 400Kcal/1646kJ; Protein 1g; Carbohydrate 0g, of which sugars 0g; Fat 7g, of which saturates 1g; Cholesterol 10mg; Calcium 10mg; Fibre 0.1g; Sodium 100mg.

p329 Roasted Garlic Sauce
Energy 184Kcal/761kJ; Protein 3g; Carbohydrate 9g, of which sugars 1g; Fat 15g, of which saturates 2g; Cholesterol 0mg; Calcium 17mg; Fibre 1.1g; Sodium 100mg.

p330 Watercress Sauce
Energy 451Kcal/1856kJ; Protein 1g; Carbohydrate 1g, of which sugars 1g; Fat 49g, of which saturates 16g; Cholesterol 98mg; Calcium 50mg; Fibre 0.4g; Sodium 300mg.

p331 Shallots in Balsamic Vinegar Energy 59Kcal/247kJ; Protein 1g; Carbohydrate 12g, of which sugars 10g; Fat 0g, of which saturates 0g; Cholesterol 0mg; Calcium 25mg; Fibre 1.2g; Sodium 100mg.

p332 Barbecue Sauce
Energy 31Kcal/132kJ; Protein 1g; Carbohydrate 7g, of which sugars 6g; Fat 0g, of which saturates 0g; Cholesterol 0mg; Calcium 42mg; Fibre 0.8g; Sodium 100mg.

p333 Mixed Herb and Peppercorn Sauce
Energy 50Kcal/207kJ; Protein 0g; Carbohydrate 0g, of which sugars 0g; Fat 6g, of which saturates 1g; Cholesterol 0mg; Calcium 15mg; Fibre 0g; Sodium 100mg.

p336 Leafy Apple Lift-off
Energy 169Kcal/719kJ; Protein 2g; Carbohydrate 41g, of which sugars 41g; Fat 1g, of which saturates 0g; Cholesterol 0mg; Calcium 69mg; Fibre 4.2g;

Sodium 100mg.

p336 Fennel Fusion
Energy 127Kcal/539kJ; Protein 3g; Carbohydrate 29g, of which sugars 29g; Fat 1g, of which saturates 0g; Cholesterol 0mg; Calcium 96mg; Fibre 7.9g; Sodium 100mg.

p338 Tropical Calm
Energy 149Kcal/633kJ; Protein 3g; Carbohydrate 34g, of which sugars 26g; Fat 1g, of which saturates 0g; Cholesterol 0mg; Calcium 118mg; Fibre 5.7g; Sodium 100mg.

p338 Strawberry Soother
Energy 111Kcal/471kJ; Protein 3g; Carbohydrate 26g, of which sugars 26g; Fat 0g, of which saturates 0g; Cholesterol 0mg; Calcium 50mg; Fibre 4.4g; Sodium 100mg.

p339 Carrot Revitalizer
Energy 232Kcal/981kJ; Protein 4g; Carbohydrate 55g, of which sugars 54g; Fat 1g, of which saturates 0g; Cholesterol 0mg; Calcium 137mg; Fibre 11.9g; Sodium 100mg.

p339 Purple Pep
Energy 136Kcal/571kJ; Protein 4g; Carbohydrate 29g, of which sugars 27g; Fat 1g, of which saturates 0g; Cholesterol 0mg; Calcium 150mg; Fibre 9.1g; Sodium 200mg.

p340 Tomato and Cucumber Juice with Basil
Energy 41Kcal/175kJ; Protein 2g; Carbohydrate 7g, of which sugars 6g; Fat 1g, of which saturates 0g; Cholesterol 0mg; Calcium 51mg; Fibre 2.2g; Sodium 100mg.

p341 Beetroot, Ginger and Orange Juice
Energy 155Kcal/666kJ; Protein 6g; Carbohydrate 34g, of which sugars 31g; Fat 1g, of which saturates 0g; Cholesterol 0mg; Calcium 134mg; Fibre 7.1g; Sodium 100mg.

p342 Melon Pick-me-up
Energy 189Kcal/799kJ; Protein 3g; Carbohydrate 45g, of which sugars 45g; Fat 1g, of which saturates 0g; Cholesterol 0mg; Calcium 95mg; Fibre 10.2g; Sodium 100mg.

p342 Apple Shiner
Energy 228Kcal/970kJ; Protein 4g; Carbohydrate 56g, of which sugars 56g; Fat 1g, of which saturates 0g; Cholesterol 0mg;

Calcium 57mg; Fibre 5.1g; Sodium 100mg.

p343 Citrus Sparkle
Energy 167Kcal/705kJ; Protein 5g; Carbohydrate 38g, of which sugars 38g; Fat 0g, of which saturates 0g; Cholesterol 0mg; Calcium 16/mg; Fibre 7.4g; Sodium 100mg.

p343 Hum-zinger
Energy 227Kcal/975kJ; Protein 3g; Carbohydrate 55g, of which sugars 51g; Fat 1g, of which saturates 0g; Cholesterol 0mg; Calcium 95mg; Fibre 8.6g; Sodium 100mg.

p344 Grapefruit and Pear Juice Energy 140Kcal/597kJ; Protein 2g; Carbohydrate 33g, of which sugars 33g; Fat 1g, of which saturates 0g; Cholesterol 0mg; Calcium 78mg; Fibre 6.9g; Sodium 100mg.

p345 Strawberry Apple Slush Energy 95Kcal/400kJ; Protein 2g; Carbohydrate 23g, of which sugars 23g; Fat 0g, of which saturates 0g; Cholesterol 0mg; Calcium 28mg; Fibre 3.5g; Sodium 100mg.

p346 Honey and Watermelon Tonic
Energy 96Kcal/399kJ; Protein 1g; Carbohydrate 22g, of which sugars 22g; Fat 0g, of which saturates 0g; Cholesterol 0mg; Calcium 19mg; Fibre 0.3g; Sodium 100mg.

p347 Cranberry, Ginger and Cinnamon Spritzer
Energy 121Kcal/512kJ; Protein 8g; Carbohydrate 29g, of which sugars 8g; Fat 0g, of which saturates 0g; Cholesterol 0mg; Calcium 3mg; Fibre 0g; Sodium 100mg.

p348 Lavender Orange Lush
Energy 133Kcal/568kJ; Protein 3g; Carbohydrate 32g, of which sugars 32g; Fat 0g, of which saturates 0g; Cholesterol 0mg; Calcium 132mg; Fibre 4.8g; Sodium 100mg.

p349 Ice Cool Currant
Energy 126Kcal/539kJ; Protein 1g; Carbohydrate 35g, of which sugars 35g; Fat 0g, of which saturates 0g; Cholesterol 0mg; Calcium 54mg; Fibre 2.3g; Sodium 100mg.

p350 Lemon Float
Energy 345Kcal/1461kJ; Protein 3g; Carbohydrate 70g, of which sugars 69g; Fat 8g, of which saturates 5g; Cholesterol 19mg; Calcium 91mg; Fibre 0.1g; Sodium 100mg.

p351 Blue Lagoon
Energy 148Kcal/630kJ; Protein 3g; Carbohydrate 36g, of which sugars 36g; Fat 0g, of which saturates 0g; Cholesterol 0mg; Calcium 127mg; Fibre 8.3g; Sodium 100mg.

p352 Strawberry and Banana Smoothie Energy

85Kcal/360kJ; Protein 4g; Carbohydrate 18g, of which sugars 17g; Fat 0g, of which saturates 0g; Cholesterol 2mg; Calcium 103mg; Fibre 1.1g; Sodium 100mg.

p352 Raspberry and Orange Smoothie Energy 110Kcal/466kJ; Protein 5g; Carbohydrate 18g, of which sugars 18g; Fat 2g, of which saturates 1g; Cholesterol 7mg; Calcium 164mg; Fibre 2.2g; Sodium 100mg.

p354 New York Egg Cream
Energy 271Kcal/1132kJ; Protein 6g; Carbohydrate 20g, of which sugars 19g; Fat 19g, of which saturates 7g; Cholesterol 7mg; Calcium 207mg; Fibre 0g; Sodium 100mg.

p355 Banana and Maple Flip
Energy 376Kcal/1573kJ; Protein 12g; Carbohydrate 58g, of which sugars 52g; Fat 12g, of which saturates 5g; Cholesterol 240mg; Calcium 141mg; Fibre 0.9g; Sodium 100mg.

p356 Chocolate Brownie Milkshake Energy 454Kcal/1899kJ; Protein 12g; Carbohydrate 50g, of which sugars 36g; Fat 24g, of which saturates 14g; Cholesterol 47mg; Calcium 344mg; Fibre 0.8g; Sodium 300mg.

p357 Peppermint Candy Crush Energy 175Kcal/743kJ; Protein 6g; Carbohydrate 32g, of which sugars 32g; Fat 3g, of which saturates 2g; Cholesterol 11mg; Calcium 227mg; Fibre 0g; Sodium 100mg.

p360 Rum and Star Anise Hot Toddy Energy 200Kcal/833kJ; Protein 0g; Carbohydrate 12g, of which sugars 12g; Fat 0g, of which saturates 0g; Cholesterol 0mg; Calcium 1mg; Fibre 0g; Sodium 100mg.

p361 Cardamom Hot Chocolate Energy 359Kcal/1567kJ; Protein 10g; Carbo-hydrate 42g, of which sugars 42g; Fat 18g, of which saturates 11g; Cholesterol 6mg; Calcium 127mg; Fibre 0g; Sodium 100mg.

p362 Atole Energy 197Kcal/838kJ; Protein 4g; Carbohydrate 44g, of which sugars 13g; Fat 2g, of which saturates 1g; Cholesterol 6mg; Calcium 127mg; Fibre 0g; Sodium 100mg.

p362 Café de Olla
Energy 149Kcal/634kJ; Protein 1g; Carbohydrate 34g, of which sugars 30g; Fat 2g, of which saturates 0g; Cholesterol 0mg; Calcium 25mg; Fibre 0g; Sodium 100mg.

p364 Vanilla Caffè Latte
Energy 545Kcal/2299kJ; Protein 15g; Carbohydrate 77g, of which sugars 76g; Fat 22g, of which saturates 13g; Cholesterol 24mg; Calcium 445mg; Fibre 1.4g; Sodium 200mg.

p365 Frothy Hot Chocolate
Energy 223Kcal/942kJ; Protein 10g; Carbohydrate 25g, of which sugars 25g; Fat 10g, of which saturates 6g; Cholesterol 16mg; Calcium 307mg; Fibre 0.5g; Sodium 100mg.

p366 Cuba Libre
Energy 109Kcal/454kJ; Protein 0g; Carbohydrate 11g, of which sugars 11g; Fat 0g, of which saturates 0g; Cholesterol 0mg; Calcium 9mg; Fibre 0g; Sodium 100mg.

p367 Tropical Fruit Royale
Energy 94Kcal/396kJ; Protein 1g; Carbohydrate 13g, of which sugars 13g; Fat 0g, of which saturates 0g; Cholesterol 0mg; Calcium 15mg; Fibre 2.0g; Sodium 100mg.

p368 Lemon Vodka
Energy 111Kcal/470kJ; Protein 0g; Carbohydrate 20g, of which sugars 20g; Fat 0g, of which saturates 0g; Cholesterol 0mg; Calcium 10mg; Fibre 0g; Sodium 100mg.

p369 Quick Bloody Mary
Energy 171Kcal/722kJ; Protein 2g; Carbohydrate 9g, of which sugars 9g; Fat 0g, of which saturates 0g; Cholesterol 0mg; Calcium 30mg; Fibre 1.8g; Sodium 1.2g.

p370 Gin Fizz
Energy 200Kcal/840kJ; Protein 0g; Carbohydrate 28g, of which sugars 7g; Fat 0g, of which saturates 0g; Cholesterol 0mg; Calcium 11mg; Fibre 0g; Sodium 100mg.

p371 Sea Breeze
Energy 135Kcal/566kJ; Protein 0g; Carbohydrate 10g, of which sugars 4g; Fat 0g, of which saturates 0g; Cholesterol 0mg; Calcium 6mg; Fibre 0g; Sodium 100mg.

p372 Perfect Manhattan
Energy 106Kcal/440kJ; Protein 0g; Carbohydrate 1g, of which sugars 1g; Fat 0g, of which saturates 0g; Cholesterol 0mg; Calcium 1mg; Fibre 0g; Sodium 100mg.

p373 Margarita Energy 90Kcal/376kJ; Protein 0g; Carbohydrate 4g, of which sugars 4g; Fat 0g, of which saturates 0g; Cholesterol 0mg; Calcium 3mg; Fibre 0g; Sodium 100mg.

Index